The Advanced Practice Nurse's Legal Handbook

The Advanced Practice Nurse's Legal Handbook

Rebecca F. Cady, RNC, BSN, JD
Associate Attorney
Grace, Brandon, Hollis, L.L.P.
San Diego, California

Consultant
Helen A. Carcio, MS, RN, CS, ANP
Nurse Practitioner
Pioneer Women's Health, Greenfield, MA
Associate Clinical Professor
University of Massachusetts

LIPPINCOTT WILLIAMS & WILKINS
A **Wolters Kluwer** Company
Philadelphia • Baltimore • New York • London
Buenos Aires • Hong Kong • Sydney • Tokyo

Acquisitions Editor: Jennifer Brogan
Assistant Editor: Susan Barta Rainey
Production Editor: Nicole Walz
Senior Production Manager: Helen Ewan
Managing Editor/Production: Erika Kors
Design Coordinator: Brett MacNaughton
Manufacturing Manager: William Alberti
Interior and Cover Designer: Melissa Olson
Indexer: Angie Wiley
Printer: Maple/Vail–Ballou Press

9 8 7 6 5 4 3 2 1

ISBN: 0-7817-2337-X

This publication is designed to provide accurate and authoritative information in regard to the subject matter covered. It is sold with the understanding that the publisher is not engaged in rendering legal, accounting, or other professional service. If legal advice or other expert assistance is required, the service of a competent professional person should be sought. (From a Declaration of Principles jointly adopted by a Committee of the American Bar Association and a Committee of Publishers and Associations.)

Care has been taken to confirm the accuracy of the information presented and to describe generally accepted practices. However, the authors, editors, and publisher are not responsible for errors or omissions or for any consequences from application of the information in this book and make no warranty, express or implied, with respect to the content of the publication.

The authors, editors, and publisher have exerted every effort to ensure that drug selection and dosage set forth in this text are in accordance with the current recommendations and practice at the time of publication. However, in view of ongoing research, changes in government regulations, and the constant flow of information relating to drug therapy and drug reactions, the reader is urged to check the package insert for each drug for any change in indications and dosage and for added warnings and precautions. This is particularly important when the recommended agent is a new or infrequently employed drug.

Some drugs and medical devices presented in this publication have Food and Drug Administration (FDA) clearance for limited use in restricted research settings. It is the responsibility of the health care provider to ascertain the FDA status of each drug or device planned for use in his or her clinical practice.

To my newborn daughter,
Elizabeth Spencer Cady,
whose imminent birth was the driving force
behind the completion of this book.

Preface

This book was written to provide a comprehensive look at the legal issues affecting all categories of advanced practice nurses (APNs). While excellent resources exist with respect to nurse practitioners and the law, there were no similar resources for the CNM, CNS, or CRNA. Originally, this book was to have covered all the laws of every state regarding advanced practice nurses. It quickly became apparent, however, that doing so would have resulted in a cumbersome and voluminous text. As a result, the beginning chapters cover the big picture of the laws in all states, while the remaining chapters focus on the states with the heaviest population of nurses. This text is intended not as a legal reference, but to provide APNs with information about the legal context in which they conduct their practices. Every effort has been made to keep the information in this book as up-to-date and accurate as possible, but because laws can and do change, this book is not a substitute for the advice of an attorney, nor is it intended to function as such. It is my hope that this book will provide a user-friendly map of how APN practice differs among the states and that it will provide a starting point for the APN who wishes to understand how the law will impact his or her practice.

Acknowledgments

I would like to thank Jennifer Brogan and Susan Rainey at Lippincott Williams & Wilkins for their support and patience. Helen Carcio has provided an invaluable sounding board and has ensured that this text is user friendly. This book was a family project. My dad, Mahlon Fiscel, spent hours at the library helping me with my research. My mom, Jane Freeman, watched my girls while I worked on the book. My husband Bob, and daughters Ginny and Maggie, have given me infinite patience and encouragement, without which this project would never have come to fruition. Lastly, to the faculty at Georgetown University School of Nursing, for teaching me that it is the duty of nurses to ask questions and think independently, and to Mike Grace, Esq., who taught me everything I know about defending malpractice cases, for his example of dedication, integrity, and compassion.

Contents

Defining Advanced Practice Nursing

Vignette: Law in Real Life

Why is it important from a legal standpoint to be able to clearly define what an advanced practice nurse is and the accepted role of an advanced practice nurse? Consider the following hypothetical scenario: Jamie Smith is licensed as a family nurse practitioner. She works in a clinic providing obstetric and gynecologic care to indigent women and well baby care to their children. One of her patients decides to sue her regarding alleged negligence in not providing adequate informed consent for a Depo-Provera injection. The patient claims that she was not made aware of the risk of breakthrough bleeding and that she was not counseled regarding the potential of weight gain as a side effect. The patient had insisted on getting the shot at her first visit with the nurse practitioner (NP); she also insists that at the time of her visit she thought the NP was a physician.

At the trial, the jury will need to be educated by the nurse practitioner's attorney regarding the nature of her qualifications, the laws regarding her scope of practice, and the applicable standard of care in order to reach a decision about the question of negligence.

Defining the Advanced Practice Nurse

Although nurses have been engaged in advanced practice for decades, the definitions vary about what an advanced practice nurse (APN) is and what role advanced practice nurses have in the health care system. Hodson, 1998, notes that advanced nursing practice and titles have been inconsistently defined in the literature: the APN title is a general term for master's prepared nurses who provide clinical care; the nurse practitioner title is a generic term for advance practice nurses who traditionally have engaged in direct care in primary care settings; the clinical nurse specialist (CNS) term applies to nurses who traditionally serve as role models for staff nurses in acute care settings through the subroles of expert practice, education, consultation, and research; acute care nurse practitioners (ACNPs) are APNs who provide care to acutely ill patients, regardless of setting; the ACNP role also has been referred to as inpatient nurse practitioner, nurse specialist, advanced practice nurse, and tertiary nurse practitioner.

Brent, 1997, defines an advanced practice nurse as a registered nurse who has completed an additional course of study in a nursing specialty that provides specialized knowledge and skills to function in an expanded role. The American Nurses' Association (ANA) states that advanced practice nurses are advanced registered nurses who provide direct patient care in the roles of nurse practitioner, clinical nurse specialist, certified nurse midwife, and certified registered nurse anesthetist and are nurses who have acquired the knowledge base and practice experiences to prepare them for specialization, expansion, and advancement in selected roles (ANA, 1994). The ANA definition of advanced practice nurse states that the APN

- Possesses a master's degree.
- Is competent to manage client health and illness status.
- Coaches disease prevention and health promotion.
- Conducts comprehensive health assessments.
- Functions in collegial relationships with other nurses, physicians, and providers who influence the health environment.
- Formulates clinical decisions to manage acute and chronic illnesses by assessing, diagnosing, and prescribing treatment modalities, including pharmacological agents.
- Integrates clinical practice, education, research, management, leadership, and consultation into a single role (Hodson, 1998).

Others have defined advanced practice nursing as any additional training of nurses beyond the diploma or associates degree level (Faherty, 1995) and any additional training beyond the basic requirements for licensure (Rooks, 1986). Advanced practice nurses typically function as primary care providers in a variety of clinical settings. There are many different types of advanced practice nurses including nurse practitioners, nurse midwives, nurse anesthetists, and clinical nurse specialists. Among nurse practitioners, one can find pediatric nurse practitioners, womens' health care nurse practitioners, perinatal nurse practitioners, geriatric nurse practitioners, psychiatric nurse practitioners, and family nurse practitioners. As the titles suggest, these nurse practitioners function as primary care providers within their given clinical area.

Growth and Practice Trends in the Profession

In 1986, the congressional Office of Technology Assessment conducted a study that found process and outcome measures were equivalent between advanced practice nurses and physicians. This study also found that advanced practice nurses scored higher than the physicians in patient communication and preventive care (O'Flynn, 1996), and that 50% to 90% of primary care provided by physicians could be provided by APNs at approximately one third the cost (Hodson, 1998). In 1990, the U.S. Department of Health and Human Services (DHHS) assessed the supply of nurse practitioners as primary care providers and concluded that 45% of states had a shortage of nurse practitioners (DHHS, 1990). As of 1998, there were 2.2 million registered nurses in the United States, approximately 100,000 of whom were classified as advanced practice nurses (Hodson, 1998). At that time, DHSS estimated that 200,000 nurses with advanced degrees would be needed by the year 2000 to accommodate increasing patient acuity, decreased lengths of stay, and advanced technology (Hodson, 1998). Figure 1-1 illustrates the status of APN need predicted in 1998. Despite the documented need for advanced practice nurses and the high quality and cost-effective care they provide, in many areas advanced practice nurses are not major players in the health care system. Spatz, 1996, noted that multiple barriers prohibit more wide scale use of advanced practice nurses including

- Second licensure
- Limits on prescriptive authority

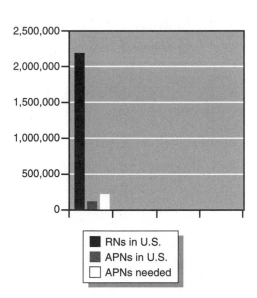

FIGURE 1-1. 1998 Number of advanced practice nurses (APNs) and projected need by 2000.

- Problems with reimbursement from insurance companies
- Inconsistencies in educational preparation and job functions among those who call themselves advanced practice nurses.

These barriers remain ingrained in the system despite the fact that patients overwhelmingly prefer advanced practice nurses to physicians and appear to be more satisfied with care received from advanced practice nurses than that received from physicians. A 1998 survey indicated that 100% of respondents would seek health care from a NP for themselves and their family members (AWHONN, 1998).

As of 1998, 85% of nurses not currently working in an advanced role planned to obtain an advanced degree (AWHONN, 1998). As of fall 1998, graduations of new nurse practitioners rose by 15.8%, enrollment in master's degree nurse practitioner programs grew by 1 %, and more than half of master's degree students in nursing schools were pursuing study in nurse practitioner tracks (AWHONN, 1999). Figure 1-2 illustrates 1998 growth in the number of APN graduates.

Exploring the Various Types of Advanced Practice Nursing

Because each of the various types of advanced practice nursing have specific requirements and roles, it is important to recognize the differences among them. There remains a wide variety in the requirements and education necessary to become an advanced practice nurse. Although the American Association of Colleges of Nursing (AACN) insists that advanced practice nurses must be master's or doctoral prepared (AACN,

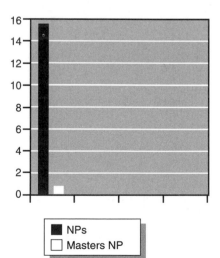

■ NPs
□ Masters NP

FIGURE 1-2. 1998 growth in advanced practice nurse graduates (amounts in percents).

1995), many states do not require this level of education for licensure as an APN. Figure 1-3 illustrates the states that currently require master's degrees from at least one category of advanced practice nursing. Even among graduate nursing programs, there are variations in curricula. The AACN recommends three content areas: the core courses, the advanced clinical core, and the specialty area courses (AACN, 1995). The National Organization of Nurse Practitioner Faculties (NONPF) has also published curriculum guidelines for advanced nurse practitioners (NONPF, 1995). There are four currently recognized types of advanced practice nurses: certified nurse anesthetists (CRNAs), certified nurse midwives (CNMs), nurse practitioners (NPs), and clinical nurse specialists (CNSs). Also included in this text is the certified registered nurse first assistant (CRNFA), a role that may become nationally recognized within the next 5 years as a fifth category of advanced practice nurse.

NURSE ANESTHETIST

History

Garde, 1996, provides a comprehensive history of nurse anesthesia in the United States. Box 1-1 illustrates the key dates in the history of nurse anesthesia. The earliest recorded nurse anesthetist was Sister Mary Bernard, a Catholic nun who administered anesthesia at St. Vincent's Hospital in Erie, Pennsylvania, in 1877. By 1889, nine other nuns had become nurse anesthetists. The popularity of nurse anesthetists grew and the profession flourished until 1915 when the Ohio State Medical Board

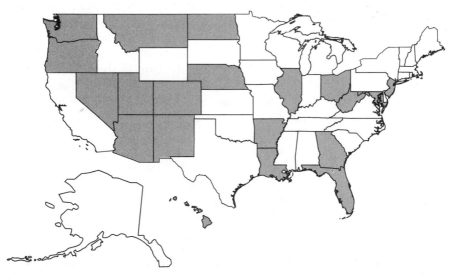

FIGURE 1-3. States that require master's degrees from at least one category of advanced practice nursing.

BOX 1-1	Key Dates in the History of Nurse Anesthesia

1877	The earliest recorded administration of anesthesia by a nurse.
1919	The first mention of nurse anesthetists in a state statute.
1931	The National Association of Nurse Anesthetists is formed.
1945	The first certification exam in nurse anesthesia is given.
1986	Nurse anesthesia becomes the first nursing specialty to be given direct reimbursement rights under the Medicare program.

decided that no one other than a registered physician was permitted to administer anesthesia and the state attorney general concurred. In 1917 the Medical Board was persuaded to lift the order. In 1919 an exemption was granted within the Medical Practice Act for nurses appropriately educated in anesthesia to administer anesthesia under the supervision of a physician. This was the first mention of nurse anesthetists in a state statute.

By the end of World War I, the demand for nurse anesthetists increased rapidly. In 1942 there were 17 nurse anesthetists for every one anesthesiologist. In 1917 the Kentucky Medical Society issued an ethical policy that sanctioned by expulsion any member of the society who used nurse anesthetists or practiced in hospitals that employed nurse anesthetists. Membership in the society was often essential to acquire medical staff membership. The Society was taken to court over this policy, which was overturned by the Appellate Court in 1917. The last case to address the subject of whether or not nurse anesthetists were practicing medicine was *Chalmers-Francis et al. v. Nelson et al.*, 1936; here the California Supreme Court ruled in favor of the nurse anesthetist.

The National Association of Nurse Anesthetists was formed in 1931, making it the oldest specialty nursing organization in the United States. In 1939 it was renamed the American Association of Nurse Anesthetists (AANA). According to the AANA, ever since World War I nurse anesthetists have been the principal anesthesia providers in combat areas of every war in which the United States has been engaged (AANA, 2000a).

The first certification examination was given in 1945, making nurse anesthesia the first specialty for which certification was available. In 1955, the U.S. Department of Health, Education, and Welfare recognized the AANA as the accrediting agency for schools of nurse anesthesia. In 1986 Medicare direct reimbursement legislation for CRNAs was signed into law, making nurse anesthesia the first nursing specialty to be given direct reimbursement rights under the Medicare program. Presently, more than 27,000 CRNAs provide anesthesia services (AANA, 2000b).

Education/Training

As defined by the American Association of Nurse Anesthetists, a nurse anesthetist is a registered nurse who has successfully completed an approved nurse anesthetist program from an accredited program (Eskreis, 1985). Educational programs in Nurse Anesthesia range from 24 to 36 months in length. The academic curriculum requires a minimum of 30 credit hours in an anesthesia component that includes advanced anatomy, physiology, and pathophysiology; biochemistry and physics related to anesthesia; advanced pharmacology; principles of anesthesia practice; research methodology and statistical analysis; and research or other scholarly endeavor. In addition, each student must complete a minimum of 450 cases (AANA, 2000c). Admission requirements for nurse anesthesia educational programs include a bachelor of science degree in nursing or other appropriate baccalaureate degree, licensure as an RN, and a minimum of 1 year acute care nursing experience (AANA, 2000c). In order to become certified as a nurse anesthetist, the nurse must pass a national qualifying examination and fulfill continuing education requirements every 2 years for recertification. See Box 1-2 for the requirements to become and remain a certified nurse anesthetist.

BOX 1-2   **Requirements to Become and Remain a CRNA**

To become and remain a CRNA, requirements include:

1. Licensure as a registered nurse and completion of at least 1 year of experience in an acute care setting.
2. Graduation from an approved school of nursing and current state licensure as a registered nurse.
3. Graduation from a nurse anesthesia educational program accredited by the Council on Accreditation of Nurse Anesthesia Educational Programs or its predecessor.
4. Successful completion of the certification examination administered by the Council on Certification of Nurse Anesthetists or its predecessor.
5. Compliance with criteria for biennial recertification as defined by the Council on Recertification of Nurse Anesthetists. These criteria include evidence of (1.) current licensure as a registered nurse, (2.) active practice as a CRNA, (3.) appropriate continuing education, and (4.) verification of the absence of mental, physical, and other problems that could interfere with the practice of anesthesia.
6. Continued compliance with the state legal requirements for practice (Garde, 1996).

Garde, 1996, notes that as of 1998 all nurse anesthesia programs must offer a master's degree upon successful completion. The clinical component of the nurse anesthesia educational program mandates that each student administer a minimum of 450 anesthetic agents to patients, representing at least 800 hours of anesthesia time. Currently all nurse anesthesia educational programs offer a master's degree; depending on the particular program, the degree obtained is in nursing, allied health, or biological and clinical sciences (AANA, 2000d).

Garde, 1996, notes that nurse anesthetists are prepared to administer all types of anesthesia including general, regional, selected local, and conscious sedation; to use all currently available anesthesia and adjunctive drugs; to determine need and manage fluid and blood therapy; monitor, and interpret data from sophisticated monitoring devices; to insert invasive catheters (including intravenous, central venous, and pulmonary artery catheters); to recognize and correct complications during the course of anesthesia with the use of consultation as necessary; to provide airway and ventilatory support; to manage resuscitation efforts for cardiopulmonary arrest or serious injury; and to provide pain management services.

Practice Roles

CRNAs administer more than 65% of the 26 million anesthetics given to patients in the United States each year (Garde, 1996). CRNAs administer anesthesia for all types of surgical cases, use all anesthetic techniques (ie, local, regional and general anesthesia), and practice in every setting in which anesthesia is delivered (eg, traditional hospital suites and obstetric delivery rooms; offices of dentists, podiatrists, ophthalmologists, and plastic surgeons; ambulatory surgical centers; health maintenance organizations; preferred provider organizations; U.S. military and public health services; and Veterans Administration medical facilities). CRNAs provide services as employees of hospitals, physicians and/or as private practitioners either on the basis of clinical privileging and/or as contractors. CRNAs are the sole anesthesia providers in more than 70% of rural hospitals in the United States, thereby providing access to anesthesia for 70 million rural Americans. They also provide a significant percentage of anesthesia care in inner cities (Garde, 1996). A CRNA provides for patients' anesthesia needs before, during, and after surgery or the delivery of a baby by

- Performing a physical assessment.
- Participating in preoperative teaching.
- Preparing for anesthetic management.
- Administering anesthesia intraoperatively.
- Overseeing recovery from anesthesia.
- Following the patient's postoperative course from recovery room to patient care unit (AANA, 2000d).

The reported average annual salary for CRNAs in 1997 was approximately $87,000 (AANA, 2000d).

NURSE MIDWIVES

History of Nurse Midwifery

Burkhardt, 1996, reminds us that midwifery as a profession has existed since biblical times, that until the 1500s and 1600s midwifery enjoyed a public perception that midwives were vital and integral to the community. At that time, the Church weakened the place of midwives through claims of witchcraft (Ehrenrich, 1973). By the end of the 1700s in Europe, physicians began to perform midwifery. By the start of the 20th century, medicine had a firm grip on midwifery practice. However, the demand for maternity care was greater than what available physicians could provide, and some states legalized midwives in order to provide this needed care (Burkhardt, 1996). One court has noted that licensure law in this area may have developed as a market control device; midwives were depriving new obstetricians of the opportunity for training, and elimination of midwifery would allow the science of obstetrics to grow into a mature medical specialty (*State Board of Nursing v. Ruebke*, 1996). Also around this time, British nurse midwives were introduced into the United States in Kentucky (Varney, 1989). In May of 1955, the American College of Nurse Midwifery was formed. This group has set standards for practice and education to assure safe and satisfying care of women and their babies and has developed the process and structure for implementing and evaluating these standards (Varney, 1989; Burkhardt, 1996).

Until 1910 approximately 50% of births in this country were midwife-assisted. By 1930, however, births attended by non-physicians had declined to 15% of all births. By 1975 the percentage of births attended by midwives had dropped to less than 1% (*State Board of Nursing v. Ruebke*, 1996). Fortunately for the profession, this trend has reversed itself. According to a report from CNN, 1999, babies these days are more likely to be delivered by midwives, with an increase in midwife-attended deliveries from 3.7% in 1989 to 7% in 1997. However, the report also indicated that the use of midwives varies considerably from state to state, from less than 1% of births in Missouri to 20% in New Mexico to 55% in the Virgin Islands. Figure 1-4 illustrates the fluctuation in the percentage of midwife-assisted births in the United States from 1910 to 1997. According to the American College of Nurse Midwives, as of 1998 there were approximately 5,500 CNMs in practice in the United States (ACNM, 2000a). Box 1-3 illustrates the advantages to patients who utilize the services of CNMs over physicians. Burkhardt, 1996, questions whether or not, given the history of midwifery's evolution in the United States, midwifery is truly advanced nursing practice. She notes that midwifery in the

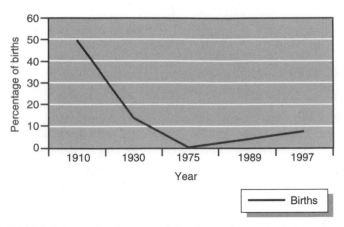

FIGURE 1-4. Midwife-assisted births in the United States.

United States grew out of nursing for two reasons: the founding group of women was comprised of nurses and the natural candidates to become midwives were nurses (Burkhardt, 1996).

Today much tension and confusion still exist about the role of non-nurse or lay midwives. In 1995, the American College of Nurse-Midwives (ACNM) began developing criteria for accreditation of direct entry or non-nurse midwifery programs and began work on expanding its certification definitions to include the graduates of these programs, thus creating the category of Certified Midwife (CM) (Burst, 1995). Currently, the ACNM recognizes two routes to practice midwifery in the United States: CNMs and certified midwives (CMs)(ACNM, 2000a). CMs are midwives who have a background in a health-related field other than nursing and who have completed certain education and testing requirements but who are not RNs. CNMs are recognized by all 50 states and U.S. territories; CMs are characterized as a new and growing group of professionals in the field of midwifery and are not yet practicing in all U.S. states and territories (ACNM, 2000a).

BOX 1-3	Advantages to Patients Using CNMs Rather Than Physicians

- CNMs use fetal monitoring less frequently.
- CNMs use fewer medications.
- CNMs perform fewer technical procedures.
- CNMs are less likely to induce labor.
- CNMs demonstrate infant clinical outcomes that are equivalent to physicians' results.

Education/Training

The first midwifery education program began in New York City in 1932 in conjunction with the Maternity Center Association, which adapted its curriculum from the British curricula. By 1965, there were nine nurse midwifery education programs in major universities such as Columbia University, Johns Hopkins University, Yale University, Catholic University, and Utah University (Burkhardt, 1996, ACNM, 1995a).

To practice as a nurse midwife, one must graduate from an ACNM accredited education program and pass a national certification examination. The mechanism of program accreditation began in 1962 and is required of all nurse midwifery programs for their graduates to be eligible for certification. A variety of programs can be completed to qualify as a nurse midwife. Box 1-4 lists the current available programs that can lead to a career in nurse midwifery. The successful completion of the nurse midwifery or midwifery portion of any of these options enables the graduate to take the certification examination to become either a CNM or a CM (ACNM, 2000b). The ACNM describes each of the program options as follows:

1. Diploma or associates degree RN to CNM graduate program: for the individual who is a licensed RN with either a diploma or an associates degree in nursing. The program offers several options including earning a baccalaureate degree and certificate in nurse midwifery; earning a baccalaureate degree and master's degree in nurse midwifery; or earning a master's degree in nurse midwifery.
2. BA/BS to RN/CNM graduate program: for individuals who are not licensed RNs but who have a baccalaureate degree in a field other than nursing. These individuals apply to become an RN then continue in the nurse midwifery education program. Some programs

BOX 1-4	Program Options for Nurse-Midwifery

1) Nurse midwifery education programs
2) Midwifery education programs
3) Diploma or associates degree RN to CNM graduate programs
4) BA/BS to RN/CNM graduate programs
5) Certificate programs
6) Distance education programs
7) Master's completion programs
8) Post-master's certificate

(ACNM, 2000b).

require students to work as an RN for a period of time before beginning the nurse midwifery part of the program.

3. Certificate program: This program offers a certificate in nurse midwifery or midwifery for people who want to become a CNM or a CM but do not want to complete the master's degree requirements beyond the midwifery education requirements.
4. Distance education program: These programs have been designed to allow students to complete either a portion or the entire program at a distance from the campus of the program.
5. Master's completion program: This is for CNMs or CMs who are graduates of a certificate program and would like to pursue a master's degree.
6. Post-master's certificate program: This is for people who have a master's degree or higher and want to become a CNM or CM without completing another graduate degree program (ACNM, 2000c).

Nurse midwifery education occurs in a variety of educational settings. As of 1996, there were 43 basic nurse midwifery programs in the United States: 32 were in schools of nursing, 3 in schools of allied health sciences, 1 each in a college of medicine and a school of public health, with the remaining 6 located either in a medical center or in a stand-alone program (ACNM, 1995a). The ACNM, 2000d, notes that the number of states and employers who require nurse midwives to be master's prepared in order to practice is increasing.

For a foreign educated nurse midwife (FENM) to be eligible to enter U.S. nurse midwifery education programs, he or she must (1.) be a licensed registered nurse in one of the 50 states, the District of Columbia, or U.S. territories; (2.) have a baccalaureate degree before beginning the program or attend a program that grants no less than a baccalaureate degree; (3.) be prepared to submit a Test of English as a Foreign Language (TOEFL) score if English is not a first language. In addition, the FENM may be asked to provide evidence of formal recognition as a midwife in the country or state of preparation, provide transcripts of education from the country of preparation or education received in the United States, and submit scores from the Graduate Record Examination (GRE) (ACNM, 2000e).

The ACNM Certification Council developed and has administered the certifying examination since 1971 (Burkhardt, 1996). Certification obtained after January 1996 is good for 8 years; a certification maintenance program must be completed in order to renew the certification at the end of the 8-year period (ACNM, 2000f). The maintenance program consists of completing one module in each of the three areas of practice: antepartum, intrapartum/newborn and postpartum/gynecology as well as accrue 20 contact hours of ACNM or ACCME Category 1 approved activities. Otherwise, the test must be retaken to maintain certification (ACNM, 2000g).

To sit for the certification examination, a U.S.-prepared nurse midwife must be licensed as an RN in one of the 50 states, the District of Columbia or a U.S. territory; satisfactorily complete a program in nurse midwifery accredited by or with pre-accreditation status from the Division of Accreditation of the ACNM; and provide a signature by the director of the nurse midwifery educational program on the test application form attesting that the candidate has satisfactorily completed the nurse midwifery component of the program. (ACNM, 2000f).

To sit for the certification exam, a foreign prepared nurse midwife must be licensed as an RN in one of the 50 states, the District of Columbia, or a U.S. territory; provide written evidence of formal recognition as a midwife in the applicant's country of preparation; and satisfactorily complete a precertification program accredited by or with pre-accreditation status from the division of accreditation of the ACNM (ACNM, 2000f).

Practice Roles

The ACNM defines nurse midwifery practice as the "independent management of care of essentially normal newborns and women, antepartally, intrapartally, postpartally, and/or gynecologically, occurring within a health care system. . . ." (ACNM, 1995a). Nurse midwifery encompasses obstetrics, gynecology, neonatal pediatrics, and medical management (Varney, 1989). Nurse midwives provide both low- and high-risk obstetric care, including prenatal, intrapartum, and postpartum care, as well as routine gynecologic care and family planning counseling (Spatz, 1996). According to the ACNM, CNMs practice in public, private, university, and military hospitals; health maintenance organizations; private practice; and birth centers. Many work in public health clinics; others provide home birth services (ACNM, 2000h). The ACNM, 2000h, notes that nurse midwives practice in collaboration with physicians and that the degree of collaboration depends on the medical needs of the patient and the practice setting. Of all visits to CNMs, 90% are for primary preventive care; 70% for care during pregnancy and after birth; and 20% for care outside the maternity cycle (ACNM, 2000h). On average, nurse midwives devote about 10% of their time to direct care of birthing women and their newborns (ACNM, 2000h). The ACNM notes that CNM salaries average from $40,000-$70,000 per year depending on the practice setting, geographic location, benefits, and type of care provided (ACNM, 2000d).

NURSE PRACTITIONERS

The role of nurse practitioner was conceived to increase access to primary health care and to address physician shortages (Page & Arena, 1994). The nurse practitioner's client is the patient and the focus of the nurse practitioner is to provide direct patient care (Page & Arena, 1994).

Nurse practitioners provide a full range of primary healthcare services with a holistic patient and family focus (Page & Arena, 1994). Traditional medical functions such as writing histories and physicals and prescribing medication are within the nurse practitioner's scope of practice (Page & Arena, 1994). Studies show that nurse practitioners achieve equal or better outcomes than physicians and that nurse practitioner patients demonstrate higher scores on patient compliance and satisfaction with care (Spatz, 1996). According to the U.S. Government's Health Resources and Services Administration (1997), an estimated 71,000 registered nurses had formal preparation to practice as nurse practitioners in March 1996.

Education/Training

Page and Arena 1994, note that a nurse practitioner can earn a certificate from a community hospital program or a master's degree in a university setting and that practice settings have traditionally been in public schools, occupational settings, correctional facilities, and primary care with recent trends showing an increase in NPs in acute care settings. In a study by Beal et al. in 1999, 20 out of 22 nurse practitioners working at five Neonatal Intensive Care Units (NICUs) in Massachusetts and Rhode Island had master's degrees. Hodson, 1998, notes that recent changes in graduate education are merging the CNS and NP curricula to create a reconceptualized role in advanced clinical practice and that issues regarding the titling, role definition, and education of this merged role are being developed. Effective January 1, 2000, the Health Care Financing Administration (HCFA) requires all nurse practitioners to hold a Master's in Nursing degree (NAPNAP, 1999).

Practice Roles

Nurse practitioners work in various settings, from the community to tertiary care settings, homeless shelters, and on-the-job sites (Spatz, 1996). Callahan, 1996, notes that currently, nurse practitioners are moving into acute care in growing numbers and cites several factors driving this trend. Changes in health care over recent years have resulted in the need for new ways to care for hospitalized patients. In the mid-1980s, medical residency programs came under review as the numbers of hours worked and the level of supervision were adjusted. Reduced numbers of residents in training have resulted from changes in funding for residency programs. Health care reform has resulted in the need for more efficient and cost-effective patient care. Studies have shown that advanced practice nurses may be a capable substitute for resident house staff (Callahan, 1996). Nurse practitioners can function in a wide variety of clinical areas.

Spatz, 1996, notes that some practitioners advocate the nurse practitioner for care of chronically mentally ill patients. Callahan, 1996, describes a nurse practitioner's cardiac surgery practice, which involves preoperative assessment and education, postoperative management and discharge planning, and postoperative follow-up.

Beal et al., 1999, note that due to the decreasing availability of resident physicians providing care in critical care settings such as the NICU, NICUs across the country are hiring more nurse practitioners. The neonatal nurse practitioner was one of the first NPs to practice in tertiary care settings (Keane et al., 1994).

Hunsberger et al., 1992, were among the first to define role activities of the neonatal nurse practitioner (NNP). Their definition included immediate and ongoing assessment and diagnosis; ongoing clinical management of the infant including the performance of selected diagnostic and therapeutic skills during emergent and non-emergent situations; parent support; research participation; administrative activities; role evaluation; and education of self and colleagues. Beal et al., 1999, found that NP responsibilities at NICUs varied, however, all were involved in the immediate assessment and diagnosis as well as the ongoing clinical management of the infant, which included collaborating with other health providers to initiate and continue a treatment regimen; ordering and performing a variety of diagnostics and therapeutics; providing parent support; educating nurses and medical students; and participating in research and in the administration of patient care services in the NICU. Beal et al., 1999, also found that all NPs were involved in or ran family meetings and frequently consulted with other providers to plan an infant's care. Activities that varied were attending deliveries and admitting infants from the delivery room to the NICU, providing antepartum consultation, performing transport, and providing outpatient follow-up to infants discharged from the NICU. Beal, 2000, notes that the majority of nurse practitioners who work in the NICU are neonatal nurse practitioners, however, in some states, pediatric and family nurse practitioners also practice in the NICU. Box 1-5 summarizes the settings in which nurse practitioners currently work.

BOX 1-5	Settings in Which Nurse Practitioners Currently Work

- Nursing homes
- Incontinence centers
- Infertility clinics
- Homeless shelters
- Corporate offices
- Cardiac surgery
- Mental health clinics
- NICU
- Public schools
- Correctional facilities
- Acute care
- Primary care

CLINICAL NURSE SPECIALISTS

History

O'Flynn, 1996, notes that in 1954 Hildegarde Peplau started the first clinical master's program at Rutgers University. Shortly thereafter, the first clinical nurse specialist examination in psychiatric and mental health nursing was developed. Page and Arena, 1994, note that the clinical nurse specialist (CNS) role was established to improve the quality of nursing care delivered to patients, as well as to keep the expert, specialized nurse at the bedside. The CNS's client is the nurse, and the CNS's focus is on nursing staff education, system analysis, and providing direct and indirect nursing care (Page & Arena, 1994). Clinical nurse specialists consult to address both patient care and system issues, consult and educate others who provide direct care to patients, facilitate changes in nursing care delivery, and influence the quality of care through interactions with healthcare providers and with patients; their ultimate goal is to improve quality by providing direct care or through work with other nurses at the bedside (Page & Arena, 1994). The American Nurses Association (ANA) describes a CNS as an expert clinician in a specialty area exhibiting a high level of expertise in dealing with complex responses to actual or potential health problems, preventing illness, maintaining wellness, and providing comfort with the addition of prescriptive authority, and the responsibilities of education, research, and consultation (ANA, 1996).

Education/Training

In its 1980 Social Policy Statement, the ANA stated that the educational preparation of all clinical nurse specialists is at the master's level and above (O'Flynn, 1996). Traditionally, nurses have educated clinical nurse specialists, with a master's degree required for entry (Page & Arena, 1994). The core content is based on the five CNS subroles of expert clinician, consultant, researcher, educator, and manager (Page & Arena, 1994). Clinical education typically occurs in secondary and tertiary care sites (Page & Arena, 1994). De Villers, 1998, notes that despite opposition from some specialty organizations, the consensus is that graduate education at the master's level should be the minimum entry-level preparation.

Practice Roles

Clinical nurse specialists provide care in a wide variety of clinical settings including obstetrics, surgery, mental health, and critical care. De Villers, 1998, notes that the CNS role as a caregiver in the obstetrical/gynecological setting directly overlaps the duties and functions traditionally carried out by nurse midwives. Box 1-6 summarizes the clinical settings in which CNSs currently work.

BOX 1-6	Clinical Settings in Which CNSs Currently Work

- High risk obstetrics
- Maternal/infant health services
- Surgery
- Mental health
- Critical care

RN First Assistant

The RN first assistant (RNFA) role was officially recognized by the Association of Operating Room Nurses (AORN) in 1983, and the scope of practice for RNFAs is now regulated by individual state nurse practice acts (Hodson, 1998). As of 1998 there were approximately 2,195 AORN member RNFAs providing services in this expanded practice role (Hodson, 1998). The surgical APN role is to coordinate, collaborate, and merge hospital care with physician practice partners (Hodson, 1998). Hodson, 1998, notes that the advanced practice certified RNFA role in surgical arenas has many similarities to the advanced practice nurse and acute care nurse practitioner designations, however, it as yet has not been fully recognized by educators, surgical directors, and health care administrators. In 1980, the American College of Surgeons affirmed its support for RNFAs as providers of assistant services in surgery (Hodson, 1998). By 1983, RNFAs were able to assist in 17 states. By 1998 RNFAs were recognized in all 50 states and by the ANA (Hodson, 1998). The CRNFA examination was created by AORN in 1993. To be eligible to take the exam, one must be a CNOR; have 2000 hours of preoperative, intraoperative, and postoperative practice as an RNFA; and have a Bachelor of Science degree in Nursing (Hodson, 1998).

RNFAs perform a variety of pre, intra, and postoperative tasks, which are outlined in Box 1-7.

Hodson, 1998, notes that RNFAs are hospital-based, physician-employed, or in independent practice. As of 1998, only Florida and Minnesota had specific state legislation to support RNFA reimbursement through private insurers (Hodson, 1998). RNFAs are not currently eligible for direct Medicare payment (Hodson, 1998).

DIFFERENTIATING THE ADVANCED PRACTICE NURSE FROM THE PHYSICIAN ASSISTANT

Some confusion remains as to the differences between the advanced practice nurse and the physician assistant (PA) on the part of patients and on the part of some nurses. Physician assistants are defined as health care professionals licensed to practice medicine with physician supervi-

BOX 1-7	Tasks of the Certified RN First Assistant (CRNFA)

Preoperative: Managing preadmission (including ordering lab tests, providing consultation, performing outpatient examinations); taking patient histories and physical assessments; conducting interviews; providing education; reviewing charts for completeness; and communicating care plans including special patient or surgeon needs to OR staff members

Intraoperative: Handling tissue; providing exposure and hemostasis; and suturing

Postoperative: Assisting with initial postoperative assessments; writing postoperative orders; dictating progress or discharge summaries; performing daily rounds and wound management; directing nutritional, electrolyte, and IV therapies; providing discharge education; collaborating and consulting with social services for health maintenance; and performing physician office visits that may include any of these activities (Hodson, 1998)

sion (American Association of Physician Assistants, 2000a). Physician assistants conduct physical exams, diagnose and treat illnesses, order and interpret tests, counsel on preventive health care, assist in surgery, and in most states can write prescriptions (AAPA, 2000a). This ancillary profession was developed in the mid-1960s at Duke University Medical Center in North Carolina to address the shortage and uneven distribution of primary care physicians (AAPA, 2000a). Physician assistants do not necessarily have any college degree but are required to complete PA programs, which last approximately 111 weeks (AAPA, 2000b). According to the American Association of Physician Assistants (AAPA), most PA programs require applicants to have previous health care experience and some college education (AAPA, 2000b). Upon completion of the PA program, applicants must pass a national certification examination in order to practice. Graduation from an accredited PA program and passage of the examination are required for state licensure (AAPA, 2000a).

Table 1-1 summarizes the major differences between the advanced practice nurse and the physician assistant (PA). According to the AAPA, 41,421 people were eligible to practice as PAs as of March 1, 1999 (AAPA, 2000c). All jurisdictions in the United States except Mississippi have enacted statutes and regulations that define PAs, describe their scope of practice, discuss supervision, designate the agency that will administer the law, set application and renewal criteria, and establish disciplinary measures for violations of the law (AAPA, 2000d). A complete summary of each state's law regarding PAs can be found on the AAPA's website at http://www.aapa.org. Nurses who work with PAs need to be aware of the laws regarding physician assistants in their particular state of practice.

TABLE 1-1. Differences Between the Advanced Practice Nurse and the Physician Assistant

ADVANCED PRACTICE NURSE	PHYSICIAN ASSISTANT
Practices under own license	Practices under physician's license
May not be required to practice with physician supervision	Physician supervision always required
Can make independent nursing judgments	No provision for independent judgment
Physician not responsible for acts of APN	Physician directly responsible for acts of PA

This is important, for example, in determining whether a NP is able to carry out an order written by a physician assistant. In states that allow PAs to write orders, the NP would be permitted to carry out those orders.

Though the daily activities of the advanced practice nurse and the physician assistant may be nearly identical, there are important legal differences between the two professions. Physician assistants may never practice independently, and their supervising physician is totally responsible for their performance. APNs, on the other hand, practice under their own licenses and work in collaboration with physicians, not under physician supervision. Physicians who collaborate with an APN are not responsible for any of the APN's actions.

ENHANCE YOUR LEARNING

1. Design a study to identify patient perceptions regarding APN care in your area.
2. Based on the results of the above study, develop a marketing plan for your practice that addresses any patient misperceptions discovered in the study.
3. Interview other APNs who practice in your clinical area but who have a different certification. What areas of your practice overlap; which are different?
4. Review your state's laws regarding physician assistants.

TEST YOUR COMPREHENSION

1. Differentiate between the various education options available to become a nurse midwife; list benefits and drawbacks to each option.
2. List the functions of a RNFA.
3. List the functions of a CRNA.
4. Compare and contrast the roles of a nurse practitioner and that of a physician assistant.

REFERENCES

American Association of Colleges of Nursing Task Force on the Essentials of Master's Education for Advanced Practice Nursing. (1995). *The essentials of master's education for advanced practice nursing.* Washington, DC: American Association of Colleges of Nursing.

American Association of Nurse Anesthetists. (2000a). History of nurse anesthesia practice. Available online at http://www.aana.com/library/history.asp.

American Association of Nurse Anesthetists. (2000b). Nurse anesthesia . . . no longer the best kept secret in health care. Available online at http://www.aana.com/information.

American Association of Nurse Anesthetists. (2000c). Nurse anesthesia education. Available online at http://www.aana.com/library/naeducation.asp.

American Association of Nurse Anesthetists. (2000d). Questions and answers about a career in nurse anesthesia, 1/29/2000. Available online at http://www.aana.com/information/careerqa.asp.

American Association of Physician Assistants. (2000a). General information. Available online at http://aapa.org/geninfo1.html.

American Association of Physician Assistants. (2000b). Physician assistant education. Available online at http://www.aapa.org/edinfo.html.

American Association of Physician Assistants. (2000c). Data and statistics. Available online at http://www.aapa.org/index.html.

American Association of Physician Assistants. (2000d). State regulation of physician assistant practice. Available online at http://www.aapa.org/statelaw.html.

American College of Nurse Midwives. (1995). Essential documents. Washington, DC: Author.

American College of Nurse Midwives. (2000a). Routes to the midwifery profession. Available online at http://www.acnm.org/educ/doaroutes.html.

American College of Nurse Midwives. (2000b). Nurse midwifery and midwifery education options at a glance. Available online at http://www.acnm.org/educ/glance.html.

American College of Nurse Midwives. (2000c). Explanation of options. Available online at http://www.acnm.org/educ/options.htm.

American College of Nurse Midwives. (2000d). Frequently asked questions. Available online at http://www.midwife.org/educ/Femfqa.htm.

American College of Nurse Midwives. (2000e). Information for foreign educated midwives & nurse midwives who seek to practice in the United States. Available online at http://www.midwife.org/educ/Feminfo.htm.

American College of Nurse Midwives. (2000f). The ACNM Certification Council, Inc. Available online at http://www.midwife.org/educ/fenmacc.htm.

American College of Nurse Midwives. (2000g). The ACNM Certification Council, Inc. Certificate maintenance program. Available online at http://www.midwife.org/educ/cmp_ihtr.htm.

American College of Nurse Midwives. (2000h). CNM Practice. Available online at http://www.midwife.org/educ/doacnmpr.htm.

American Nurses Association. (1994). *Nursing: A social policy statement.* Kansas City, MO: American Nurses Association.

American Nurses Association. (1996). *Scope and standards of advanced practice registered nursing.* (pp. 2–3). Washington, DC: American Nurses Publishing.

Association of Women's Health, Obstetric, and Neonatal Nurses (AWHONN). (1999, June/July). NP Programs hit popularity stride: RN enrollments decline. *Lifelines, 3*(3), 15.

Association of Women's Health, Obstetric, and Neonatal Nurses (AWHONN). (1998, August). Nurses speak out survey results. *Lifelines, 2*(4), 23.

Beal, J. (2000). A nurse practitioner model of practice in the neonatal intensive care unit. *MCN, 25*(1), 18–24.

Beal, J., Richardson, D.K., Dembinski, S., et al. (1999). Responsibilities, roles and staffing patterns of nurse practitioners in the neonatal intensive care unit. *MCN, The American Journal of Maternal Child Nursing, 24*(4), 169–175.

Brent, Nancy J. (1997). *Nurses and the law, a guide to principles and applications.* Philadelphia: WB Saunders.

Burkhardt, P. (1996, September). Nurse midwifery: Advanced practice nursing? *Nursing Clinics of North America, 31*(3), 439–448.

Burst, H. V. (1995). An update on the credentialing of midwives by the ACNM. J *Nurse Midwifery, 40*(3), 290–6.

Callahan, M. (1996, September). The advanced practice nurse in an acute care setting: The nurse practitioner in adult cardiac surgery care. *Nursing Clinics of North America, 31*(3), 487–493.

Cable News Network (CNN). (1999, December 1). *Both midwives and induced labors on the rise.* Available online at http://www.cnn.com/1999/HEALTH/women/ 12/01/american.births.ap/index.html.

DeVillers, M. (1998). The clinical nurse specialist as expert practitioner in the obstetrical/gynecological setting. *Clinical Nurse Specialist, 12*(5), 193–198.

Eherenrich, B, & English, D. (1973). *Witches, midwives and nurses: A history of women healers.* New York: The Feminist Press.

Eskreis, T., (1986, June). Health law—the legal implications in utilizing the nurse anesthetist in place of the anesthesiologist. *Specialty Law Digest Health Care (Mon), 8*(4), 7–32.

Faherty, B. (1995). Advanced practice nursing: What's all the fuss? *Journal of Nursing Law, 2.*

Garde, J. F. (1996, September). The nurse anesthesia profession: A past, present and future perspective. *Nursing Clinics of North America, 31*(3), 567–580.

Health Resources and Services Administration, Division of Nursing Nurse Practitioners. (1997, June). *Selected facts about nurse practitioners.* Available online at http://www.hrsa.dhhs.gov/bhpr/DN/npnmdata.htm.

Hodson, D. (1998, May). The evolving role of advanced practice nurses in surgery. *Association of Operating Room Nurses (AORN) Journal, 67*(5), 998–1006.

Hunsberger, M. et al. (1992). Definition of an advanced nursing practice role in the NICU: The clinical nurse specialist/neonatal nurse practitioner. *Clinical Nurse Specialist, 6*(2), 91–96.

Keane, A. et al. (1994). Critical care nurse practitioners: Evolution of the advanced practice nursing role. *American Journal of Critical Care, 3*(3), 232–237.

National Association of Pediatric Nurse Associates & Practitioners. (1999). *Master's degree for NPs*, Legislative News. Available online at http://www.napnap.org/archives/legnews-archive/legnews-19990924.html.

National Organization of Nurse Practitioner Faculties Curriculum Guidelines Task Force. (1995). *Advanced nursing practice: Curriculum guidelines and program standards for nurse practitioner education* (2nd ed.). Washington, DC: National Organization of Nurse Practitioner Faculties.

O'Flynn, A. (1996, September). The preparation of advanced practice nurses: Current issues. *Nursing Clinics of North America, 31*(3), 429–438.

Page, N., & Arena, D. (1994). Rethinking the merger of the clinical nurse specialist and the nurse practitioner roles. *Image: Journal of Nursing Scholarship, 26*(4), 315–318.

Rooks, J. P. (1986). *Nurse-midwifery in America: A report of the American college of nurse midwives foundation*. Washington, DC: American College of Nurse Midwives.

Spatz, D. (1996). Women's health: The role of advanced practice nurses in the 21st century. *Nursing Clinics of North America, 31*(2), 269–277.

U.S. Department of Health and Human Services. (1989). *States' assessment of health personnel shortages: Issues and concerns*. DHHS Publication No. HRS-P-OD-90-6. Rockville, MD.

Varney, H. (1989). *Nurse midwifery*. Boston, MA: Blackwell Scientific.

Cases

Chalmers-Francis et al. v. Nelson et al., 57 P.2d 1312 (CA. 1936).
State Board of Nursing v. Ruebke, 913 P.2d 142 (KS. 1996).

State Nurse Practice Acts

State Nurse Practice Acts: What Are They and Why Are They Important?

Mannino, 1996, defines the nurse practice act as the prevailing state law that defines the practice of registered professional nurses. State laws are important because they define the requirements for licensure, the scope of practice, and the disciplinary measures for nurses in the state. It is imperative that advanced practice nurses (APNs) obtain and read (and understand!) the nurse practice act in all states in which they practice. Thanks to the Internet, most state nurse practice acts can now be obtained free from various websites. The National Council of State Boards of Nursing (NCSBN) website http://www.ncsbn.org has full-text state nurse practice acts for the following states: Alabama, Alaska, Arizona, Arkansas, Florida, Georgia, Idaho, Illinois, Iowa, Kansas, Louisiana, Massachusetts, Minnesota, Mississippi, Missouri, Montana, Nevada, New Hampshire, New Mexico, New York, North Carolina, North Dakota, Ohio, Oklahoma, Oregon, Pennsylvania, South Carolina, Texas, Virginia, Wisconsin, and Wyoming. It also has links to websites where state rules and regulations regarding nursing can be found. Ideally, you should annually check the laws and regulations of any states in which you practice. Keeping up with professional reading will also alert you to potential or actual changes in your state's laws. Appendix 2-1 lists the addresses and web site addresses, if available, for the boards of nursing of each state and U.S. territory. This information is also available on the NCSBN's web site.

Tables 2-1 through 2-4 provide a summary of the variations in state laws pertaining to certified nurse midwives (CNMs), nurse practitioners (NPs), clinical nurse specialists (CNSs), and certified nurse anesthetists (CRNAs). Currently, the regulation and control of APNs vary widely from state to state. For example, as of 1999, 38 states placed nurse midwives under the state board of nursing; 2 states put them under the medical

TABLE 2-1. Summary of State Laws Regarding Nurse Midwives

STATE	GOVERNING AUTHORITY	PROTOCOLS REQUIRED	PRESCRIPTION PRIVILEGES GRANTED	CONTROLLED SUBSTANCES	MASTER'S DEGREE REQUIRED
Alabama	BON	Yes	Yes	No	Yes
Alaska	BON	No	Yes	Yes	No
Arizona	BON	No	Yes	Yes	Yes
Arkansas	BON	Yes (rx only)	Yes	Yes	No
California	BON	Yes	Yes	No	No
Colorado	BON	No	Yes	Yes	Yes (rx)
Connecticut	BON	Yes	Yes	Yes	No
Delaware	BON/BOM	No	Yes	Yes	No
District of Columbia	BON	No	Yes	Yes	No
Florida	BON	Yes	Yes	Yes	Yes
Georgia	BON	Yes	Yes	Yes	Yes
Hawaii	BON	No	Yes	No	Yes (rx)
Idaho	BON	No	Yes	Yes	No
Illinois	BON	Yes	Yes	Yes	Yes
Indiana	BON	Yes (rx only)	Yes	Yes	No
Iowa	BON	Yes	Yes	Yes	Yes
Kansas	BON	Yes (rx only)	Yes	Yes	No
Kentucky	BON	Yes	Yes	No	No
Louisiana	BON	Yes	Yes	No	Yes
Maine	BON	No	Yes	No	No
Maryland	BON	No	Yes	Yes	No
Massachusetts	BON/BOM	Yes	Yes	Yes	Yes
Michigan	BON	No	Yes	Yes	No
Minnesota	BON	Yes	Yes	Yes	No
Mississippi	BON	Yes	Yes	No	Yes
Missouri	BON	Yes (rx only)	Yes	No	Yes
Montana	BON	No	Yes	Yes	Yes
Nebraska	BON/BOM	Yes	Yes	Yes	Yes
Nevada	BON	Yes	Yes	No	No
New Hampshire	BON	No	Yes	Yes	No
New Jersey	BOME	Yes	Yes	Yes	No
New Mexico	Dept. of Health	No	Yes	Yes	No
New York	Dept. of Education	Yes	Yes	No	No
North Carolina	Midwifery Committee	No	No	No	No
North Dakota	BON	Yes (rx only)	Yes	Yes	Yes

(continued)

TABLE 2-1. Summary of State Laws Regarding Nurse Midwives (Continued)

STATE	GOVERNING AUTHORITY	PROTOCOLS REQUIRED	PRESCRIPTION PRIVILEGES GRANTED	CONTROLLED SUBSTANCES	MASTER'S DEGREE REQUIRED
Ohio	BON	Yes	No	No	No
Oklahoma	BON	No	Yes	Yes	No
Oregon	BON	No	Yes	No	Yes
Pennsylvania	BOM	Yes	No	No	No
Rhode Island	Dept. of Health	No	Yes	Yes	No
South Carolina	BON	Yes	Yes	No	Yes
South Dakota	BOM/BON	No	Yes	Yes	No
Tennessee	BON	No	No	No	No
Texas	BNE	Yes	Yes	No	No
Utah	CNM Board	Yes (rx only)	Yes	Yes	No
Vermont	BON	Yes	Yes	Yes	No
Virginia	BOM/BON	Yes	Yes	No	No
Washington	NCQAC	No	Yes	Yes	Yes
West Virginia	BON	Yes (rx only)	Yes	Yes	Yes
Wisconsin	BON	Yes	Yes	Yes	Yes (rx)
Wyoming	BON	No	Yes	Yes	No

TABLE 2-2. Summary of State Laws Regarding Nurse Practitioners

STATE	GOVERNING AUTHORITY	PROTOCOLS REQUIRED	PRESCRIPTION PRIVILEGES GRANTED	CONTROLLED SUBSTANCES	MASTER'S DEGREE REQUIRED
Alabama	BON	Yes	Yes	No	Yes
Alaska	BON	No	Yes	Yes	No
Arizona	BON	No	Yes	Yes	Yes
Arkansas	BON	Yes (rx)	Yes	Yes	No
California	BON	Yes	Yes	Yes	No
Colorado	BON	No	Yes	Yes	Yes (rx)
Connecticut	BON	Yes (rx only)	Yes	Yes	Yes (rx)
Delaware	BON/BOM	No	Yes	Yes	No
District of Columbia	BON	No	Yes	Yes	No
Florida	BON	Yes	Yes	Yes	Yes
Georgia	BON	Yes	Yes	Yes	Yes
Hawaii	BON	No	Yes	No	Yes (rx)
Idaho	BON	No	Yes	Yes	No

(continued)

TABLE 2-2. Summary of State Laws Regarding Nurse Practitioners
(Continued)

STATE	GOVERNING AUTHORITY	PROTOCOLS REQUIRED	PRESCRIPTION PRIVILEGES GRANTED	CONTROLLED SUBSTANCES	MASTER'S DEGREE REQUIRED
Illinois	BON	Yes	Yes	Yes	Yes
Indiana	BON	Yes (rx only)	Yes	Yes	No
Iowa	BON	Yes	Yes	Yes	No
Kansas	BON	Yes (rx only)	Yes	Yes	No
Kentucky	BON	Yes	Yes	No	No
Louisiana	BON	Yes	Yes	No	Yes
Maine	BON	No	Yes	Yes	No
Maryland	BON	Yes	Yes	Yes	No
Massachusetts	BON	Yes	Yes	Yes	Yes
Michigan	BON	No	Yes	Yes	No
Minnesota	BON	Yes	Yes	Yes	No
Mississippi	BON/BOM	Yes	Yes	Yes	Yes
Missouri	BON	Yes (rx only)	Yes	No	Yes
Montana	BON	No	Yes	Yes	Yes
Nebraska	APRN Board	Yes	Yes	Yes	Yes
Nevada	BON	Yes	Yes	No	No
New Hampshire	BON	No	Yes	Yes	No
New Jersey	BON	Yes (rx only)	Yes	Yes	Yes
New Mexico	BON	No	Yes	Yes	Yes
New York	BON	Yes	Yes	Yes	No
North Carolina	BON/BOM	Yes	Yes	Yes	No
North Dakota	BON	Yes (rx only)	Yes	Yes	Yes
Ohio	BON	Yes	Yes	No	No
Oklahoma	BON	No	Yes	Yes	No
Oregon	BON	No	Yes	Yes	Yes
Pennsylvania	BOM/BON	Yes	Yes	No	No
Rhode Island	BON	Yes (rx only)	Yes	Yes	Yes
South Carolina	BON	Yes	Yes	Yes	Yes
South Dakota	BOM/BON	No	Yes	Yes	No
Tennessee	BON	Yes	Yes	Yes	Yes (rx)
Texas	BNE	Yes	Yes	No	No
Utah	BON	Yes (rx only)	Yes	Yes	Yes
Vermont	BON	Yes	Yes	Yes	No
Virginia	BOM/BON	Yes	Yes	Yes	No
Washington	NCQAC	No	Yes	Yes	Yes
West Virginia	BON	Yes (rx only)	Yes	Yes	Yes
Wisconsin	BON	Yes	Yes	Yes	Yes (for rx)
Wyoming	BON	No	Yes	Yes	No

TABLE 2-3. Summary of State Laws Regarding Clinical Nurse Specialists

STATE	GOVERNING AUTHORITY	PROTOCOLS REQUIRED	PRESCRIPTION PRIVILEGES GRANTED	CONTROLLED SUBSTANCES	MASTER'S DEGREE REQUIRED
Alabama	BON	No	No	No	Yes
Alaska	Not recognized	—	—	—	—
Arizona	BON	No	No	No	Yes
Arkansas	BON	Yes (rx only)	Yes	Yes	Yes
California	BON	Yes	No	No	Yes
Colorado	BON	No	Yes	Yes	Yes (rx)
Connecticut	BON	Yes (rx)	Yes	Yes	Yes (rx)
Delaware	BON/BOM	No	Yes	Yes	No
District of Columbia	BON	No	Yes	Yes	No
Florida	BON	Yes	Yes	Yes	Yes
Georgia	BON	Yes	Yes	Yes	Yes
Hawaii	BON	No	Yes	No	Yes (rx)
Idaho	BON	No	Yes	Yes	Yes
Illinois	BON	Yes	Yes	Yes	Yes
Indiana	BON	Yes (rx only)	Yes	Yes	Yes
Iowa	BON	Yes	Yes	Yes	No
Kansas	BON	Yes (rx only)	Yes	Yes	Yes
Kentucky	BON	Yes	Yes	No	No
Louisiana	BON	Yes	Yes	No	Yes
Maine	BON	No	No	No	Yes
Maryland	BON	No	No	No	Yes
Massachusetts	BON/BOM	Yes	Yes	Yes	Yes
Michigan	Not recognized	—	—	—	—
Minnesota	BON	Yes	Yes	Yes	No
Mississippi	BON	Yes	No	No	Yes
Missouri	BON	Yes (rx only)	Yes	No	Yes
Montana	BON	No	Yes	Yes	Yes
Nebraska	Not recognized	—	—	—	—
Nevada	BON	Yes	Yes	No	Yes
New Hampshire	BON	No	Yes	Yes	No
New Jersey	BON	Yes (rx only)	Yes	No	Yes
New Mexico	BON	No	Yes	Yes	Yes
New York	BON	No	No	No	Yes
North Carolina	BON	No	No	No	Yes
North Dakota	BON	Yes (rx only)	Yes	Yes	Yes
Ohio	BON	Yes	No	No	Yes
Oklahoma	BON	No	Yes	Yes	No

(continued)

TABLE 2-3. **Summary of State Laws Regarding Clinical Nurse Specialists** (Continued)

STATE	GOVERNING AUTHORITY	PROTOCOLS REQUIRED	PRESCRIPTION PRIVILEGES GRANTED	CONTROLLED SUBSTANCES	MASTER'S DEGREE REQUIRED
Oregon	BON	No	No	No	No
Pennsylvania	Not recognized	—	—	—	—
Rhode Island	BON	Yes (rx only)	Yes	Yes	Yes
South Carolina	BON	Yes	Yes	No	Yes
South Dakota	BON	No	No	No	Yes
Tennessee	Not recognized	—	—	—	—
Texas	BNE	Yes	Yes	No	Yes
Utah	Professional Licensing Board	Yes (rx only)	Yes	Yes	Yes
Vermont	BON	Yes	Yes	Yes	No
Virginia	BON	No	No	No	Yes
Washington	NCQAC	No	Yes	Yes	Yes
West Virginia	BON	Yes (rx only)	Yes	Yes	Yes
Wisconsin	BON	Yes	Yes	Yes	Yes (for rx)
Wyoming	BON	No	Yes	Yes	No

TABLE 2-4. **Summary of State Laws Regarding Certified Registered Nurse Anesthetists**

STATE	GOVERNING AUTHORITY	PROTOCOLS REQUIRED	PRESCRIPTION PRIVILEGES GRANTED	CONTROLLED SUBSTANCES	MASTER'S DEGREE REQUIRED	DIRECT PHYSICIAN SUPERVISION REQUIRED
Alabama	BON	No	No	No	No	Yes
Alaska	BON	No	Yes	Yes	No	No
Arizona	BON	No	Yes (only for admin to patient)	Yes	No	Yes
Arkansas	BON	Yes (rx only)	Yes (only for admin to patient)	Yes	No	No
California	BON	Yes	No	No	No	No
Colorado	BON	No	Yes	Yes	Yes (rx)	No
Connecticut	BON	Yes (rx)	Yes	Yes	Yes (rx)	Yes
Delaware	BON/BOM	No	Yes	Yes	No	No
District of Columbia	BON	No	Yes	Yes	No	No

(continued)

TABLE 2-4. Summary of State Laws Regarding Certified Registered Nurse Anesthetists (Continued)

STATE	GOVERNING AUTHORITY	PROTOCOLS REQUIRED	PRESCRIPTION PRIVILEGES GRANTED	CONTROLLED SUBSTANCES	MASTER'S DEGREE REQUIRED	DIRECT PHYSICIAN SUPERVISION REQUIRED
Florida	BON	Yes	Yes	Yes	Yes	No
Georgia	BON	Yes	Yes	Yes	Yes	No
Hawaii	BON	No	Yes	No	Yes (rx)	No
Idaho	BON	No	Yes	Yes	No	No
Illinois	Dept. of Prof. Regulation	No	No	No	No	Yes
Indiana	BON	No	No	No	No	Yes
Iowa	BON	Yes	Yes	Yes	No	No
Kansas	BON	Yes (rx only)	Yes	Yes	No	No
Kentucky	BON	Yes	Yes	No	No	Yes
Louisiana	BON	Yes	No	No	Yes	No
Maine	BON	No	No	No	Yes	No
Maryland	BON	No	No	No	No	No
Massachusetts	BON/BOM	Yes	Yes	Yes	No	No
Michigan	BON	No	Yes	No	No	No
Minnesota	BON	Yes	Yes	Yes	No	No
Mississippi	BON	Yes	Yes	No	Yes	No
Missouri	BON	Yes (rx only)	Yes	No	Yes	No
Montana	BON	No	Yes	Yes	Yes	No
Nebraska	BON/BOM	No	Yes	Yes	No	No
Nevada	BON	No	No	No	No	No
New Hampshire	BON	No	Yes	Yes	No	No
New Jersey	BON	Yes	No	No	No	Yes
New Mexico	BON	No	No	No	Yes	Yes
New York	BON	No	No	No	No	Yes
North Carolina	BON	No	No	No	No	No
North Dakota	BON	Yes (rx only)	Yes	Yes	Yes	No
Ohio	BON	No	No	No	No	Yes
Oklahoma	BON	No	Yes	Yes	No	No
Oregon	BON	No	No	No	Yes	Yes
Pennsylvania	BON	No	No	No		No
Rhode Island	BON	No	No	No	No	Yes
South Carolina	BON	Yes	No	No	Yes	No
South Dakota	BON	No	No	No	No	No
Tennessee	BON	Yes	Yes	No	No	No
Texas	BNE	Yes	Yes	No	No	Yes
Utah	Professional Licensing Board	No	No	No	No	Yes
Vermont	BON	Yes	Yes	Yes	No	No
Virginia	BOM/BON	Yes	Yes	Yes	No	Yes
Washington	NCQAC	No	Yes	Yes	Yes	No
West Virginia	BON	Yes (rx only)	Yes	Yes	Yes	Yes
Wisconsin	BON	Yes	Yes	Yes	Yes (rx)	No
Wyoming	BON	No	Yes	Yes	No	No

board; 7 states provided joint regulation by the board of nursing and the board of medicine; 1 state regulated nurse midwives within the department of public health; the remaining 3 states regulated midwives from various obscure state agencies (Pearson, 1999). As of January 1999, 17 states required midwives to have a registered nurse (RN) credential to legally practice. At least 16 states regulate midwifery as a profession and do not require midwives to be registered nurses. In 13 more states, midwifery practice by non-nurses is legal but unregulated. In at least 5 states, the legal status of midwives other than CNMs is in dispute (ACNM, 2000). The two primary areas of difference from state to state are the degree of professional autonomy and the range of drugs that the APN is authorized to prescribe (Spatz, 1996).

As of 1999, in 19 states NPs can practice independently without physician collaboration, direction, or supervision; in 16 states NPs are required to practice with physician collaboration, and in 9 states NPs are required to practice under the supervision of a physician (Pearson, 1999). Figure 2-1 illustrates the level of independence for NPs in the various states. Arkansas is the only state that has two different types of NPs: the registered nurse practitioner (RNP) and the ANP. The RNP is not required to have national certification, must practice with protocols, and has no prescriptive authority. The ANP is required to have national certification, needs protocols only for prescribing, and has prescriptive authority for both legend and controlled substances.

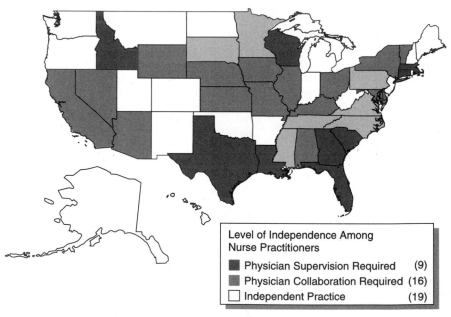

Level of Independence Among Nurse Practitioners

■ Physician Supervision Required (9)
■ Physician Collaboration Required (16)
□ Independent Practice (19)

FIGURE 2-1. Level of independence among nurse practitioners.

DEVELOPMENT OF STATE LAWS REGARDING APN PRACTICE

Over the last 20 years, the laws in each state have developed gradually regarding advanced practice nursing. Some states have taken a very hands-off approach, allowing great freedom of practice to APNs, while others have made the practice of APNs highly regulated. At this point, it is unlikely that major changes will occur in any of the states' laws within the next several years because all states have addressed prescriptive authority for APNs. Additionally, changes in state law can take several years to become final due to the somewhat lengthy legislative process. 1998 was the first year in which NPs had independent or dependent statutory or regulatory prescriptive authority in all 50 states and the District of Columbia (Pearson, 1999).

Pearson, 1999, notes that the legislative progress of autonomous practice for APNs is most dramatic in those states where APNs are statutorily regulated by the board of nursing. Lamm, 1996, notes that there is a growing feeling that state legislatures are using licensure laws for purposes other than consumer protection and quality assurance, which are widely believed to be the only legitimate goals of occupational regulation. Lamm, 1996, describes the changes made in licensing law in Ontario, Canada in 1991, which basically consolidated regulation of all health professionals under a single law. This law, called the Regulated Health Professions Act (RHPA), set out 13 controlled acts that are listed in Box 2-1. The legislation regulated a total of 25 different health professions, listed in Box 2-2. The legislation covered professional scopes of practice for each of the professions and listed which of the controlled acts, if any, may be performed by that profession. Examples of the allowed acts for medicine, nursing, and midwives are included in Box 2-3. As a result of the reforms undertaken in Ontario, five U.S. states (Colorado, Maine, Virginia, Nebraska, and Washington) are reforming their own health professions' regulations. Lamm, 1996, notes a growing feeling that an efficient health care system must explore how the various professions overlap and can substitute for each other.

In 1993, the NCSBN approved a proposal recommending that APNs possess two separate licenses: the current one for basic practice and a separate one for advanced practice (Spatz, 1996). This recommendation has not been implemented by all states. Figure 2-2 illustrates the changes over the last 6 years in the way states regulate APN practice.

INTERSTATE COMPACT

At the present time, there is a move afoot to enact an interstate nurse licensure compact. This compact, finalized in 1998, has as its purposes:

- To facilitate the states' responsibility to protect the public's health and safety

BOX 2-1	Controlled Acts Set Forth by the RHPA

1. Communicating to the individual or his or her personal representative a diagnosis identifying a disease or disorder as the cause of symptoms in the individual in circumstances in which it is reasonably foreseeable that the individual or his or her personal representative will rely on the diagnosis
2. Performing a procedure on tissue below the dermis, below the surface of a mucous membrane, in or below the surface of the cornea, or in or below the surfaces of the teeth, including the scaling of teeth
3. Setting or casting a fracture of a bone or a dislocation of a joint
4. Moving the joints of the spine beyond the individual's usual physiological range of motion, using a fast, low amplitude thrust
5. Administering a substance by injection or inhalation
6. Putting an instrument, hand, or finger:

    Beyond the external ear canal
    Beyond the point in the nasal passages where they normally narrow
    Beyond the larynx
    Beyond the opening of the urethra
    Beyond the labia majora
    Beyond the anal verge
    Into an artificial opening into the body

7. Applying or ordering the application of a form of energy prescribed by the regulations under the RHPA
8. Prescribing, dispensing, selling, or compounding a drug as defined in clause 113(1) (d) of the Drug and Pharmacies Regulation Act, or supervision of the part of the pharmacy where such drugs are kept
9. Prescribing or dispensing, for vision or eye problems, subnormal vision devices, contact lenses, or eyeglasses other than simple magnifiers
10. Prescribing a hearing aid for a person with hearing impairment
11. Fitting or dispensing a dental prosthesis, orthodontic or periodontal appliance, or device used inside the mouth to protect teeth from abnormal functioning
12. Managing labor or conducting the delivery of an infant
13. Allergy challenge testing of a kind in which a positive test result is a significant allergic response

- To ensure and encourage the cooperation of party states in the areas of nurse licensure and regulation
- To facilitate the exchange of information between party states in the areas of nurse regulation, investigation, and adverse actions
- To promote compliance with the laws governing the practice of nursing in each jurisdiction
- To invest all party states with the authority to hold a nurse accountable for meeting all state practice laws in the state where

BOX 2-2	Professionals Covered by the RHPA

Audiologists	Speech-language pathologists
Chiropodists	Naturopaths
Chiropractors	Occupational therapists
Dental hygienists	Ophthalmic dispensers
Dental technicians	Optometrists
Dentists	Osteopaths
Denture therapists	Pharmacists
Dietitians	Physicians
Massage therapists	Physiotherapists
Medical laboratory technologists	Podiatrists
Midwives	Psychologists
Registered nurses and registered	Radiological technicians
practical nurses	Respiratory technologists

the patient is located at the time care is rendered through the mutual recognition of party state licenses (Nurse Licensure Compact, Article I[b]).

The compact provides that a license to practice registered nursing issued by any participating state will be recognized by all other participating states. The state that originally grants the license is referred to as the home state; participating states other than the home state are referred to as party states. Party states may limit or revoke the multistate licensure privilege of any nurse to practice in that state and may take other actions under their state's law as needed to protect the health and safety of their citizens. If such actions are taken, the party state must promptly notify the home state of the action taken. This compact requires that nurses practicing in any party state must comply with the state practice laws of the state where the patient is located at the time care is rendered. The compact does not limit the definition of practice of nursing to patient care but indicates that it includes all nursing practice as defined by the laws of the individual state. The compact does not affect additional requirements imposed by states for advanced practice registered nursing. However, a multistate licensure privilege to practice registered nursing granted by a party state will be recognized by other party states as a license to practice

BOX 2-3	Examples of Authorized Acts Under the RHPA

Medicine: All acts except number 11
Nurses: Acts 2, 5, and 6
Midwives: Acts 2, 5, 6, 8, and 12

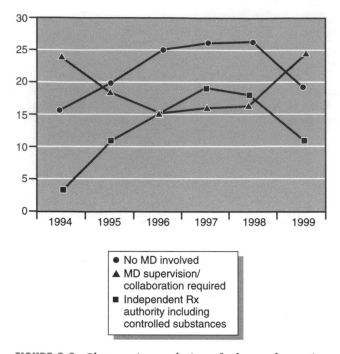

FIGURE 2-2. Changes in regulation of advanced practice nursing from 1994–1999.

registered nursing if the licensure priviledge is required by state law as a precondition for qualifying for advanced practice registered nurse authorization (Nurse Licensure Compact, Article III[a-d]).

Under the compact, a state that is not the home state may take adverse action affecting the multistate licensure privilege to practice within that state. However, only the home state has the power to impose adverse action against the license issued by the home state (Nurse Licensure Compact Article V[c]). The compact gives party state nurse licensing boards the authority

- To recover from the affected nurse the costs of investigations and disposition of cases resulting from any adverse action taken against that nurse
- To issue subpoenas for both hearings and investigations that require the attendance and testimony of witnesses and the production of evidence
- To pay any witness fees, travel expenses, mileage, and other fees required by law of the state where the witnesses and or evidence are located
- To issue cease and desist orders to limit or revoke a nurse's authority to practice in that state

- To promulgate uniform rules and regulations to facilitate and coordinate implementation of the compact (Nurse Licensure Compact Article VI[a-d]).

All states signing on to the compact will participate to create a coordinated data base of all licensed RNs and licensed practical nurses (LPNs) that will include information on the licensure and disciplinary history of each nurse, as contributed by the individual states, to assist in the coordination of nurse licensure and enforcement efforts. All licensing boards will promptly report adverse actions, actions against multistate licensure privileges, any current significant investigative information yet to result in adverse action, denials of applications, and the reasons for the denials to the coordinated licensure information system (Nurse Licensure Compact Article VII[a-b]).

There has been a huge uproar in response to this compact, with strong feelings on both sides of the pro-con debate. Many questions have been raised about the practicality of administering this licensure information system including privacy and due process concerns. Another problem with this compact is that it requires nurses practicing telemedicine to be aware of the laws in the state where the *patient* is located. For nurses who work at national or regional facilities that provide telephonic consultations to patients, this aspect of the compact is quite troubling. From a legal viewpoint, the compact doesn't stand firm as the law has long held that the standard of care applicable to a given patient care situation is based not upon local conventions but on a nationally recognizable standard for patient care. Nevertheless, as of July 26, 2001, 15 states have enacted legislation adopting the compact (Arkansas, Arizona, Delaware, Iowa, Idaho, Maine, Maryland, Mississippi, North Carolina, North Dakota, Texas, Utah, Nebraska, South Dakota, and Wisconsin). Three more states (Georgia, Illinois, and New Jersey) have introduced legislation regarding the compact (NCSBNa). Figure 2-3 illustrates the states that, at press time, have adopted this compact.

SELECTED CASES

In the case of *Lange-Kessler v. Department of Education*, 1997, the U.S. Court of Appeals, Second District, held that because the right to privacy does not encompass the right to choose a direct-entry midwife to assist with childbirth, New York's Professional Midwifery Practice Act need only be rationally related to a legitimate state interest. Insuring that midwives will be qualified to handle the medical risks associated with pregnancy and childbirth is rationally related to the state's legitimate interest in protecting the health and welfare of mothers and infants, therefore, the law is constitutional. The New York law does not permit "direct entry" midwifery; only registered nurses may be midwives in this state.

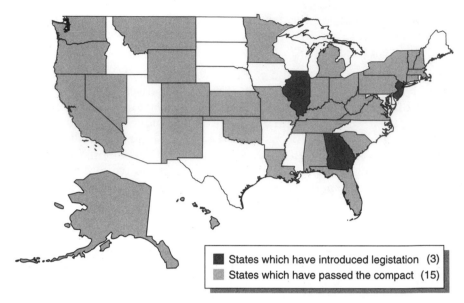

States which have introduced legistation (3)
States which have passed the compact (15)

FIGURE 2-3. Interstate compact.

The plaintiffs in this case, a direct entry midwife and several of her potential clients sued the New York Department of Education alleging that the law deprived the midwife of the ability to earn a living in her chosen profession in violation of the 14th amendment to the U.S. constitution by precluding the legal practice of direct entry midwives in that state. The patients alleged that the law violated their right to privacy under the first and 14th amendments of the U.S. constitution by restricting their right to choose a birthing style and a qualified attendant. The New York law defines the practice of midwifery as the management of normal pregnancies, child birth, and postpartum care as well as primary preventive reproductive health care of essentially healthy women as specified in the written practice agreement and includes newborn evaluation, resuscitation and referral for infants (New York Education Law, § 6951.1).

In the case of *Firman v. State Board of Medicine*, 1997, the court upheld an order of Pennsylvania's medical and nursing boards that suspended the plaintiff's nurse midwife and registered nurse licenses as a result of her guilty plea to felony counts of obtaining a Schedule IV controlled substance by fraud and possession of a Schedule IV controlled substance in Maryland. The relevant Pennsylvania law provided that "the license shall be automatically suspended upon . . . conviction of a felony under the Controlled Substance, Drug Device, and Cosmetic Act, or conviction of an offense under the laws of another jurisdiction, which, if committed in the Commonwealth, would be a felony under the Controlled Substance, Drug, Device and Cosmetic Act" (63 Pa. Stats. §422.40[b]). In its decision the court found that the law was not unconstitutional even though it mandated automatic suspension because the board has an important interest in preventing a potential harm caused by a drug-impaired practitioner. Therefore, the state interest served by the summary procedure outweighed the interests of the health care provider involved. Also, irreparable harm could result from the imposition of additional procedural safeguards prior to the board being allowed to suspend a license due to drug-related felonies.

In *State v. Mountjoy*, 1995, the Supreme Court of Kansas reviewed a criminal prosecution of midwives for practicing the healing arts without a license. The court held that the practice of the healing arts without a license is a strict liability crime not requiring criminal intent, and the court refused to consider the defendants' constitutionality issue for a lack of statutory authority to do so.

ENHANCE YOUR LEARNING

1. Participate in lobbying activities when your state's legislature is considering laws affecting APN practice.
2. Read your state's nurse practice act and compare it with the nurse practice act of one state that borders yours.
3. Find out if any politicians in your state are nurses and interview one of them regarding her or his views on APN practice in your state.
4. Interview an APN who has been practicing for at least 10 years regarding the changes that have taken place in his or her practice over time.

TEST YOUR COMPREHENSION

1. List the purposes of the Interstate Licensure Compact.
2. Identify at least two states that do not recognize the Clinical Nurse Specialist role.
3. Identify which state has two different types of Nurse Practitioners.
4. Identify three states that have passed the Interstate Licensure Compact.

REFERENCES

American College of Nurse-Midwives. (1995). *Nurse midwifery today, a handbook of state legislation.* Washington, DC: American College of Nurse-Midwives.
American College of Nurse-Midwives. (2000). *Information for foreign educated midwives & nurse midwives who seek to practice in the United States.* Available online at http://www.midwife.org/educ/Feminfo.htm.

Association of Women's Health, Obstetric, and Neonatal Nurses (AWHONN). (1998). NPs: the growing solution in health care delivery? *Lifelines, 2*(3) 19.

Iowa Board of Nursing Website. (2000). *Scope of practice of the advanced registered nurse practitioner*, available at http://www.state/ia.us/government/nursing/arnp.html.

Lamm, R. (1996). Regulating the health professions: A tale of two jurisdictions, *Advanced Practice Nursing Quarterly, 1*(4) 1–7.

Mannino, M. (1996, September). Legal aspects of nurse anesthesia practice. *Nursing Clinics of North America, 31*(3), 581–589.

National Council of State Boards of Nursing. (2000). Contact information. Available online at http://www.ncsbn.org/files/boards/boardscontact.asp.

National Council of State Boards of Nursing. (2001). *State compact bill status*. Available online at http://www.ncsbn.org/files/mutual/billstatus.asp.

Nurse Licensure Compact Final Version. (1998). Available online at http://www.ncsbn.org/files/mutual/compact.asp.

Pearson, L. (1999). Annual update of how each state stands on legislative issues affecting advanced nursing practice. *The Nurse Practitioner, 24*(1) 16–83.

Pearson, L. (1998). Annual update of how each state stands on legislative issues affecting advanced nursing practice. *The Nurse Practitioner, 23*(1), 14–66.

Pearson, L. (1997). Annual update of how each state stands on legislative issues affecting advanced nursing practice. *The Nurse Practitioner, 22*(1), 18–86.

Pearson, L. (1996). Annual update of how each state stands on legislative issues affecting advanced nursing practice. *The Nurse Practitioner,21*(1) 10–70.

Pearson, L. (1995). Annual update of how each state stands on legislative issues affecting advanced nursing practice. *The Nurse Practitioner, 20*(1), 13–51.

Pearson, L. (1994). Annual update of how each state stands on legislative issues affecting advanced nursing practice. *The Nurse Practitioner, 19*(1), 11–53.

Spatz, D. (1996). Women's health: The role of advanced practice nurses in the 21st century. *Nursing Clinics of North America, 31*(2), 269–277.

Tadych, R. Advanced practice nursing and collaborative practice: A regulatory perspective. Available online at: http://www.ecodev.state.mo.us/pr/nursing/ADVCTICE.htm.

Thornton, C. (1996). Nurse practitioner in a rural setting. *Nursing Clinics of North America 31*(3), 495–505.

Cases

Firman v. State Board of Medicine, 697 A.2d 291 (Pa. 1997).
Lange-Kessler v. Department of Education, 109 F.3d 137 (2d D. 1997).
State Board of Nursing v. Ruebke, 913 P.2d 142 (Kans. 1996).

State Boards of Nursing Addresses and Website Information

Alabama:
Alabama Board of Nursing
RSA Plaza, Suite 250
770 Washington Avenue
Montgomery, AL 36130-3900
Phone: (334) 242-4060
Fax: (334) 242-4360
Website: *http://www.abn.state.al.us*

Alaska:
Alaska Board of Nursing
Department of Comm. & Econ. Development
Division of Occupational Licensing
3601 C Street, Suite 722
Anchorage, AK 95503
Phone: (907) 269-8161
Fax: (907) 269-8196
Website: *http://www.dced.state.ak.us/occ/pnur.htm*

American Samoa:
American Samoa Health Services
Regulatory Board
LBJ Tropical Medical Center
Pago Pago, AS 96799
Phone: (684) 633-1222
Fax: (684) 633-1869

Arizona:
Arizona State Board of Nursing
1651 E. Morten Avenue, Suite 150
Phoenix, AZ 85020
Phone: (602) 331-8111
Fax: (602) 906-9365
Website: *http://www.azboardofnursing.org*

Arkansas: Arkansas State Board of Nursing
University Tower Building
1123 S. University, Suite 800
Little Rock, AR 72204
Phone: (501) 686-2700
Fax: (501) 686-2714
Website: *http://www.state.ar.us/nurse*

California: California Board of Registered Nursing
400 R Street, Suite 4030
Sacramento, CA 95814-6239
Phone: (916) 322-3350
Fax: (916) 327-4402
Website: *http://www.rn.ca.gov*

Midwifery Licensing Program
Medical Board of California
1426 Howe Avenue
Sacramento, CA 95825

Colorado: Colorado Board of Nursing
1560 Broadway, Suite 880
Denver, CO 80202
Phone: (303) 894-2430
Fax: (303) 894-2821
Website: *http://www.dora.state.co.us/nursing*

Connecticut: Connecticut Board of Examiners for Nursing
Division of Health Systems Regulation
410 Capitol Avenue, MS#12HSR
P.O. Box 340308
Hartford, CT 06134-0328
Phone: (860) 509-7624
Fax: (860) 509-7553
Website: *http://www.state.ct.us/dph*

Delaware: Delaware Board of Nursing
861 Silver Lake Blvd.
Cannon Building, Suite 203
Dover, DE 19904
Phone: (302) 739-4522
Fax: (302) 739-2711

District of Columbia: District of Columbia Board of Nursing
Department of Health
825 N. Capitol Street, N.E., 2nd Floor
Room 2224
Washington, DC 20002
Phone: (202) 442-4778
Fax: (202) 442-9431

Florida: Florida Board of Nursing
4080 Woodcock Drive, Suite 202
Jacksonville, FL 32207
Phone: (904) 858-6940
Fax: (904) 858-6964
Website: *http://www.doh.state.fl.us/mqa/nursing/
rnhome.htm*

Georgia: Georgia Board of Nursing
237 Coliseum Drive
Macon, GA 31217-3858
Phone: (912) 207-1640
Fax: (912) 207-1660
Website: *http://www.sos.state.ga.us/ebd-rn*

Guam: Guam Board of Nurse Examiners
P.O. Box 2816
1304 East Sunset Boulevard
Agana, GU 96910
Phone: (671) 475-0251
Fax: (671) 477-4733

Hawaii: Hawaii Board of Nursing
Professional and Vocational Licensing Division
P.O. Box 3469
Honolulu, HI 96801
Phone: (808) 586-3000
Fax: (808) 586-2689

Idaho: Idaho Board of Nursing
280 N. 8th Street, Suite 210
P.O. Box 83720
Boise, ID 83720
Phone: (208) 334-3110
Fax: (208) 334-3262
Website: *http://www.state.id.us/ibn/ibnhome.htm*

Illinois: Illinois Department of Professional Regulation
James R. Thompson Center
100 West Randolph, Suite 9-300
Chicago, IL 60601
Phone: (312) 814-2715
Fax: (312) 814-3145
Website: *http://www.state.il.us/dpr*

Indiana: Indiana State Board of Nursing
Health Professions Bureau
402 W. Washington Street, Room W041
Indianapolis, IN 46204
Phone: (317) 232-2960
Fax: (317) 233-4236
Website: *http://www.ai.org/hpb*

Iowa: Iowa Board of Nursing
River Point Business Park
400 S.W. 8th Street, Suite B
Des Moines, IA 50309-4685
Phone: (515) 281-3255
Fax: (515) 281-4825
Website: *http://www.state.ia.us/government/nursing*

Kansas: Kansas State Board of Nursing
Landon State Office Building
900 S.W. Jackson, Suite 551-S
Topeka, KS 66612
Phone: (785) 296-4929
Fax: (785) 296-3929
Website: *http://www.ink.org/public/ksbn*

Kentucky: Kentucky Board of Nursing
312 Whittington Parkway, Suite 300
Louisville, KY 40222
Phone: (502) 329-7000
Fax: (502) 329-7011
Website: *http://www.kbn.state.ky.us*

Louisiana: Louisiana State Board of Nursing
3510 N. Causeway Boulevard, Suite 501
Metairie, LA 70003
Phone: (504) 838-5332
Fax: (504) 838-5349
Website: *http://www.lsbn.state.la.us*

Maine: Maine State Board of Nursing
158 State House Station
Augusta, ME 04333
Phone: (207) 287-1133
Fax: (207) 287-1149
Website: *http://www.state.me.us/pfr/auxboards/nurhome.htm*

Maryland: Maryland Board of Nursing
4140 Patterson Avenue
Baltimore, MD 21215
Phone: (410) 585-1900
Fax: (410) 358-3530
Website: *http://dhmhld.dhmh.state.md.us/mbn*

Michigan: Michigan CIS/Office of Health Services
Ottawa Towers North
611 W. Ottawa, 4th Floor
Lansing, MI (NEED ZIP)
Phone: (517) 373-9102
Fax: (517) 373-2179
Website: *http://www.cis.state.mi.us/bhser/genover.htm*

Minnesota: Minnesota Board of Nursing
2829 University Avenue, S.E.
Suite 500
Minneapolis, MN 55414
Phone: (612) 617-2270
Fax: (612) 617-2190
Website: *http://www.nursingboard.state.mn.us*

Mississippi: Mississippi Board of Nursing
1935 Lakeland Drive, Suite B
Jackson, MS 39216
Phone: (601) 987-4188
Fax: (601) 364-2352

Missouri: Missouri State Board of Nursing
3605 Missouri Boulevard
P.O. Box 656
Jefferson City, MO 65102-0656
Phone: (573) 751-0681
Fax: (573) 751-0075
Website: *http://www.ecodev.state.mo.us/pr/nursing*

Montana: Montana State Board of Nursing
Arcade Building, Suite 4C
111 North Jackson
Helena, MT 59620-0513
Phone: (406) 444-2071
Fax: (406) 444-7759
Website: *http://www.com.state.mt.us/License/POL/
    index.htm*

Nebraska: Nebraska Health and Human Services System
Dept. of Regulation and Licensure, Nursing Section
301 Centennial Mall South, P.O. Box 94986
Lincoln, NE 68509-4986
Phone: (402) 471-4376
Fax: (402) 471-3577
Website: *http://www.hhs.state.ne.us/crl/nns.htm*

Nevada: Nevada State Board of Nursing
1755 East Plumb Lane, Suite 260
Reno, NV 89502
Phone: (775) 688-2620
Fax: (775) 688-2628
Website: *http://www.state.nv.us/boards/nsbn*

New Hampshire: New Hampshire Board of Nursing
78 Regional Drive, Bldg. B
P.O. Box 3898
Concord, NH 03302
Phone: (603) 271-2323
Fax: (603) 271-6605
Website: *http://www.state.nh.us/nursing*

New Jersey: New Jersey Board of Nursing
124 Halsey Street, 6th Floor
P.O. Box 45010
Newark, NJ 07101
Phone: (973) 504-6586
Fax: (973) 648-3481
Website: *http://www.state.nj.us/lps/ca/medical.htm*

New Mexico: New Mexico Board of Nursing
4206 Louisiana Boulevard, NE
Suite A
Albuquerque, NM 87109
Phone: (505) 841-8340

Fax: (505) 841-8347
Website: *http://www.state.nm.us/clients/nursing*

New York: New York State Board of Nursing
State Education Department
Cultural Education Center, Room 3023
Albany, NY 12230
Phone: (518) 474-3845
Fax: (518) 474-3706
Website: *http://www.nysed.gov/prof/nurse.htm*

North Carolina: North Carolina Board of Nursing
3724 National Drive
Raleigh, NC 27602
Phone: (919) 782-3211
Fax: (919) 781-9461
Website: *http://www.ncbon.com*

North Dakota: North Dakota Board of Nursing
919 South 7th Street, Suite 504
Bismark, ND 58504
Phone: (701) 328-9777
Fax: (701) 328-9785
Website: *http://www.ndbon.org*

Ohio: Ohio Board of Nursing
17 South High Street, Suite 400
Columbus, OH 43215-3413
Phone: (614) 466-3947
Fax: (614) 466-0388
Website: *http://www.state.oh.us/nur*

Oklahoma: Oklahoma Board of Nursing
2915 N. Classen Boulevard, Suite 524
Oklahoma City, OK 73106
Phone: (405) 962-1800
Fax: (405) 962-1821

Oregon: Oregon State Board of Nursing
800 N.E. Oregon Street, Box 25
Suite 465
Portland, OR 97232
Phone: (503) 731-4745
Fax: (503) 731-4755
Website: *http://www.osbn.state.or.us*

Pennsylvania: Pennsylvania State Board of Nursing
124 Pine Street
P.O. Box 2649
Harrisburg, PA 17101
Phone: (717) 783-7142
Fax: (717) 783-0822
Website: *http://www.dos.state.pa.us/bpoa/nurbd.htm*

Puerto Rico: Commonwealth of Puerto Rico
Board of Nurse Examiners
800 Roberto H. Todd Avenue
Room 202, Stop 18
Santurce, PR 00908
Phone: (787) 725-8161
Fax: (787) 725-7903

Rhode Island: Rhode Island Board of Nurse Registration and
Nursing Education
Cannon Health Building
Three Capitol Hill, Room 104
Providence, RI 02908
Phone: (401) 222-3855
Fax: (401) 222-2158

South Carolina: South Carolina State Board of Nursing
110 Centerview Drive
Suite 202
Columbia, SC 29210
Phone: (803) 896-4550
Fax: (803) 896-4525
Website: *http://www.llr.state.sc.us/bon.htm*

South Dakota: South Dakota Board of Nursing
4300 South Louise Avenue, Suite C-1
Sioux Falls, SD 57106-3124
Phone: (605) 362-2760
Fax: (605) 362-2768
Website: *http://www.state.sd.us/dcr/nursing*

Tennessee: Tennessee State Board of Nursing
426 Fifth Avenue North
Cordell Hull Building, 1st Floor
Nashville, TN 37247
Phone: (615) 532-5166

Fax: (615) 741-7899
Website: *http://170.142.76.180/bmf-bin/BMFproflist.pl*

Texas:

Texas Board of Nurse Examiners
333 Guadalupe, Suite 3-460
Austin, TX 78701
Phone: (512) 305-7400
Fax: (512) 305-7401
Website: *http://www.bne.state.tx.us*

Utah:

Utah State Board of Nursing
Heber M. Wells Building, 4th Floor
160 East 300 South
Salt Lake City, UT 84111
Phone: (801) 530-6628
Fax: (801) 530-6511
Website: *http://www.commerce.state.ut.us/*

Vermont:

Vermont State Board of Nursing
109 State Street
Montpelier, VT 05609-1106
Phone: (802) 828-2396
Fax: (802) 828-2484
Website: *http://vtprofessionals.org/nurses*

Virgin Islands:

Virgin Islands Board of Nurse Licensure
Veterans Drive Station
St. Thomas, VI 00803
Phone: (340) 776-7397
Fax: (340) 777-4003

Virginia:

Virginia Board of Nursing
6606 W. Broad Street, 4th Floor
Richmond, VA 23230
Phone: (804) 662-9909
Fax: (804) 662-9512
Website: *http://www.dhp.state.va.us*

Washington:

Washington State Nursing Care Quality Assurance
  Commission
Department of Health
1300 Quince Street, S.E.
Olympia, WA 98504-7864
Phone: (360) 236-4740

Fax: (360) 236-4738
Website: *http://www.doh.wa.gov/hsqa/hpqad/Nursing*

West Virginia: West Virginia Board of Examiners for Registered Professional Nurses
101 Dee Drive
Charleston, WV 25311
Phone: (304) 558-3596
Fax: (304) 558-3666
Website: *http://www.state.wv.us/nurses/rn*

Wisconsin: Wisconsin Department of Regulation and Licensing
1400 E. Washington Avenue
P.O. Box 8935
Madison, WI 53708
Phone: (608) 266-2112
Fax: (608) 267-0644
Website: *http://www.state.wi.us*

Wyoming: Wyoming State Board of Nursing
2020 Carey Avenue, Sutie 110
Cheyenne, WY 82002
Phone: (307) 777-7601
Fax: (307) 777-3519
Website: *http://commerce.state.wy.us/b%26c/nb*

Scope of Practice and Standard of Care

This chapter will explore the legal scope of practice generally permitted of advanced practice nurses and will outline relevant law regarding the standard of care to be applied to the advanced practice nurse (APN). Scope of practice answers the question "what can APNs do" and standard of care answers the question "how are APNs expected to perform." Due to the many legal implications of what APNs are allowed to do and how they are expected to do it, these subjects are among the most important for the APN to learn.

Scope of Practice

Each state has the ability to establish the scope of APN practice and does so via laws and regulations that outline the accepted scope of APN practice. These laws vary in their specificity and broadness of scope of practice they establish for the various categories of APN. Some state laws limit the APN's scope of practice by setting limits on the number of APNs with whom a physician can collaborate. In one state, that practice was challenged and found to be invalid. Box 3-1 discusses the case of *Arkansas State Nurses Association v. Arkansas State Medical Board*, 1984.

Other states regulate APN practice by requiring direct supervision of certified nurse anesthetists (CRNAs) while administering anesthesia. In one case, the violation of such a law was used to hold the providers liable for injuries to the patient when this requirement was not followed. Box 3-2 discusses the cases of *Central Anesthesia Associates, P.C. et al. v. Worthy et al., Castro v. Worthy et al., Moorehead v. Worthy et al., Executive Committee of the Baptist Convention of the State of Georgia d/b/a Georgia Baptist Medical Center v. Worthy et al.*, 1985.

In addition to state laws, some federal laws impact the APN's scope of practice. For example, federal law regarding Medicare used to require

BOX 3-1	Limits on the Number of APNs With Whom a Physician Can Collaborate

In the case of *Arkansas State Nurses Association v. Arkansas State Medical Board* (1984), the Arkansas Supreme Court invalidated the Medical Board's Regulation 10 as an unauthorized and illegal attempt to regulate registered nurse practitioners. The Medical Board's Regulation 10 provided that "No physician licensed to practice medicine in the State of Arkansas shall employ more than two (2) licensed Registered Nurse Practitioners at any one time; nor shall such physician assume responsibility for collaborating with or directing the activities of more than two (2) Registered Nurse Practitioners at any one time. Violation of this regulation shall constitute "malpractice" within the meaning of the Arkansas State Medical Practices Act and shall subject the violator to all penalties provided therein." The court found the regulation to be invalid insofar as it restricted the number of RNPs that may be employed by a physician or a group of physicians and insofar as it declared that a violation of the restriction is malpractice. The court felt that at a time when there is a need for additional medical care in some parts of the state, the effect of Regulation 10 would be to discourage registered nurses from becoming nurse practitioners, for the regulation would undeniably limit the number of jobs available to them.

that physicians supervise CRNAs. As of June 2000, the Health Care Financing Administration (HCFA) removed the federal requirement that nurse anesthetists be supervised by physicians when administering anesthesia to Medicare patients. However, this regulation is currently threatened by President George W. Bush's hold on all pending federal regulations issued late in the previous administration. In addition, bills have been introduced in the U.S. House and Senate to reinstate physician oversight of nurse anesthetists (AWHONN, 2001). Presently, the nursing statutes and boards of nursing in 29 states don't require physician supervision of CRNAs (AWHONN, 2000b). JCAHO does not require anesthesiologist supervision of CRNAs (AANA, 2000).

Professional associations also help to frame the scope of APN practice. For example, AWHONN, 1997, identifies three distinct but overlapping general roles in neonatal nursing care: the neonatal nurse, the APN in neonatal care, and the certified nurse midwife (CNM). The APN in the neonatal setting may provide direct patient care, staff, or patient education, or act as a neonatal case manager (AWHONN, 1997). The neonatal nurse practitioner manages a caseload of neonates with consultation, collaboration, and general supervision from a physician while exercising independent judgment in assessment, diagnosis, initiation of delegated medical procedures, and evaluation, (AWHONN, 1997). The clinical nurse specialist (CNS) in this setting provides continuity of care for high

BOX 3-2	Direct Supervision of CRNAs

In the cases of *Central Anesthesia Associates, P.C. et al. v. Worthy et al., Castro v. Worthy et al., Moorehead v. Worthy et al., Executive Committee of the Baptist Convention of the State of Georgia d/b/a Georgia Baptist Medical Center v. Worthy et al.* (1985), the state supreme court affirmed the lower court judgments finding the defendants negligent per se based upon OCGA § 43-26-9 (b). Mrs. Brenda Worthy gave birth to a baby boy without anesthesia at Georgia Baptist Hospital in September 1981, and the next day had a tubal ligation, a form of sterilization, performed by her obstetrician-gynecologist, Dr. Moorehead. Central Anesthesia Associates, P.C. (CAA), a professional corporation of eight anesthesiologists, three of whom were individual defendants, administered the anesthesia through Bonnie Gayle Castro, a registered nurse enrolled as a senior student nurse anesthetist in the school of anesthesia operated at the hospital by CAA.

At the time of induction, Castro was under the supervision of David Krencik, a physician assistant employed by CAA. Allegedly as the result of improper anesthesia procedure, Mrs. Worthy suffered a cardiac arrest with consequent brain damage and, at the time of trial, remained in a coma. Mr. and Mrs. Worthy sued CAA, student nurse anesthetist Castro, physician assistant Krencik, the three CAA anesthesiologists, Dr. Moorehead, intern Moore, and Georgia Baptist Hospital. Discovery disclosed that at the time of the occurrence in question, Dr. Moorehead, Dr. Moore and nurse Castro were in the seventh floor operating room where the surgery was being conducted. Physician assistant Krencik had been present when nurse Castro began administering the anesthesia but left for 10 to 15 minutes, during which time Mrs. Worthy's complications arose. At the time in question, four of CAA's eight anesthesiologists were not at the hospital. Dr. Cortes was CAA's officer of the day and was in his office on the second floor of the hospital. He denied assigning Castro or Krencik to conduct the procedure and denied having any knowledge of the case until he entered the seventh floor operating room in response to the emergency alarm. Nurse Castro decided that anesthesia should be administered by mask and authored the anesthesia plan. She placed Dr. Shantha's name on the preoperative consultation that prescribed the anesthesia plan and that must be approved by an anesthesiologist, but Dr. Shantha denied having signed or approved the plan. Nurse Castro placed Dr. Mani's name on the anesthesia record as the responsible anesthesiologist, but Dr. Mani denied having any involvement with Mrs. Worthy's treatment.

Plaintiffs' expert found that Mrs. Worthy's treatment and care failed to meet the proper standard of care in, among other things, the performance of a postpartum sterilization by administering anesthesia using a mask instead of an endotracheal tube, permitting an unlicensed student to administer anesthesia under the supervision of a physician assistant, and failure to properly oxygenate the patient during the administration of anesthesia. The plaintiffs moved for partial summary judgment on the issue of negligence

(continued)

BOX 3-2	Direct Supervision of CRNAs (Continued)

per se for violating OCGA § 43-26-9 (b). The court of appeals affirmed as to CAA, nurse Castro, physician assistant Krencik, and the three named anesthesiologists, holding that all of these defendants had breached their statutory duty by allowing an uncertified student nurse anesthetist to administer anesthesia while not "under the direction and responsibility" of an anesthesiologist as required by OCGA § 43-26-9 (b). The Court of Appeals also held that the hospital, which used a surgical consent form stating that anesthesia would be administered under the direct supervision of an anesthesiologist of CAA and which contracted with CAA to operate the school of anesthesia to which it lent its name, facilities, funding, and services and which contemplated use of student anesthetists, had also violated its legal duty by knowingly permitting CAA to violate OCGA § 43-26-9. OCGA § 43-26-9 (b) provides: "In any case where it is lawful for a duly licensed physician practicing medicine under the laws of this state to administer anesthesia, such *anesthesia may also lawfully be administered by a certified registered nurse anesthetist, provided that such anesthesia is administered under the direction and responsibility of a duly licensed physician with training or experience in anesthesia.*" (Emphasis supplied.) It was uncontradicted in the record that nurse Castro was a student, not a certified registered nurse anesthetist (CRNA). Moreover, each of the available anesthesiologists denied that nurse Castro was administering anesthesia under his direction and responsibility. The Supreme Court therefore agreed that the defendants violated OCGA § 43-26-9 (b) as a matter of law. The court held that the standard of conduct established by OCGA § 43-26-9 (b) is that anesthesia may not lawfully be administered by a certified registered nurse anesthetist except under the direction and responsibility of a duly licensed physician with training and experience in anesthesia. In this case, nurse Castro was not certified and such direction and responsibility were absent. In addition, the court rejected nurse Castro's contention that she should not be held to the standard of care and skill of a certified registered nurse anesthetist, but only to the standard of care and skill of a second year student nurse anesthetist.

risk neonates and infants and their families through direct patient care and nursing case management and may also provide consultation and education to families and staff, as well as initiating and participating in research projects and implementing research findings (AWHONN, 1997). The certified nurse midwife (CNM) in this setting manages low risk neonates in consultation and collaboration with physicians and other APNs and provides education about the neonate to the family and specialty education to other members of the health care community (AWHONN, 1997). AWHONN (1996) notes that the role of the women's health care nurse practitioner is dynamic and provides comprehensive health care, including wellness promotion and primary care in a variety of settings.

With varying results, physicians' organizations have also attempted to play a role in shaping the scope of practice of APNs. For example, in a 1991 policy statement the American College of Emergency Physicians expressed the opinion that nurse practitioners (NPs) may only render care "under the supervision of an emergency physician who is ultimately responsible for the patient's medical care. . . . Written protocols . . . should be carefully developed by the medical director of the emergency department" (American College of Emergency Physicians, 1991). Despite these pronouncements, Curry, 1994, notes that many NPs practicing in the emergency department do not face this issue and are able to practice under protocols without physician oversight on each patient.

Many states define the scope of practice of APNs by specific reference to definitions of scope of practice set forth by APN professional organizations. One that is frequently cited is the definition by the American Association of Nurse Anesthetists (AANA, 2000). Box 3-3 contains the AANA's definition of the CRNA's scope of practice.

BOX 3-3 | **AANA Definition of CRNA Scope of Practice**

The scope of practice of CRNAs includes but is not limited to:

- Performing and documenting a pre-anesthetic assessment and evaluation of the patient, including requesting consultations and diagnostic studies; selecting, obtaining, ordering, and administering pre-anesthetic medications and fluids; and obtaining informed consent for anesthesia
- Developing and implementing an anesthetic plan
- Initiating the anesthetic technique, which may include general, regional, local, and sedation
- Selecting, applying, and inserting appropriate non-invasive and invasive monitoring modalities for continuous evaluation of the patient's physical status
- Selecting, obtaining, and administering the anesthetics and adjuvant and accessory drugs and fluids necessary to manage the anesthetic
- Managing the patient's airway and pulmonary status using current practice modalities
- Managing emergence and recovery from anesthesia by selecting, obtaining, ordering, and administering medications, fluids, and ventilatory support
- Discharging the patient from a post anesthesia care area and providing post anesthesia follow-up evaluation and care
- Implementing acute and chronic pain management modalities
- Responding to emergency situations by providing airway management, administration of emergency fluids and drugs, and using basic or advanced cardiac life support techniques

(AANA, 2000)

According to one author, NP scope of practice includes conducting physical examinations, taking medical histories, diagnosing and treating common acute minor illness or injuries, managing long-term chronic illnesses, ordering and interpreting diagnostic tests, and counseling and educating clients (Curry, 1994). As a practical matter, actual NP scope of practice varies widely depending upon the state of practice, due to the variations in the laws of the individual states regarding APN practice. Curry, 1994, identifies the following hindrances that NPs face in providing care: statutory and regulatory requirements for formal practice relationships with physicians; requirements for physician direction and supervision of practice; and restrictions of practice to certain sites, facilities, or geographic areas.

It is important for APNs to know about and document the scope of their practice not only for purposes of complying with the law, but also to enhance their status as professionals. Herman, 1998, describes several reasons for documenting acute care nurse practitioner (ACNP) practice: providing evidence of experience with procedures to be presented in the credentialing process; negotiating contracts with managed care organizations to calculate per capita cost of ACNP care; providing information that can be used to negotiate individual contracts with an employer as a way to demonstrate productivity; monitoring quality of practice and making appropriate changes as needed; and fulfilling professional obligations to clarify and validate role characteristics.

Standard of Care

What is the standard of care for APNs? Unfortunately there is no simple answer to this question. In general, the nursing statutes do not address this question, so it has been left up to the courts to determine. In several instances courts have determined that the standard of care for nurse practitioners is the same as that for a physician. Box 3-4 discusses the case of *Fein v. Permanente Medical Group, Inc.,* 1981.

In *Planned Parenthood v. Vines,* 1989, a patient sued Planned Parenthood and one of its nurse practitioners for injuries resulting from the NP's insertion of an IUD. In discussing the issue of which standard of care applied to the NP, the court noted that by the terms of the nursing statutes, a nurse practitioner is a specialist and as such must be held to the standard of care appropriate to persons of such superior knowledge and skill. The court went on to note that even though a nurse practitioner works under standing orders or a protocol established by a physician, that nurse must meet the standard of care to which nurses practicing that profession in the community are held, which must be established by expert testimony. At trial, expert testimony was given that the standard of care for nurse practitioners inserting IUDs was the same standard

BOX 3-4	Nurse Practitioner Standard of Care

In *Fein v. Permanente Medical Group, Inc.* (1981), a patient sued Kaiser Permanente Medical Group, alleging that a nurse practitioner and other providers employed by Kaiser had failed to diagnose his heart attack. The patient's expert witness testified at trial that the symptoms described by the patient should have indicated to the NP and to the Kaiser physicians who saw him several hours later that an EKG needed to be performed. In appealing the approximately 1 million dollar verdict to the California Supreme Court, the defendant contended, among other things, that the trial court misinstructed the jury on the standard of care by which the NP's conduct should be judged. In addition to the general BAJI jury instruction on the duty of care of a graduate nurse, the court told the jury "the standard of care required of a nurse practitioner is that of a physician and surgeon ... when the nurse practitioner is examining a patient or making a diagnosis." The relevant instruction read in full: "It is the duty of one who undertakes to perform the service of a trained or graduate nurse to have the knowledge and skill ordinarily possessed, and to exercise the care and skill ordinarily used in like cases, by trained and skilled members of the nursing profession practicing their profession in the same or similar locality and under similar circumstances. Failure to fulfill either of these duties is negligence. I instruct you that the standard of care required of a nurse practitioner is that of a physician and surgeon duly licensed to practice medicine in the state of California when the nurse practitioner is examining a patient or making a diagnosis."

The initial paragraph of this instruction tracks California's standard jury instruction BAJI No. 6.25; the second paragraph was an added instruction given at plaintiff's request. The Supreme Court agreed with defendant that this instruction was inconsistent with legislation setting forth general guidelines for the services that may properly be performed by registered nurses in this state. The court noted that Section 2725 of the Business and Professions Code, as amended in 1974, explicitly declared a legislative intent "to recognize the existence of overlapping functions between physicians and registered nurses and to permit additional sharing of functions within organized health care systems which provide for collaboration between physicians and registered nurses." Section 2725 also included, among the functions that properly fall within "the practice of nursing" in California, the "[observation] of signs and symptoms of illness, reactions to treatment, general behavior, or general physical condition, and . . . determination of whether such signs, symptoms, reactions, behavior or general appearance exhibit abnormal characteristics. . . ."

In light of these provisions, the court felt that the "examination" or "diagnosis" of a patient couldn't in all circumstances be said—as a matter of law—to be a function reserved to physicians, rather than registered nurses or nurse practitioners. The court went on to note that although plaintiff was

(continued)

BOX 3-4	Nurse Practitioner Standard of Care (Continued)

certainly entitled to have the jury determine (1) whether defendant medical center was negligent in permitting a nurse practitioner to see a patient who exhibited the symptoms of which plaintiff complained and (2) whether the NP met the standard of care of a reasonably prudent nurse practitioner in conducting the examination and prescribing treatment in conjunction with her supervising physician, the court should not have told the jury that the nurse's conduct in this case must—as a matter of law—be measured by the standard of care of a physician or surgeon. Despite this error in instruction, however, the Supreme Court felt that there was no prejudice to the defendant Kaiser Permanente as the negligence of a Kaiser physician who saw the patient several hours after the NP was enough to support a finding for the plaintiff in this case.

applicable to physicians. Thus in this case it was established that the NP was held to the standard of care applicable to a physician performing the same medical task. Similarly, the court in *Berdyck v. Shinde*, 1993, noted ". . . the fact that a particular act is within a physician's duty of care does not necessarily exclude it from the duty of care owed to the patient by the nurse. Depending on the facts and circumstances, the same act may be within the scope of their separate duties of care because it is, coincidentally, within their respective standards of conduct. Whether it is or is not is a question of fact to be determined by the standard of conduct required, which is proved by expert testimony."

In *Jenkins v. Payne*, 1996, the court ruled that based upon expert testimony, all the defendants (including a nurse practitioner, a family practice physician, and a gynecologist) were negligent in failing to diagnose plaintiff's breast cancer, and that all the defendants were subject to the same standard of care. The court in *Lane v. Otts*, 1982, recognized that the standard to be applied is not limited to what local practitioners would do but is rather the national standard. (The locality rule has been all but abandoned by courts in modern times.) In this case, an anesthesiology group was sued as a result of alleged negligence of a CRNA employed by the group. The CRNA failed to call for assistance when she first realized that she was having a problem ventilating the patient. The court recognized that this failure was a departure from the accepted standard of care not only in the city where this incident occurred but also in the national medical community.

As with scope of practice issues, professional associations also help to frame the standard of care to be applied to the various categories of APN. As an example, AWHONN, 1996, has developed guidelines for practice for womens' health nurse practitioners that include specific competencies in the areas of client care, nurse–client relationship, health education and counseling, professional role, managing health care delivery, and quality of care. The American College of Nurse-Midwives (ACNM), 1993, promulgated standards for the practice of nurse midwifery, which are listed in Box 3-5. The ACNM also publishes Guidelines for the Incorporation of New Procedures into Nurse-Midwifery Practice, which was last revised in 1992.

The AANA has established standards for CRNA practice including a standard for office based anesthesia practice outlined in Box 3-6.

Peer Review

Peer review systems can also shape the standard of care for APNs. Stein, 1996, provides an overview of peer review in Chapter 1 of the New York chapter of the ACNM from 1987 to 1994. In this overview Stein reminds us that the peer review process reviews care by evaluating standards, process, and outcomes by reviewing midwifery service protocols, charts, and statistics. She noted that under current New York law, nursing peer review was not specifically included in laws protecting physician peer review discussions from discovery. In performing a service peer review, there are several components that must be reviewed:

BOX 3-5	**ACNM Standards**

Standards for the practice of nurse midwifery include the following:

- Nurse midwifery care is provided by qualified practitioners.
- Nurse midwifery care supports individual rights and self-determination within boundaries of safety.
- Nurse midwifery care comprises knowledge, skills, and judgments that foster the delivery of safe and satisfying care.
- Nurse midwifery care is based upon knowledge, skills, and judgments, which are reflected in written policies/practice guidelines.
- Nurse midwifery care is provided in a safe environment.
- Nurse midwifery care occurs within the health care system of the community using appropriate resources for referrals to meet medical, psychosocial, economic, and cultural or family needs.
- Nurse midwifery care is documented in legible, complete health records.
- Nurse midwifery care is evaluated according to an established program for quality assessment that includes a plan to identify and resolve problems.

(ACNM, 1993).

BOX 3-6	AANA Standards

AANA standards for office-based CRNA practice include the following requirements:

1. Perform a thorough and complete preanesthesia assessment.
2. Obtain informed consent for the planned anesthetic intervention from the patient or legal guardian.
3. Formulate a patient-specific plan for anesthesia care.
4. Implement and adjust the anesthesia care plan based on the patient's physiological response.
5. Monitor the patient's physiologic condition as appropriate for the type of anesthesia and specific patient needs.
6. Completely, accurately, and timely document pertinent information on the patient's medical record.
7. Transfer the responsibility for care of the patient to other qualified providers in a manner that assures continuity of care and patient safety.
8. Adhere to appropriate safety precautions, as established within the institution, to minimize the risks of fire, explosion, electrical shock and equipment malfunction; document on the patient's medical record that the anesthesia machine and equipment were checked.
9. Take precautions to minimize the risk of infection to the patient, the CRNA, and other health care providers.
10. Assess anesthesia care to assure its quality and contribution to positive patient outcomes.
11. Respect and maintain the basic rights of patients.

(AANA, 2000b).

1. Credentials and legal documents including licensure, evidence of hospital privileges, and a building license
2. Additional documents including the service's philosophy, protocols, policies, consultant physician statements, charts, and mechanisms for internal review
3. Statistics from the previous year including birth information, morbidity and mortality, and complications
4. Number and method of randomization of charts (Stein, 1996).

Stein, 1996, notes that the standard of care for CNMs is the same regardless of location of the practice site. Midwifery service protocols represent the scope of practice that a CNM is allowed in that particular service and represent internal standards of care; however, CNMs may not provide less care than current standards dictate but CNMs can and usually do provide more than minimum care (Stein, 1996).

Review of Selected State Laws

According to the most recent data available from the HRSA website, the following states have the largest numbers of nurses for each of the nine geographic areas of the country (New England, Mid-Atlantic, South Atlantic, East South Central, West South Central, East North Central, West North Central, Mountain, and Pacific): Massachusetts, New York, Florida, Tennessee, Texas, Illinois, Missouri, Arizona, and California. Specific data regarding the states with the largest numbers of APNs is not currently available. Laws from these nine states will be discussed throughout the remainder of this book to provide a sampling of the laws regarding APNs in the United States.

ARIZONA

APNs

Arizona specifically defines the scope of practice of APNs as follows: (1.) examine patients and establish medical diagnosis; (2.) admit patients to health care facilities; (3.) order, perform, and interpret laboratory, radiographic, and other diagnostic tests; (4.) identify, develop, implement, and evaluate a plan of care; (5.) prescribe and dispense medications; and (6.) refer to and consult with appropriate health care providers. All acts must be performed in collaboration with a physician (Arizona State Board of Nursing Rules, Art. 5, §R4-19-505).

APNs in Arizona must practice in accordance with the standards of nursing specified in the scope of practice statements according to the APN's specialty area listed in Box 3-7.

CNSs

In Arizona, the CNS may perform the following functions (Arizona BON Rules R4-19-512):

- Provide comprehensive assessment, analysis, and evaluation of individuals, families, communities, or any combination of individuals, families, and communities with complex health needs within an area of specialization
- Direct patient care as an advanced clinician within the clinical nurse specialist's specialty area and develop, implement, and evaluate treatment plans within that specialty
- Consult with the public and professionals in health care, business, and industry in the areas of research, case management, education, and administration
- Provide psychotherapy by clinical nurse specialists with expertise in adult, or child and adolescent psychiatric, and mental health nursing.

BOX 3-7	Standards of APN Practice to be Used in Arizona

- The Scope of Practice of the Primary Health Care Nurse Practitioner, 1985, pp. 3, 4, 6–9, American Nurses Association.
- Standards of Practice for the Primary Health Care Nurse Practitioner, 1987, pp. 4–9, American Nurses Association.
- Standards of Practice for PNP/As, 1987, National Association of Pediatric Nurse Associates and Practitioners.
- Standards of Practice of Nurse-Midwifery, 1993, pp. 2–6, American College of Nurse-Midwives.
- Nurse Providers of Neonatal Care, Guidelines for Educational Development and Practice, 1990, pp. 4–5, Nurses Association of the American College of Obstetrics and Gynecology.
- The Obstetric-Gynecologic/Women's Health Nurse Practitioner, Role Definition, Competencies, and Educational Guidelines, 3rd Edition, 1990, p. 2, NAACOG.
- Standards for the Nursing Care of Women and Newborns, 4th Edition, pp. 5–13, 15–25, 27–61, 63–77, NAACOG.
- Neonatal Nurse Practitioners, Standards of Education and Practice, 1992, p. 2, National Association of Neonatal Nurses.
- Statement on Psychiatric-Mental Health Clinical Nursing Practice and Standards of Psychiatric-Mental Health Clinical Nursing Practice, 1994, pp. 25–34, American Nurses Association.
- Standards of School Nursing Practice, 1983, pp. 5–11, American Nurses Association.
- Standards of Practice, 1993, American Academy of Nurse Practitioners.
- Scope of Practice for Nurse Practitioners, 1993, American Academy of Nurse Practitioners.
- Core Competencies for Basic Nurse-Midwifery Practice, 1992, American College of Nurse Midwives.

(AZ BON Rules R4-19-505C).

CALIFORNIA

CRNAs

Regulation 22 CCR 70235 (2000) regarding hospitals indicates that anesthesia care may be provided by physicians or dentists with anesthesia privileges, nurse anesthetists, or appropriately supervised trainees in an approved educational program.

NPs

"Nurse practitioner" in this state means a registered nurse who possesses additional preparation and skills in physical diagnosis, psychosocial assessment, and management of health–illness needs in primary health care and who has been prepared in a program that conforms to the board of nursing standards (16 CCR 1480).

California Welfare & Institutions Code § 14111.5 (2000) outlines permitted tasks of nurse practitioners in long-term health care facilities. A nurse practitioner may, to the extent consistent with his or her scope of practice, perform any of the following tasks otherwise required of a physician:

1. With respect to visits required by federal law or regulations, make alternating visits or more frequent visits if the physician is not available.
2. Perform any duty or task that is consistent with federal and state law or regulation within the scope of practice of nurse practitioners, if a physician approves, in writing, the admission of the individual to the facility; the medical care of each resident is supervised by a physician; a physician performs the initial visit and alternate required visits.

All responsibilities undertaken by a nurse practitioner in a long-term care facility must be performed in collaboration with the physician and pursuant to a standardized procedure among the physician, nurse practitioner, and facility. Except for those tasks indicated above that the physician must perform, any task required by federal law or regulation to be performed personally by a physician may be delegated to a nurse practitioner who is not an employee of the long-term health care facility.

CNMs

A certificate to practice nurse midwifery in California authorizes the holder to perform and repair episiotomies and to repair first-degree and second-degree lacerations of the perineum in a licensed acute care hospital and a licensed alternate birth center only if all of the following conditions are met: (1.) The supervising physician and any backup physician are credentialed to perform obstetrical care in the facility; (2.) The episiotomies are performed pursuant to protocols developed and approved by the supervising physician; the CNM; the director of the obstetrics (OB) department or the director of the family practice (FP) or both if a physician in the OB department or the family practice department is a supervising physician or an equivalent person if there is no specifically identified OB or FP department; the interdisciplinary practices committee if applicable; the facility administrator or his or her designee. The protocols and the procedures must relate to the performance and repair of episiotomies and the repair of first- and second-degree lacerations of the perineum and must do all the following: Ensure that all complications are referred to a physician immediately; ensure immediate care of patients who are in need of care beyond the scope of practice of the CNM or emergency care for times when the supervising physician is not on the premises; and establish the number of CNMs that a supervising physician may supervise (B&P code § 2746.52). In California, the license to practice midwifery authorizes the holder, under the supervision of a licensed physician, to attend cases of normal childbirth and to provide prenatal, intrapartum, and postpartum care, including family planning care, for the mother and immediate care for the newborn (B&P code § 2507). In this state, the scope of nurse-midwifery practice includes:

- Providing necessary supervision, care, and advice in a variety of settings to women during the antepartal, intrapartal, postpartal, interconceptional periods, and family planning needs
- Conducting deliveries on his or her own responsibility and caring for the newborn and the infant, including preventive measures and the detection of abnormal conditions in mother and child
- Obtaining physician assistance and consultation when indicated
- Providing emergency care until physician assistance can be obtained
- Other practices and procedures included when the nurse-midwife and the supervising physician deem appropriate by using standardized procedures (Ca. Reg. Tit. 16, Div. 14, Art. 6, § 1463)

FLORIDA

APNs

The scope of practice for all categories of APNs in this state includes those functions that the APN has been educated to perform including the monitoring and altering of drug therapies and initiation of appropriate therapies according to the established protocol and consistent with the practice setting (64B9-4.009, F.A.C.). An APN must perform authorized functions within the framework of an established protocol. A physician must maintain supervision for directing the specific course of medical treatment. Within the established framework, an APN may

- Monitor and alter drug therapies.
- Initiate appropriate therapies for certain conditions.
- Perform additional functions as may be determined by the board.
- Order diagnostic tests and physical and occupational therapy (Fla. Stats. Ch. 464, §464.012).

CRNAs

In addition to the general functions specified above, a CRNA may, to the extent authorized by established protocol approved by the medical staff of the facility in which the anesthetic service is performed, perform any or all of the following:

- Determine the health status of the patient as it relates to the risk factors and to the anesthetic management of the patient through the performance of the general functions.
- Based on history, physical assessment, and supplemental laboratory results, determine, with the consent of the responsible physician, the appropriate type of anesthesia within the framework of the protocol.
- Order, under the protocol, preanesthetic medication.
- Perform, under the protocol, procedures commonly used to render the patient insensible to pain during the performance of surgical, obstetrical, therapeutic, or diagnostic clinical procedures. These procedures include ordering and administering regional, spinal, and general anesthesia; inhalation agents and techniques; intravenous agents and techniques; and techniques of hypnosis.
- Order or perform monitoring procedures indicated as pertinent to the anesthetic health care management of the patient.
- Support life functions during anesthesia health care including induction and intubation procedures, use of appropriate mechanical supportive devices, and management of fluid, electrolyte, and blood component balances.
- Recognize and take appropriate corrective action for abnormal patient responses to anesthesia, adjunctive medication, or other forms of therapy.
- Recognize and treat a cardiac arrhythmia while the patient is under anesthetic care.
- Participate in management of the patient while in the postanesthesia recovery area including ordering the administration of fluids and drugs.
- Place special peripheral and central venous and arterial lines for blood sampling and monitoring as appropriate (Fla. Stats. Ch. 464, §464.012).

NPs

The nurse practitioner may perform any or all of the following acts within the framework of an established protocol:

- Manage selected medical problems.
- Order physical and occupational therapy.
- Initiate, monitor, or alter therapies for certain uncomplicated acute illnesses.
- Monitor and manage patients with stable chronic diseases.
- Establish behavioral problems and diagnosis and make treatment recommendations (Fla. Stats. Ch 464, §464.012).

CNMs

The CNM may, to the extent authorized by an established protocol approved by the medical staff of the health care facility in which the midwifery services are performed or approved by the nurse midwife's physician backup when the delivery is performed in a patient's home, perform any or all of the following:

1. Perform superficial minor surgical procedures.
2. Manage the patient during labor and delivery to include amniotomy, episiotomy, and repair.
3. Order, initiate, and perform appropriate anesthetic procedures.
4. Perform postpartum examination.
5. Order appropriate medications.
6. Provide family-planning services and well-woman care.
7. Manage the medical care of the normal obstetrical patient and the initial care of a newborn patient (Fla. Stats. Ch 464, §464.012).

ILLINOIS

Regulation 225 ILCS 60/54.5 outlines physician delegation of authority. A physician with an unrestricted license to practice medicine in this state may collaborate with an APN in accordance with the requirements of the Nursing and Advanced Practice Nursing Act. Collaboration is for the purpose of providing medical direction; no employment relationship is required. A written collaborative agreement must conform to the requirements of the Nursing and Advanced Practice Nursing Act. The written collaborative agreement must be for services that the collaborating physician generally provides to his or her patients in the normal course of clinical medical practice. Physician medical direction will be adequate with respect to collaboration with certified nurse practitioners, certified nurse midwives, and clinical nurse specialists if the collaborating physician

1. Participates in the joint formulation and joint approval of orders or guidelines with the APN and periodically reviews such orders and the services provided patients under such orders in accordance with accepted standards of medical practice and advanced practice nursing practice
2. Is on site at least once a month to provide medical direction and consultation
3. Is available through telecommunications for consultation on medical problems, complications, or emergencies, or patient referral (225ILCS60154.5).

The collaborating physician must have access to the medical records of all patients attended to by an APN (225ILCS60154.5).

CRNAs

Regulation 210 ILCS 5/6.5 (2000) indicates that all ambulatory surgical treatment centers licensed by the state must comply with the following requirements (210 ILCS 85/10.7 [2000] provides identical rules for licensed hospitals):

1. No policy, rule, regulation, or practice will be inconsistent with the provision of adequate collaboration, including medical direction of licensed APNs.
2. A licensed physician, dentist, or podiatrist may be assisted by a licensed APN granted clinical privileges to assist in surgery by the consulting committee of the ambulatory surgical treatment center (ASTC).
3. The anesthesia service must be under the direction of a physician licensed to practice medicine in all its branches who has had specialized preparation or experience in the area or who has completed a residency in anesthesiology. An anesthesiologist, Board-certified or Board-eligible, is recommended. Anesthesia services may only be administered pursuant to the order of a physician licensed to practice medicine in all its branches, licensed dentist, or licensed podiatrist.
   (a) The individuals who, with clinical privileges granted by the medical staff and ASTC, may administer anesthesia services are limited to the following: an anesthesiologist; a physician licensed to practice medicine in all its branches; a dentist with authority to administer anesthesia; or a licensed CRNA.
   (b) For anesthesia services, an anesthesiologist must participate through discussion of and agreement with the anesthesia plan and must remain physically present and be available on the premises during the delivery of anesthesia services for diagnosis, consultation, and treatment of emergency medical conditions. In the absence of 24-hour availability of anesthesiologists with clinical privileges, an alternate policy (requiring participation, presence, and availability of a physician licensed to practice medicine in all its branches) must be developed by the medical staff consulting committee in consultation with the anesthesia service and included in the medical staff consulting committee policies.
   (c) A CRNA is not required to possess prescriptive authority or a written collaborative agreement to provide anesthesia services ordered by a licensed physician, dentist, or podiatrist. Licensed CRNAs are authorized to select, order, and administer drugs and apply the appropriate medical devices in the provision of anesthesia services under the anesthesia plan agreed with by the anesthesiologist or, in the absence of an available anesthesiologist with clinical privileges, agreed with by the operating physician, operating dentist, or operating podiatrist in accordance with the medical staff consulting committee policies of a licensed ambulatory surgical treatment center.

An anesthesiologist or a physician licensed to practice medicine in all its branches may collaborate with a CRNA in accordance with the Nursing and Advanced Practice Nursing Act. Medical direction for a CRNA will be adequate if

1. An anesthesiologist or a physician participates in the joint formulation and joint approval of orders or guidelines and periodically reviews the orders and the services provided patients under the orders; and
2. For anesthesia services, the anesthesiologist or physician participates through discussion of and agreement with the anesthesia plan and is physically present and available on the premises during the delivery of anesthesia services for diagnosis, consultation, and treatment of emergency medical conditions. Anesthesia services in a hospital must be conducted in accordance with the Hospital Licensing Act and in an ambulatory surgical treatment center in accordance with the Ambulatory Surgical Treatment Center Act. (210 ILCS 85/10.7 [2000]). The anesthesiologist or operating physician must agree with the anesthesia plan prior to the delivery of services.

68 Ill. Adm. Code 1220.520 indicates that a licensed dentist must hold a deep sedation or general anesthesia permit to perform dentistry while a CRNA administers deep sedation or general anesthesia. A dentist must hold a conscious parenteral sedation permit to perform dentistry while a CRNA administers parenteral conscious sedation (68 Ill. Adm. Code 1220.510).

In ambulatory surgical treatment centers, anesthesia may be administered only by the following persons, each having been granted specific anesthesia privileges by the consulting committee or a committee designated by the consulting committee:

- A qualified anesthesiologist
- A physician licensed to practice medicine in all its branches
- A dentist who has been approved to administer anesthesia for dental surgery
- A CRNA who is implementing the orders of a qualified anesthesiologist, or the physician, dentist, or podiatrist performing the procedure; the qualified anesthesiologist, physician, dentist, or podiatrist who has ordered the anesthesia must be on the premises of the facility during the administration of the anesthesia (77 Ill. Adm. Code 205.530).

The person administering anesthesia, or a person who has equivalent practice privileges, must be present in the facility during the recovery of the patient to whom anesthesia was administered (77 Ill. Adm. Code 205.530).

MASSACHUSETTS

CRNAs

The scope of practice of a nurse anesthetist in Massachusetts is the preparation of a patient for anesthesia, its administration, and the provision of postoperative care according to guidelines approved and developed in compliance with state law. The CRNA's scope of practice includes:

- Performing an immediate preoperative patient evaluation
- Selecting an anesthetic agent
- Including and maintaining anesthesia and managing intraoperative pain relief
- Supporting life functions during the induction and period of anesthesia, including intratracheal intubation, monitoring of blood loss and replacement and electrolytes, and the maintenance of cardiovascular and respiratory function
- Recognizing abnormal patient responses to anesthesia or to any adjunctive medication or other form of therapy and taking corrective action
- Providing professional observation and resuscitative care during the immediate postoperative period and until a patient has regained control of his vital functions
- Such other additional professional activities as authorized by the guidelines under which a particular nurse anesthetist practices (244 CMR 4.26).

NPs

The scope of practice of a nurse practitioner in Massachusetts includes:

- Assessing the health status of individuals and families by obtaining health and medical histories, performing physical examinations, diagnosing health and developmental problems, and caring for patients suffering from acute and chronic diseases by managing therapeutic regimens according to guidelines approved and developed in compliance with state law
- Other additional professional activities as authorized by the guidelines under which a particular nurse practitioner practices (244 CMR 4.26).

Regulation 105 CMR 130.640 requires that each hospital providing special care nursery services have on-site coverage 24 hours a day by either a pediatrician or neonatal nurse practitioner who meets the requirements listed below and who is immediately available to the special care nursery and the delivery room. The requirements for the neonatal nurse practitioner are as follows:

1. Preferably have a master's degree but at a minimum have a baccalaureate degree.
2. Be certified as a neonatal nurse practitioner by a nationally recognized organization.
3. Be licensed to practice in the expanded role by the Massachusetts Board of Registration in Nursing.

Before assignment to provide on-site coverage, each neonatal nurse practitioner must successfully complete the American Heart Association/ American Academy of Pediatrics neonatal resuscitation course or an equivalent. There must be a planned schedule for the practitioner to rotate regularly to the Level 3 service with which the Level 2 service has a collaboration agreement with frequency as to assure that the neonatal nurse practitioner has the opportunity to maintain skills in emergency procedures. At a minimum, the rotation must occur annually and the neonatal nurse practitioner (NNP) must be evaluated periodically by both Level 2 and Level 3 services. Neonatal nurse practitioners must have credentials through the hospital's nursing department and medical staff and function under approved written guidelines for practice.

According to 105 CMR 130.640, neonatal nurse practitioners must also meet the criteria for delivery room and special care nursery coverage established by the director of the special care nursery; that criteria must include the skills necessary to provide emergency care to newborns. The nurse practitioner providing Level 2 coverage must have at least one year of recent experience functioning as a neonatal nurse practitioner on a service that provides high risk obstetrical and neonatal intensive care unit services. Neonatal nurse practitioners must be part of a team providing patient care and not retained only to provide off hour or holiday coverage at the Level 2 service. The schedule for coverage of the delivery room and special care nursery must reflect that pediatricians and neonatal nurse practitioners who are members of the team share responsibility for covering all shifts and collaborate in the ongoing care of infants and their families and in professional education activities. There must be written policies and procedures outlining the specific criteria for summoning pediatrician or neonatologist back-up coverage for consultation and for on-site assistance in the delivery room and special care nursery (105 CMR 130.640).

Regulation 130 CMR 421.424 indicates that in family planning agency services, the medical director or his or her designee must perform an on-site review of all NPs within the first 3 months of employment and semiannually thereafter; written reports of the reviews must be included in the NP's personnel file. Review must include observation and assessment of the NP's clinical skills in caring for a variety of patients. In family planning agencies, NPs may perform initial, routine, or annual visits, but physicians must see patients with medical problems (130 CMR

421.412). NPs may admit patients to long-term care facilities but must consult with the supervising physician by phone prior to writing the admission order. NPs may also discharge patients but must consult the supervising physician by phone prior to discharging a patient to an acute facility for a non-emergency situation, prior to transferring a patient to another facility, or prior to discharging a patient to home (105 CMR 150.003). The NP may discharge a long-term care patient to an acute facility in an emergency without the physician's prior approval if the physician cannot be contacted immediately (105 CMR 150.003). NPs may assist physicians during cardiac catheterizations within their scope of practice (105 CMR 130.940).

CNMs

The area of practice of a nurse midwife is defined by this state as the care of women throughout the course of pregnancy, labor, and delivery periods. It provides for care to mothers and their infants in the postpartum period as well as well-woman gynecological and family planning management. This care must be provided according to the standards deemed acceptable by the Board as well as guidelines approved and developed in compliance with other state laws. CNM scope of practice includes:

1. Assessing the health status of women and infants by obtaining health and medical histories, performing physical examinations, and diagnosing health and developmental problems
2. Instituting and providing health care to patients in a continuous manner, helping patients develop and understanding of the importance of following a prescribed therapeutic regimen, and arranging patient referrals to physicians or other health care providers
3. Providing instruction and counseling to women, their families, and other patient groups about the promotion and maintenance of personal health during pregnancy and the postnatal period
4. Acting in collaboration with other health care providers and agencies to provide coordinated services to women and their families
5. Managing the care of women with normal pregnancies during the labor, delivery, and postpartum period
6. Assessing the growth and development of infants
7. Managing diagnostic and therapeutic regimens for contraception and acute and chronic gynecologic illness
8. Such other additional professional activities as authorized by the guidelines under which a particular nurse midwife practices (244 CMR 4.26).

In an advisory ruling, the Massachusetts Board of Nursing (BON), 1998, indicated that first assisting at cesarean sections may be a component of nurse midwifery practice and may include handling tissue, providing exposure, using instruments, suturing, and providing hemostasis. A nurse midwife acting as a first assistant may not concurrently function as a scrub nurse. To function as a first assistant at cesarean sections, the CNM must have current licensure as a registered nurse in Massachusetts with current authorization from the Board of Registration in Nursing to practice as a nurse midwife; demonstrated ability to apply principles of asepsis and infection control; knowledge of surgical anatomy, physiology, pathophysiology, and operative technique related to cesarean sections; ability to perform cardiopulmonary resuscitation; ability to perform effectively in stressful and emergency situations; ability to recognize safety hazards and initiate appropriate preventive and corrective action; ability to perform effectively and harmoniously as a member of the operative team; and completion of formal study, supervised practice, and comprehensive evaluation as required in the American College of Nurse-Midwives' Guidelines for the Incorporation of New Procedures into Midwifery Practice. A CNM can be the director of a free-standing birth center if the CNM has obstetrics privileges at a nearby hospital; a CNM can also be the director of a hospital-affiliated birth center (105 CMR 142.501).

CNSs

The scope of practice of a psychiatric nurse mental health clinical nurse specialist in this state is the delivery of mental health care and includes evaluative, diagnostic, consultative, and therapeutic procedures established in accordance with guidelines approved and developed in compliance with state law (244 CMR 4.26).

MISSOURI

APNs

The APN in Missouri is defined as a registered professional nurse who is a nurse anesthetist, nurse midwife, nurse practitioner, or clinical nurse specialist. Registered professional nurses recognized by the Missouri State Board of Nursing as being eligible to practice as APNs function clinically within the state of Missouri Nursing Practice Act and all other applicable rules and regulations and within the professional scope and standards of their advanced practice nursing clinical specialty area and consistent with their formal advanced nursing education and national certification, if applicable, or within their education, training, knowledge, judgment, skill, and competence as registered professional nurses (4 CSR 200-4.100).

With a collaborative practice arrangement in place, APNs in Missouri may do the following:

- Provide health care services that include the diagnosis and initiation of treatment for acutely or chronically ill or injured persons.

- Provide health care services for acute self-limited or well-defined problems.
- Provide health care services for other than acute self-limited or well-defined problems.
- Provide care to well patients or those with narrowly circumscribed conditions in public health clinics or community health settings that provide specific population-based health services.
- Provide specific population-based health services in association with public health clinics (Missouri BON, 1998).

In a Level 2 trauma center, anesthesia staffing requirements may be fulfilled when the staff anesthesiologist is promptly available and an in-house CRNA capable of assessing emergent situations in trauma patients and initiating and providing any indicated treatment is available. In a Level 3 trauma center, anesthesia requirements may be fulfilled by a CRNA with physician supervision (19 CSR 30-40.430).

NEW YORK

CRNAs

CRNAs may administer anesthesia in free-standing ambulatory surgery centers under the direct personal supervision of a qualified physician, who may be the operating surgeon; and a physician must examine each patient immediately prior to surgery to evaluate the risk to anesthesia and the procedure to be performed (10 NYCRR § 755.4). In New York, CRNAs may administer anesthesia in hospitals under the supervision of an anesthesiologist who is immediately available as needed or under the supervision of the operating physician who has been found qualified by the governing body and the medical staff to supervise the administration of anesthetics and who has accepted responsibility for the supervision of the CRNA (10 NYCRR § 405.13). Hospitals must develop written policies regarding anesthesia procedures clearly delineating pre- and postanesthesia responsibilities. These policies must include, at a minimum, the following elements:

1. Preanesthesia physical evaluations must be performed by an individual qualified to administer anesthesia and recorded within 48 hours prior to surgery.
2. Routine checks must be conducted by the anesthetist prior to every administration of anesthesia to ensure the readiness, availability, cleanliness, sterility when required, and working condition of all equipment used in the administration of anesthetic agents.
3. All anesthesia care must be provided in accordance with accepted standards of practice and must ensure the safety of the patient

during the administration, conduct of, and emergence from anesthesia.

The following continuous monitoring is required during the administration of general and regional anesthetics. This continuous monitoring is not required during the administration of anesthetics for analgesia or during the administration of local anesthetics unless medically indicated. For continuous monitoring situations,

- An anesthetist must be continuously present in the operating room throughout the administration and the conduct of all general anesthetics, regional anesthetics, and monitored anesthesia care. If there is a documented hazard to the anesthetist that prevents the anesthetist from being continuously present in the operating room, provision must be made for monitoring the patient.
- All patients must be attended by the anesthetist during the emergence from anesthesia until they are under the care of qualified postanesthesia care staff or longer as necessary to meet the patient's needs.
- During all anesthetics, the heart sounds and breathing sounds of all patients must be monitored through the use of a precordial or esophageal stethoscope.
- During the administration and conduct of all anesthesia, the patient's oxygenation must be continuously monitored to ensure adequate oxygen concentration in the inspired gas and the blood through the use of a pulse oximeter or superior equipment. During every administration of general anesthesia using an anesthesia machine, the concentration of oxygen in the patient's breathing system must be measured by an oxygen analyzer with a low oxygen concentration limit alarm.
- All patient ventilation must be continuously monitored during the conduct of anesthesia. During regional anesthesia, monitored anesthesia care, and general anesthesia with a mask, the adequacy of ventilation must be evaluated through the continual observation of the patient's qualitative clinical signs. For every patient receiving general anesthesia with an endotracheal tube, the quantitative carbon dioxide content of expired gases must be monitored through the use of endtidal carbon dioxide analysis or superior technology. In all cases where ventilation is controlled by a mechanical ventilator, there must be in continuous use an alarm capable of detecting disconnection of any components of the breathing system.
- The patient's circulatory functions must be continuously monitored during all anesthetics. This must include the continuous display of the patient's electrocardiogram, from the beginning of

anesthesia until preparation to leave the anesthetizing location, and evaluation of the patient's blood pressure and heart rate at least every 5 minutes.

- During every administration of anesthesia, there must be immediately available a means to continuously measure the patient's temperature.

4. Intraoperative anesthesia records must document all pertinent events that occur during the induction, maintenance, and emergence from anesthesia. These pertinent events include the following: intraoperative abnormalities or complications, blood pressure, pulse, dosage and duration of all anesthetic agents, dosage and duration of other drugs and intravenous fluids, administration of blood and blood components, and general condition of the patient.

5. For inpatients, a postanesthetic follow-up evaluation and report by the individual who administered the anesthesia or by another individual qualified to administer anesthesia must be written between 3 and 48 hours after surgery, must note the presence or absence of anesthesia-related abnormalities or complications, and evaluate the patient for proper anesthesia recovery and document the general condition of the patient.

6. For outpatients, a postanesthesia evaluation for proper anesthesia recovery performed in accordance with policies and procedures approved by the medical staff must be documented for each patient prior to hospital discharge (10 NYCRR § 405.13).

NPs

In New York, NPs can make orders to be executed by RNs and LPNs (8 NYCRR § 64.6). Hospital emergency services may be provided by nurse practitioners, but these services must be done in collaboration with a licensed physician whose professional privileges include approval to work in the emergency service and in accordance with written practice protocols for these services (10 NYCRR § 405.19). In addition, the NP must meet the following standards:

- NPs in the emergency room must have successfully completed a course in ACLS or have had training and experience equivalent to ACLS when determined necessary by the hospital to meet anticipated patient needs or when a nurse practitioner is serving as the sole practitioner on duty in a hospital with less than 15,000 unscheduled emergency visits per year.
- NPs in the emergency room must have had training and experience equivalent to ATLS when determined necessary by the hospital to meet anticipated patient needs or when a nurse practitioner is serving as the sole practitioner on duty in a hospital with less than

15,000 unscheduled emergency visits per year (10 NYCRR § 405.19).

Hospitals that elect to use nurse practitioners in the emergency room must develop and implement written policies and treatment protocols subject to approval by the governing body that specify patient conditions that may be treated by a nurse practitioner without direct visual supervision of the emergency services attending physician (10 NYCRR § 405.19).

TENNESSEE

CRNAs

CRNAs may provide anesthesia services in hospitals (Tenn. Comp. R. & Regs. R. 1200-8-1-.07). Policies on anesthesia procedures must include the delineation of preanesthesia and postanesthesia responsibilities and must ensure that the following are provided for each patient

1. A preanesthesia evaluation or evaluation update conducted within 48 hours prior to surgery by an individual qualified to administer anesthesia
2. An intraoperative anesthesia record
3. For each inpatient, a written postanesthesia follow-up report prepared within 48 hours following surgery by an individual qualified to administer anesthesia or by the person who administered the anesthesia and submits the report by telephone
4. For each outpatient, a postanesthesia evaluation of anesthesia recovery prepared in accordance with policies and procedures approved by the medical staff (Tenn. Comp. R. & Regs. R. 1200-8-1-.07).

CRNAs may also administer anesthesia in an ambulatory surgery center (Tenn. Comp. R & R 1200-8-10-.06).

CNMs

The Tenn. Comp. R. & Regs. R. 1200-8-1-.05 (2000) indicates that CNMs may admit patients to hospitals with the concurrence of a physician member of the medical staff.

TEXAS

In Texas the Medical Practice Act provides for physicians' use of standing delegation orders, standing medical orders, physician's order, or other orders or protocols in delegating authority to APNs at sites serving medically underserved populations, at a physician's primary practice site, or at a site described below. Regulation 22 TAC § 193.6 establishes minimum standards for supervision by physicians of APNs for provision of services at such sites. This section also provides for the signing of a prescription by an APN after the person has been designated by the delegating physician and for use of prescriptions presigned by the supervising physician that may be carried out by an APN according to protocols. These protocols may authorize diagnosis of the patient's condition and treatment including prescription of dangerous drugs. Proper use of protocols allows integration of clinical data gathered by the APN. Neither the Medical Practice Act nor these rules authorize the exercise of independent medical judgment by APNs; the supervising physician remains responsible to the board and to his or her patients for acts performed under the physician's delegated authority. APNs remain professionally responsible for acts performed under the scope and authority of their own licenses.

Physician supervision of an APN at a site serving a medically underserved population will be adequate if a delegating physician

1. Receives a daily status report to be conveyed in person, by telephone, or by radio from the APN on any complications or problems encountered that are not covered by a protocol;
2. Visits the clinic in person at least once every 10 business days during regular business hours, when the APN is on site providing care, to observe and provide medical direction and consultation to include, but not be limited to
   • reviewing with the APN case histories of patients with problems or complications encountered,
   • personally diagnosing or treating patients requiring physician follow-up
   • verifying that patient care is provided by the clinic in accordance with a written quality assurance plan on file at the clinic that includes a random review and countersignature of at least 10% of the patient charts by the supervising physician;
3. Is available by telephone or direct telecommunication for consultation, assistance with medical emergencies or patient referrals;
4. Is responsible for the formulation or approval of such physician's orders, standing medical orders, standing delegation orders, or other orders or protocols and periodically reviews such orders and the services provided patients under such orders (22 TAC § 193.6).

If the APN is located at a site other than where the physician spends the majority of the physician's time, physician supervision must be documented through a log kept at the clinic where the APN is located. The log will include the names or identification numbers of patients discussed during the daily status reports, the times when the physician is on site, and a summary of what the physician did on site. This summary must include a description of the quality assurance activities conducted and the names of any patients seen or whose case histories were reviewed with the APN. The supervising physician must sign each log at the conclusion of each site visit. A log is not required if the APN is permanently located with the physician at a site where the physician spends the majority of the physician's time (22 TAC § 193.6).

If a delegating physician will be unavailable to supervise the APN, arrangements must be made for another physician to provide that supervision. The physician providing that supervision must affirm in writing that he or she is familiar with the protocols or standing delegation orders in use at the clinic and is accountable for adequately supervising care provided pursuant to those protocols or standing delegation orders by fulfilling the requirements for registration as an alternate supervising physician (22 TAC § 193.6).

CRNAs

A physician delegating the provision of anesthesia or anesthesia-related services in an outpatient setting to a CRNA must be in compliance with American Society of Anesthesiology (ASA) standards and guidelines when the CRNA provides a service specified in the ASA standards and guidelines to be provided by an anesthesiologist. In an outpatient setting, where a physician has delegated to a CRNA the ordering of drugs and devices necessary for the nurse anesthetist to administer an anesthetic or an anesthesia-related service ordered by a physician, a CRNA may select, obtain, and administer drugs, including determination of appropriate dosages, techniques, and medical devices for their administration and for maintaining the patient in sound physiologic status. This order need not be drug-specific, dosage-specific, or administration-technique specific. Pursuant to a physician's order for anesthesia or an anesthesia-related service, the CRNA may order anesthesia-related medications during perianesthesia periods in the preparation for or recovery from anesthesia. In providing anesthesia or an anesthesia-related service, the CRNA must select, order, obtain, and administer drugs that fall within categories of drugs generally utilized for anesthesia or anesthesia-related services and provide the concomitant care required to maintain the patient in sound physiologic status during those experiences. The anesthesiologist or physician providing anesthesia or anesthesia-related services in an outpatient setting must perform a preanesthetic evaluation, counsel the patient, and prepare the patient for anesthesia per current ASA standards. If the physician has delegated the provision of anesthesia or anesthesia-related services to a CRNA, the CRNA may perform those services within the scope of practice of the CRNA. Informed consent for the planned anesthetic intervention must be obtained from the patient/legal guardian and maintained as part of the medical record. The consent must include explanation of the technique, expected results, and potential risks/complications.

Appropriate preanesthesia diagnostic testing and consults must be obtained per indications and assessment findings. Preanesthetic diagnostic testing and specialist consultation should be obtained as indicated by the preanesthetic evaluation by the anesthesiologist or suggested by the nurse anesthetist's preanesthetic assessment as reviewed by the surgeon. If responsibility for a patient's care is to be shared with other physicians or non-physician anesthesia providers, this arrangement should be explained to the patient (22 TAC § 192.2). Qualified CRNAs can administer anesthesia in a licensed ambulatory surgical center (25 TAC § 135.11).

A CRNA may not perform a nitrous oxide/oxygen inhalation conscious sedation procedure, a parenteral conscious sedation procedure, a parenteral deep sedation and/or general anesthesia procedure in a dentist's office unless the dentist holds a permit issued by the State Board of Dental Examiners for the procedure being performed. When a CRNA provides parenteral conscious sedation or parenteral deep sedation and/or general anesthesia care, he or she must be under the direct supervision of the dentist in the dental office. Delegation of personal supervision may occur if a second dentist or physician anesthesiologist is delivering the anesthesia care (22 TAC § 109.175).

In a hospital, anesthesia services may be provided by a CRNA who is under the supervision of the operating physician or of an anesthesiologist who is immediately available if needed (25 TAC § 133.41). Policies on anesthesia procedures must include the delineation of preanesthesia and postanesthesia responsibilities that must ensure the following are provided for each patient:

1. A preanesthesia evaluation by an individual qualified to administer anesthesia must be performed within 48 hours prior to surgery.
2. An intraoperative anesthesia record must be provided that must include any complications or problems occurring during the anesthesia including time, description of symptoms, review of affected systems, and treatments rendered. The record must correlate with the controlled substance administration record.
3. A postanesthesia follow-up report must be written by the person administering the anesthesia before transferring the patient from the recovery room and must include evaluation for recovery from anesthesia, level of activity, respiration, blood pressure, level of consciousness, and patient color. With respect to inpatients, a postanesthesia evaluation for proper anesthesia recovery must be performed after transfer from recovery and within 48 hours after surgery by the person administering the anesthesia, registered nurse (RN), or physician in accordance with policies and procedures approved by the medical staff and using criteria written in the medical staff bylaws for postoperative monitoring of anesthesia. With respect to outpatients, immediately prior to discharge, a postanesthesia evaluation for proper anesthesia recovery must be

performed by the person administering the anesthesia, RN, or physician in accordance with policies and procedures approved by the medical staff and using criteria written in the medical staff bylaws for postoperative monitoring of anesthesia (25 TAC § 133.41).

22 TAC § 221.14 Provision of Anesthesia Services by Nurse Anesthetists in Outpatient Settings requires (after August 31, 2000) that CRNAs comply with § § 221.14(b)-221.14(e) of this title to be authorized to provide general anesthesia, regional anesthesia, or monitored anesthesia care in outpatient settings. However, 221.14(b)(3)-221.14 do not apply to the registered nurse anesthetist who practices in the following:

1. An outpatient setting in which only local anesthesia, peripheral nerve blocks, or both are used
2. An outpatient setting in which only anxiolytics and analgesics are used and only in doses that do not have the probability of placing the patient at risk for loss of the patient's life-preserving protective reflexes
3. A licensed hospital, including an outpatient facility of the hospital that is separately located apart from the hospital
4. A licensed ambulatory surgical center
5. A clinic located on land recognized as tribal land by the federal government and maintained or operated by a federally recognized Indian tribe or tribal organization as listed by the United States Secretary of the Interior under 25 U.S.C. § 479-1 or as listed under a successor federal statute or regulation
6. A facility maintained or operated by a state or governmental entity
7. A clinic directly maintained or operated by the United States or by any of its departments, officers, or agencies
8. An outpatient setting accredited by the Joint Commission on Accreditation of Healthcare Organizations relating to ambulatory surgical centers, the American Association for the Accreditation of Ambulatory Surgery Facilities, or the Accreditation Association for Ambulatory Health Care.

Under this law, CRNAs have the following roles and responsibilities:

1. CRNAs must follow current, applicable standards, and guidelines as put forth by the American Association of Nurse Anesthetists (AANA) and other relevant national standards regarding the practice of nurse anesthesia as adopted by the AANA or the board.
2. CRNAs must know and conform to the Texas Nurse Practice Act and the Board's Rules and Regulations relating to Professional Nurse Education, Licensure and Practice as well as all federal, state, and local laws, rules, or regulations affecting the practice of nurse anesthesia. Compliance with all building, fire, and safety

codes must also be maintained. A two-way communication source not dependent on electrical current must be available. Each location should have sufficient electrical outlets to satisfy anesthesia machine and monitoring equipment requirements including clearly labeled outlets connected to an emergency power supply. Sites must also have a secondary power source as appropriate for equipment in use in case of power failure.

3. In an outpatient setting where a physician has delegated to a CRNA the ordering of drugs and devices necessary for the nurse anesthetist to administer an anesthetic or an anesthesia-related service ordered by a physician, a certified registered nurse anesthetist may select, obtain, and administer drugs including determination of appropriate dosages, techniques, and medical devices for their administration and maintaining the patient in sound physiologic status. This order need not be drug-specific, dosage specific, or administration-technique specific. Pursuant to a physician's order for anesthesia or an anesthesia-related service, the CRNA may order anesthesia-related medications during perianesthesia periods in the preparation for or recovery from anesthesia. In providing anesthesia or an anesthesia-related service, the CRNA must select, order, obtain, and administer drugs that fall within categories of drugs generally utilized for anesthesia or anesthesia-related services and provide the concomitant care required to maintain the patient in sound physiologic status during those experiences (22 TAC § 221.14).

CRNA standards of practice under this law include the following:

1. The CRNA must perform a preanesthetic assessment, counsel the patient, and prepare the patient for anesthesia per current AANA standards. Informed consent for the planned anesthetic intervention must be obtained from the patient/legal guardian and maintained as part of the medical record. The consent must include explanation of the technique, expected results, and potential risks/complications. Appropriate preanesthesia diagnostic testing and consults must be obtained per indications and assessment findings.

2. Physiologic monitoring of the patient must be determined by the type of anesthesia and individual patient needs. Minimum monitoring must include continuous monitoring of ventilation, oxygenation, and cardiovascular status. Monitors must include, but not be limited to, pulse oximetry and EKG with continuous and non-invasive blood pressure to be measured at least every 5 minutes. If general anesthesia is utilized, then an O_2 analyzer and end-tidal CO_2 analyzer must also be used. A means to measure temperature must be readily available and utilized for continuous

monitoring when indicated per current AANA standards. An audible signal alarm device capable of detecting disconnection of any component of the breathing system must be utilized. The patient must be monitored continuously throughout the duration of the procedure by the CRNA. Postoperatively, the patient must be evaluated by continuous monitoring and clinical observation until stable by a licensed health care provider. Monitoring and observations must be documented per current AANA standards. In the event of an electrical outage that disrupts the capability to continuously monitor all specified patient parameters, at a minimum, heart rate and breath sounds will be monitored on a continuous basis using a precordial stethoscope or similar device, and blood pressure measurements will be reestablished using a non-electrical blood pressure measuring device until electricity is restored.

3. All anesthesia-related equipment and monitors must be maintained to current operating room standards. Prior to the administration of anesthesia, all equipment/monitors must be checked using the current FDA recommendations as a guideline. Records of equipment checks must be maintained in a separate, dedicated log that must be made available upon request. Documentation of any criteria deemed to be substandard must include a clear description of the problem and the intervention. If equipment is utilized despite the problem, documentation must clearly indicate that patient safety is not in jeopardy. All documentation relating to equipment must be maintained for a period of time as determined by board guidelines.

4. CRNAs must maintain current competency in advanced cardiac life support and must demonstrate proof of continued competency upon re-registration with the Board. Competency in pediatric advanced life support must be maintained for those CRNAs whose practice includes pediatric patients. CRNAs must verify that at least one person in the setting other than the person performing the operative procedure maintains current competency in basic life support (BLS) at a minimum.

5. CRNAs must verify that the appropriate policies or procedures are in place. Policies, procedures, or protocols must be evaluated and reviewed at least annually. Agreements with local emergency medical service (EMS) must be in place for purposes of transfer of patients to the hospital in case of an emergency. EMS agreements must be evaluated and re-signed at least annually. Policies, procedures, and transfer agreements must be kept on file in the setting where procedures are performed and made available upon request. Policies or procedures must include, but are not limited to:
   a. Management of outpatient anesthesia. At a minimum, these must address

- patient selection criteria
- patients/providers with latex allergy
- pediatric drug dosage calculations, where applicable
- ACLS algorithms
- infection control
- documentation and tracking use of pharmaceuticals including controlled substances, expired drugs, and wasting of drugs
- discharge criteria

b. Management of emergencies to include, but not be limited to cardiopulmonary emergencies, fire, bomb threat, chemical spill, natural disasters, power outage.

c. EMS response and transport requires delineation of responsibilities of the CRNA and person performing the procedure upon arrival of EMS personnel. This policy should be developed jointly with EMS personnel to allow for greater accuracy.

d. Adverse reactions/events, including but not limited to those resulting in a patient's death intraoperatively or within the immediate postoperative period, must be reported in writing to the board and other applicable agencies within 15 days. Immediate postoperative period is defined as 72 hours (22 TAC § 221.14).

Beginning April 1, 2000, each CRNA who intends to provide anesthesia services in an outpatient setting must register with the board and submit the required, non-refundable registration fee. The information provided on the registration form must include but not be limited to the name and business address of each outpatient setting and proof of current competency in advanced life support (22 TAC § 221.14).

ENHANCE YOUR LEARNING

1. Compare and contrast the laws of California and New York as they pertain to CNM practice.
2. Identify the state covered in this text with the least restrictive laws regarding CRNA practice.
3. Interview an APN who has practiced in two different states regarding the differences, if any, in his or her everyday practice.
4. Research the laws regarding APN practice of a state not covered in this chapter.

TEST YOUR COMPREHENSION

1. Discuss one aspect of physician supervision of CRNAs in the state of Texas.

2. Identify two components of APN practice in the state of Missouri.
3. Discuss the cases covered in this chapter that address the standard of care of APNs.
4. Compare and contrast the laws of Massachusetts and California regarding NP practice.

REFERENCES

American Association of Nurse Anesthetists. (2000a). CRNA scope of practice. Available online at http://www.aana.com/library/proscope.asp.

American Association of Nurse Anesthetists (2000b). Standards for office-based anesthesia practice. Available on line at http://www.aana.com/library/obStandards.asp.

American Association of Nurse Anesthetists (2000c). Cost Effectiveness of Nurse Anesthesia Practice. Available online at http://www.aana.com/library/costeffect.asp.

American College of Emergency Physicians. (1991). *Policy statement: Guidelines on the role of nurse practitioners in emergency departments*. Dallas: ACEP.

American College of Nurse Midwifery (1993). Standards for the Practice of Nurse-Midwifery. Available online at http://www.midwife.org/prof/standard.htm.

AANA. CRNA Scope of Practice. (2000). Available online at http://www.aana.com/library/proscope.asp.

Association of Women's Health, Obstetric, and Neonatal Nurses (AWHONN). (2001). Legislative News and Views. Washington, DC: AWHONN.

AWHONN. (1997). *Orientation and Development for registered and advanced practice nurses in basic and intensive care settings*. Washington, DC: AWHONN.

AWHONN. (1996). *The women's health nurse practitioner: Guidelines for practice and education*. Washington, DC: AWHONN.

AWHONN Conversations with Colleagues. (2000b). *Lifelines, 4*(4), 25.

Curry, J. (1994). Nurse practitioners in the emergency department: Current issues. *Journal of Emergency Nursing, 20*(3), 207–212.

Herman, J. (1998). Documenting acute care nurse practitioner practice characteristics. *American Association of Colleges of Nursing Clinical Issues, 9*(2), 277–282.

Massachusetts Board of Nursing. (1998). Advisory Ruling 9902 Nurse Midwives as First Assistants at Cesarean Section.

Missouri Board of Nursing. (1998). Collaborative practice arrangement checklist. Available online at http://www.ecodev.state.mo.us/pr/nursing/arrang.htm.

Stein, E. (1996). Peer review in a New York chapter of the ACNM 1987–1994. *Journal of Nurse Midwifery, 41*(5), 401–404.

Tye, C. (1997). The emergency nurse practitioner role in major accident and emergency departments: Professional issues and the research agenda. *Journal of Advanced Nursing, 26*, 364–370.

Cases

Arkansas State Nurses Association v. Arkansas State Medical Board, 283 Ark. 366 (1984).

Berdyck v. Shinde, 613 N.E.2d 1014 (Ohio, 1993).

Central Anesthesia Associates, P.C. et al. v. Worthy et al., Castro v. Worthy et al., Moorehead v. Worthy et al., Executive Committee of the Baptist Convention of the State of Georgia d/b/a Georgia Baptist Medical Center v. Worthy et al., 254 Ga. 728; 333 S.E.2d 829 (1985).

Fein v. Permanente Medical Group, 121 Cal.App.3d 135 (1981).

Jenkins v. Payne, 251 Va. 122 (1996).

Lane v. Otts, 412 So.2d 254 (Ala. 1982).

Planned Parenthood v. Vines, 543 NE.2d 654 (Ind. 1989).

Licensure, Credentialing, and Hospital Privileges

Licensure

As discussed in Chapter 2, the laws in the individual states vary widely in terms of the requirements for licensure and the types of certification required for each advanced practice nurse (APN) specialty. Chapter 2 outlined the general requirements for certification and licensure in the various APN specialties. This chapter outlines specific licensure requirements for the selected states and discusses issues surrounding credentialing and hospital privileges. Tables 4-1 through 4-4 summarize licensure requirements for all states. The National Council of State Boards of Nursing (NCSBN) has proposed uniform standards and terms for the licensure of APNs that can be accessed on the NCSBN's website (http://www.ncsbn.org).

A REVIEW OF SELECTED STATE REQUIREMENTS

Arizona

Clinical nurse specialists (CNSs) must have at least a master's degree in nursing or a master's degree with a specialization in a clinical area of nursing practice, must be currently licensed in the state as a registered nurse (RN), and must be currently certified by a national nursing credentialing agency in a clinical area of nursing practice. A certificate to practice as a CNS is granted by the board of nursing (Ariz. State Board of Nursing (BON) Rules, Art. 5, §R4-19-511). In order to be a nurse practitioner (NP) in this state, you must have a current Arizona license as an RN, have completed successfully a registered NP course of study in a regionally accredited college or university that was at least 9 months in length and included theory and clinical experience to prepare the applicant as an NP; nurse midwives must be currently certified by the Ameri-

TABLE 4-1. Licensure Requirements for CRNAs

STATE	MASTER'S DEGREE	RN LICENSURE	NATIONAL CERTIFICATION
Alabama	No	Yes	Yes
Alaska	No	Yes	Yes
Arizona	No	No	Yes
California	No	Yes	Yes
Colorado	Yes (rx)	Yes	Yes
Connecticut	Yes (rx)	Yes	Yes
Delaware	No	Yes	Yes
District of Columbia	No	Yes	Yes
Florida	Yes	Yes	Yes
Georgia	Yes	Yes	Yes
Hawaii	Yes (if not certified)	Yes	No (with Master's)
Idaho	No	Yes	Yes
Illinois	Yes	Yes	Yes
Indiana	No	Yes	Yes
Iowa	No	Yes	Yes
Kansas	No	Yes	No
Kentucky	No	Yes	Yes
Louisiana	Yes	Yes	Yes
Maine	Yes	Yes	Yes
Maryland	No	Yes	Yes
Massachusetts	No	Yes	Yes
Michigan	No	Yes	Yes
Minnesota	No	Yes	Yes
Mississippi	Yes	Yes	Yes
Missouri	Yes	Yes	Yes
Montana	Yes	Yes	Yes
Nebraska	No	Yes	Yes
Nevada	No	Yes	Yes
New Hampshire	No	Yes	Yes
New Jersey	No	Yes	Yes
New Mexico	Yes	Yes	Yes
New York	No	Yes	Yes
North Carolina	No	Yes	Yes
North Dakota	Yes	Yes	Yes
Ohio	Yes	Yes	Yes
Oklahoma	No	Yes	Yes
Oregon	Yes	Yes	Yes
Pennsylvania	No	Yes	No

(continued)

TABLE 4-1. Licensure Requirements for CRNAs (Continued)

STATE	MASTER'S DEGREE	RN LICENSURE	NATIONAL CERTIFICATION
Rhode Island	No	Yes	Yes
South Carolina	Yes	Yes	Yes
South Dakota	No	Yes	Yes
Tennessee	Yes (rx)	Yes	Yes
Texas	No	Yes	Yes
Utah	No	Yes	Yes
Vermont	No	Yes	Yes
Virginia	No	Yes	Yes
Washington	Yes	Yes	Yes
West Virginia	Yes	Yes	Yes
Wisconsin	Yes (rx)	Yes	Yes
Wyoming	No (if certified)	Yes	Yes (if no Master's)

TABLE 4-2. Licensure Requirements for CNMs

STATE	MASTER'S DEGREE	RN LICENSURE	NATIONAL CERTIFICATION
Alabama	Yes	Yes	Yes
Alaska	No	Yes	Yes
Arizona	Yes	Yes	Yes
Arkansas	Yes	Yes	Yes
California	No	Yes	No
Colorado	Yes (rx)	Yes	Yes
Connecticut	No	Yes	Yes
Delaware	No	Yes	Yes
District of Columbia	No	Yes	Yes
Florida	Yes	Yes	Yes
Georgia	Yes	Yes	Yes
Hawaii	Yes (rx)	Yes	Yes
Idaho	No	Yes	Yes
Illinois	Yes	Yes	Yes
Indiana	No	Yes	Yes
Iowa	Yes	Yes	Yes
Kansas	No	Yes	No

(continued)

TABLE 4-2.   Licensure Requirements for CNMs (Continued)

STATE	MASTER'S DEGREE	RN LICENSURE	NATIONAL CERTIFICATION
Kentucky	No	Yes	Yes
Louisiana	Yes	Yes	Yes
Maine	No	Yes	Yes
Maryland	No	Yes	Yes
Massachusetts	Yes	Yes	Yes
Michigan	No	Yes	Yes
Minnesota	No	Yes	Yes
Mississippi	Yes	Yes	Yes
Missouri	Yes	Yes	Yes
Montana	Yes	Yes	Yes
Nebraska	Yes	Yes	Yes
Nevada	No	Yes	Yes (if no BSN)
New Hampshire	No	Yes	Yes
New Jersey	No	Yes	Yes
New Mexico	No	Yes	Yes
New York	No	No	Yes
North Carolina	No	Yes	Yes
North Dakota	Yes	Yes	Yes
Ohio	Yes	Yes	Yes
Oklahoma	No	Yes	Yes
Oregon	Yes	Yes	No
Pennsylvania	No	Yes	Yes
Rhode Island	No	Yes	Yes
South Carolina	Yes	Yes	Yes
South Dakota	No	Yes	Yes
Tennessee	No	Yes	Yes
Texas	No	Yes	Yes
Utah	No	Yes	Yes
Vermont	No	Yes	Yes
Virginia	No	Yes	Yes
Washington	Yes	Yes	Yes
West Virginia	No	Yes	Yes
Wisconsin	Yes (rx)	Yes	Yes
Wyoming	No (if certified)	Yes	Yes (if no Master's)

TABLE 4-3. Licensure Requirements for NPs

STATE	MASTER'S DEGREE	RN LICENSURE	NATIONAL CERTIFICATION
Alabama	Yes	Yes	Yes
Alaska	No	Yes	Yes
Arizona	Yes	Yes	No
Arkansas	No	Yes	Yes
California	No	Yes	No
Colorado	No	Yes	Yes
Connecticut	Yes	Yes	Yes
Delaware	No	Yes	Yes
District of Columbia	No	Yes	Yes
Florida	Yes	Yes	Yes
Georgia	Yes	Yes	Yes
Hawaii	Yes (if no certification)	Yes	Yes (if no Master's)
Idaho	No	Yes	Yes
Illinois	Yes	Yes	Yes
Indiana	Yes (if no certification)	Yes	Yes (if no Master's)
Iowa	No	Yes	Yes
Kansas	No	Yes	No
Kentucky	No	Yes	Yes
Louisiana	Yes	Yes	Yes
Maine	No	Yes	Yes
Maryland	No	Yes	Yes
Massachusetts	No	Yes	Yes
Michigan	No	Yes	Yes
Minnesota	No	Yes	Yes
Mississippi	Yes	Yes	Yes
Missouri	Yes	Yes	Yes
Montana	Yes	Yes	Yes
Nebraska	Yes	Yes	Yes
Nevada	No	Yes	Yes (if no BSN)
New Hampshire	No	Yes	Yes
New Jersey	Yes	Yes	Yes
New Mexico	Yes	Yes	Yes
New York	No	Yes	No
North Carolina	No	Yes	Yes
North Dakota	Yes	Yes	Yes
Ohio	Yes	Yes	Yes
Oklahoma	No	Yes	Yes
Oregon	Yes	Yes	No

(continued)

(TABLE 4-3. Licensure Requirements for NPs (Continued)

STATE	MASTER'S DEGREE	RN LICENSURE	NATIONAL CERTIFICATION
Pennsylvania	No	Yes	No
Rhode Island	No	Yes	Yes
South Carolina	Yes	Yes	Yes
South Dakota	No	Yes	Yes
Tennessee	Yes	Yes	Yes
Texas	No	Yes	Yes
Utah	Yes	Yes	Yes
Vermont	No	Yes	Yes
Virginia	No	Yes	Yes
Washington	Yes	Yes	Yes
West Virginia	Yes	Yes	Yes
Wisconsin	Yes	Yes	Yes
Wyoming	No (if certified)	Yes	Yes (if no Master's)

TABLE 4-4. Licensure Requirements for CNSs

STATE	MASTER'S DEGREE	RN LICENSURE	NATIONAL CERTIFICATION
Alabama	Yes	Yes	No
Alaska	Not licensed separately from RN license		
Arizona	Yes	Yes	Yes
Arkansas	Yes	Yes	Yes
California	Yes	Yes	No
Colorado	Yes	Yes	No
Connecticut	Yes	Yes	Yes
Delaware	No	Yes	Yes
District of Columbia	No	Yes	Yes
Florida	No	Yes	Yes
Georgia	Yes	Yes	Yes
Hawaii	Yes (if not certified)	Yes	Yes (if no Master's)
Idaho	Yes	Yes	Yes
Illinois	Yes	Yes	Yes
Indiana	Not licensed separately from RN license		

(continued)

TABLE 4-4.   Licensure Requirements for CNSs (Continued)

STATE	MASTER'S DEGREE	RN LICENSURE	NATIONAL CERTIFICATION
Iowa	No	Yes	Yes
Kansas	Yes	Yes	No
Kentucky	No	Yes	Yes
Louisiana	Yes	Yes	Yes
Maine	Yes	Yes	Yes
Maryland	Yes	Yes	Yes
Massachusetts	No	Yes	Yes
Michigan	Not recognized	—	—
Minnesota	No	Yes	Yes
Mississippi	Yes	Yes	No
Missouri	Yes	Yes	Yes
Montana	Yes	Yes	Yes
Nebraska	Not recognized	—	—
Nevada	No	Yes	Yes (if no BSN)
New Hampshire	Not recognized	—	—
New Jersey	Yes	Yes	Yes
New Mexico	Yes	Yes	Yes
New York	Yes	Yes	Yes
North Carolina	Yes	Yes	Yes
North Dakota	Yes	Yes	Yes
Ohio	Yes	Yes	Yes
Oklahoma	Yes	Yes	Yes
Oregon	Not recognized	—	—
Pensylvania	Not recognized	—	—
Rhode Island	Yes	Yes	Yes
South Carolina	Yes	Yes	Yes
South Dakota	Yes	Yes	Yes
Tennessee	Not recognized	—	—
Texas	Yes	Yes	Yes
Utah	Yes	Yes	Yes
Vermont	No	Yes	Yes
Virginia	Yes	Yes	Yes
Washington	Yes	Yes	Yes
West Virginia	Yes	Yes	Yes
Wisconsin	Yes	Yes	Yes
Wyoming	No (if certified)	Yes	Yes (if no Master's)

can College of Nurse-Midwives (ACNM). After January 1, 2001, all applicants will be required to have a master's degree in nursing or a master's degree in a health-related area. The Board of Nursing issues a certificate to practice as an NP to nurses who meet the criteria, as opposed to issuing a second license (Ariz. BON rules, Art 5, §R4-19-504).

California

To be certified to practice midwifery in California, the applicant must be licensed as an RN in the state and be a graduate of a board-approved program in nurse-midwifery (16 CCR 1460 [2000]). An RN applicant not meeting the above requirements may still be eligible for certification if (1.) the applicant is a graduate of a nurse-midwifery program not meeting Board of Registered Nursing standards but who shows evidence satisfactory to the board that deficiencies have been corrected in a board-approved nurse-midwifery program, or have been corrected through successful completion of specific courses that have been approved by the board; or (2.) the applicant is certified as a nurse midwife by a national or state organization whose standards are satisfactory to the board (16 CCR 1460 [2000]).

In order to "hold oneself out" as a NP in California, the nurse must be actively licensed as an RN in the state; have successfully completed a program of study conforming to board standards or be certified by a national or state organization whose standards meet board requirements; or if the nurse has not completed a NP program of study that meets board approval the nurse is able to provide documentation of remediation of areas of deficiency in course content and or clinical experience and provide verification by a NP and by a physician who meet requirements for NP faculty members of clinical competence in the delivery of primary health care (CCR Tit. 16, Div. 14, Art. 8, § 1482).

To be credentialed as a certified nurse anesthetist (CRNA) in California, one must be certified by the Council on Certification of Nurse Anesthetists (B&P code §2830.6). As of July 1, 1998 an RN who meets one of the following requirements may apply to become a CNS: (1.) possession of a master's degree in a clinical field of nursing, (2.) possession of a master's degree in a clinical field related to nursing with course work in the major role components, (3.) prior to July 1, 1998 nurses who were licensed as RNs and performing the role of a CNS as described above could apply for certification as a CNS (B&P § 2838.2).

Florida

Florida House Bill 591, enacted in June of 2000, created §455.56503, Florida Statutes, which requires applicants seeking licensure as APNs to provide the names of the schools they have attended as well as a description of all graduate professional education, the name of each location at which the applicant practices, the address at which the applicant will primarily conduct his or her practice, national certifications received, the year the applicant was initially certified, the year the applicant began practicing in any jurisdiction, any faculty appointments, any criminal offenses, any disciplinary action taken against professional licenses and or staff privileges; and requires APNs to update information within 45 days if any such events occur after licensure. Fingerprints must also be submitted for a national criminal history check. All this information must also be submitted by APNs seeking to renew their licenses.

Advanced registered nurse practitioners (ARNPs) in this state must:

1. Hold a current unencumbered license to practice professional nursing in Florida.
2. Submit proof of national advanced practice certification from a nursing specialty board as required.
3. Professional or national nursing specialty boards recognized by the board include, but are not limited to Council on Certification of Nurse Anesthetists, or Council on Recertification of Nurse Anesthetists, or their predecessors; American College of Nurse-Midwives; American Nurses Association (American Nurses Credentialing Center) NP level examinations only; National Certification Corporation for OB/GYN, Neonatal Nursing Specialties (NP level examination only); National Board of Pediatric Nurse Practitioners and Associates (Pediatric Nurse Associate/Practitioner level examinations only) (64B9-4.002, F.A.C.).

Additional requirements include:

• Satisfactory completion of a formal post-basic educational program of at least 1 academic year, the primary purpose of which is to prepare nurses for advanced or specialized practice.
• Graduation from a program leading to a master's degree in a nursing clinical specialty area with preparation in specialized practitioner skills. For applicants graduating on or after October 1, 1998, graduation from a master's degree program will be required for initial certification as a NP. For applicants graduating on or after October 1, 2001, graduation from a master's degree program will be required for initial certification as a registered nurse anesthetist (Fla. Stats, Ch 464, §464.012)

RN First Assistants (RNFAs) are recognized in this state's nurse practice act. RNFAs must be licensed as an RN, hold certification in perioperative nursing, and have completed a program that addresses all content of the Association of Operating Room Nurses Core Curriculum for the RNFA and includes 1 academic year (45 hours of didactic instruction and 120 hours of clinical internship or its equivalent of 2 college semesters) (NPA § 464.027).

Illinois

By 2001, all new applicants must have a graduate degree in their APN specialty. Currently certified APNs will be grandfathered (Pearson, 1999). APN licensure requires:

1. The applicant to have a current license to practice as a RN in Illinois
2. The applicant to have successfully completed requirements to practice as, and hold a current, national certification as a nurse midwife (NM), CNS, or NP from the appropriate national certifying body as determined by the State
3. The applicant to have successfully completed a post-basic advanced practice formal education program in the area of nursing specialty
4. The applicant for initial licensure, effective this year, must have a graduate degree appropriate for national certification in a clinical advanced practice nursing specialty (Title 15 section 65/15-10).

Title 15 section 65/15-45 dictates that 50 hours of continuing education be required for each 2-year license renewal cycle.

Massachusetts

RNs who apply for initial authorization in advanced nursing practice must prove that they have received either a degree for preparation in advanced nursing practice from a graduate school approved by a national accrediting body acceptable to the board or have received a certificate of completion of an educational program in advanced nursing practice approved by a national accrediting body acceptable to the board. The applicant must also provide evidence of current certification in advanced nursing practice from a national professional or specialty certifying organization acceptable to the board (Mass. Ann. Laws ch. 112, § 80B [2000]). The requirements governing authorization as a nurse practicing in an expanded role consist of active licensure as an RN in the Commonwealth and compliance with the following requirements:

Nurse Midwife

1. Satisfactory completion of a formal educational program that has as its objective the preparation of nurses to perform as nurse midwives and that the board has recognized as such
2. Current certification by a nationally recognized accrediting body approved by the board for nurse midwives

Nurse Practitioner

1. Satisfactory completion of a formal educational program for NPs that has been approved by a national professional nurses' accrediting body the board recognizes; the program must have as its

objective the preparation of professional nurses to practice in an expanded role as NPs; the board will accept in satisfaction of this requirement only those educational programs whose attendance and training requirements are the equivalent of at least one academic year

2. Current certification by a nationally recognized accrediting body approved by the board for NPs

Psychiatric Nurse Mental Health Clinical Specialist

1. Satisfactory completion of a formal educational program (whose attendance and training requirements are the equivalent of 1 academic year) in addition to generic nursing preparation approved by a national professional nursing accrediting body that the board recognizes; the program must have as its objective the preparation of nurses to practice as psychiatric nurse mental health clinical specialists

2. Current certification by a nationally recognized accrediting body approved by the board for psychiatric nurse mental health clinical specialists

Nurse Anesthetist

1. Satisfactory completion of a formal education program in addition to generic nursing preparation that meets the standards of the Council on Accreditation of Nurse Anesthesia Programs and that has as its objective the preparation of nurses to perform as nurse anesthetists

2. Current certification by a nationally recognized accrediting body approved by the board for nurse anesthetists (244 CMR 4.13 [2000])

Qualifications in Massachusetts for a RNFA include:

- Current licensure as a RN in Massachusetts
- Documentation of proficiency in perioperative nursing practice as both a scrub and circulating nurse
- Demonstrated ability to apply principles of asepsis and infection control
- Knowledge of surgical anatomy, physiology, pathophysiology and operative technique related to the operative procedures in which the RNFA assists
- Ability to perform cardiopulmonary resuscitation
- Ability to perform effectively in stressful and emergency situations
- Ability to recognize safety hazards and initiate appropriate preventive and corrective action
- Ability to perform effectively and harmoniously as a member of the operative team

- Ability to demonstrate skill in behaviors unique to the RNFA
- Successful completion of a post-basic nursing education program whose intent is the preparation of RNs to practice as first assistants at surgery (Mass BON advisory ruling #9901, 9/9/98).

Missouri

Missouri Regulations 4 CSR 200-4.100 defines the requirements for APNs in this state. After July 1, 1998, completion of a graduate degree from an accredited college or university with a concentration in an advanced practice nursing clinical specialty area that includes advanced nursing theory and clinical nursing practice is required to practice as an APN in Missouri. In addition, if specialty certification is available, the APN applicant must be certified in her or his advanced practice specialty as well as hold a current RN license in the state and provide evidence of satisfactory, active, up-to-date certification/recertification/maintenance and or continuing education/competency status (4 CSR 200-4.100).

Certification examinations by FNP (family nurse practitioner) organizations other than the American Nurses Credentialing Center are not recognized in Missouri (Thornton, 1996). Under 4 CSR 200-4.100 (2000), registered professional nurses seeking licensure by endorsement and recognition as advanced practice nurses in Missouri may receive such recognition if

1. Prior to July 1, 1998, they had completed a formal post-basic education program from or formally affiliated with an accredited college, university, or hospital, of at least 1 academic year that included advanced nursing theory and clinical nursing practice, leading to a graduate degree or a certificate with a concentration in an advanced practice nursing clinical specialty area and
2. Prior to July 1, 1998, they were certified by a nationally recognized certifying body acceptable to the board of nursing and have continuously maintained active, up-to-date recertification status

Certified APNs must maintain active, up-to-date recertification status and continuing competency in the advanced practice nursing clinical specialty area by actively participating in and satisfactorily meeting recertification/maintenance terms and/or continuing education/competency requirements of their nationally recognized certifying body. It is the responsibility of the APN to submit evidence to the board of active, satisfactory recertification and/or continuing competency status prior to the expiration date to prevent removal of recognition as advanced practice nurses by the board of nursing (4CSR200-4.100). Noncertified APNs recognized by the board of nursing as being eligible to practice as APNs must, within every 2 years following recognition by the board, submit documented evidence of a minimum of 1500 hours of clinical practice in their advanced practice nursing clinical specialty area and a minimum of 20 contact hours in their advanced practice nursing clinical specialty area offered by an accredited college or university (4CSR200-4.100).

New York

NP applicants must provide evidence of completion of an educational program registered by the department or a program determined by the department to be equivalent to a registered program that is designed and conducted to prepare graduates to practice as NPs; or certification as a NP by a national certifying body acceptable to the department; and completion of not less than 3 semester hours or the equivalent in pharmacology either in an acceptable NP program or after other educational requirements for certification as NP have been satisfied (8 NYCRR § 64.4 [2000]). The applicant must also be licensed as an RN in the state (139 NYCL 6910). To qualify for a license as a midwife in New York, an applicant must meet the following requirements:

1. Satisfactorily complete educational preparation (degree or diploma granting) for the practice of nursing followed by or concurrently with educational preparation for the practice of midwifery; or submit evidence of license or certification, the educational preparation for which is determined by the department to be equivalent from any state or country, or complete a program determined by the department to be equivalent and in accordance with the commissioner's regulations.
2. Pass an examination satisfactory to the department and in accordance with the commissioner's regulations.
3. Be at least 21 years of age.
4. Be of good moral character as determined by the department.
5. Be a United States citizen or an alien lawfully admitted for permanent residence in the United States (140 NYCL 6955).

Tennessee

To be issued a certificate of fitness as a NP with privileges to write and sign prescriptions and/or issue noncontrolled legend drugs, a nurse must meet all of the following requirements:

1. Current licensure as a RN
2. Graduation from a program conferring a master's or doctoral degree in nursing
3. Preparation in specialized practitioner skills at the master's, post-master's, doctoral, or post-doctoral level. These specialized practitioner skills education must include, but not be limited to, at least 0.75 hours of pharmacology instruction or its equivalent
4. Current national certification in the appropriate nursing specialty area

Applicants intending to prescribe, issue, dispense, and/or administer controlled substances must maintain their Drug Enforcement Administration Certificate to Prescribe Controlled Substances at their practice location to be inspected by the board or its authorized representative (Tenn. Comp. R. & Regs. R. 1000-4-.03 [2000]).

Texas

The Board of Nursing's Rules and Regulations §221.3 indicates that to be eligible to apply for authorization as an APN, the RN must have completed an advanced educational program of study appropriate for practice in an advanced nursing specialty and role recognized by the board. Applicants for authorization as APNs must submit verification of completion of all requirements of an advanced educational program that meets the following criteria:

1. Advanced educational programs in the State of Texas must be accredited by the board or a national accrediting body recognized by the board.
2. Programs in states other than Texas must be accredited by a national accrediting body recognized by the board or by the appropriate licensing body in that state. A state licensing body's accreditation process must meet or exceed the requirements of accrediting bodies specified in board policy.
3. Programs of study must be at least 1 academic year in length and may include a formal preceptorship.
4. Beginning January 1, 2003, the program of study must be at the master's degree level.

Applicants for authorization as CNSs must submit verification of the following requirements in addition to those specified above:

1. Completion of a master's degree in the discipline of nursing
2. Completion of a minimum of 9 semester credit hours or the equivalent in a specific clinical major; clinical major courses must include didactic content and offer clinical experiences in a specific clinical specialty/practice area (BON R & R § 221.3)

Applicants who completed NP or CNS programs on or after January 1, 1998 must demonstrate evidence of completion of the following requirements:

1. Separate courses in pharmacotherapeutics, advanced assessment, and pathophysiology and/or psychopathology, which must be advanced level academic courses with a minimum of 45 clock hours per course
2. Evidence of theoretical and clinical role preparation
3. Evidence of clinical major courses in the specialty area and

4. Evidence of a practicum/preceptorship/internship to integrate clinical experiences as reflected in essential content and the clinical major courses (BON R & R § 221.3)

Applicants who complete NP or CNS programs on or after January 1, 2003 must demonstrate evidence of completion of a minimum of 500 clinical hours within the advanced educational program (BON R & R § 221.3).

The Board of Nursing's Rules and Regulations §221.4 lists other requirements for APN licensure in Texas. These requirements include:

1. Hold a current, valid, unencumbered license as a RN in the State of Texas or reside in any party state and hold a current, valid, unencumbered RN license in that state.
2. Submit to the board evidence of having met the educational requirements outlined above.
3. Meet the minimum requirement of 400 hours of current practice within the preceding 2 years unless the applicant has completed an advanced educational program within the preceding 2 years.
4. Obtain 20 contact hours of continuing education in the advanced specialty and role recognized by the board every 2 years. The 20 contact hours required for RN licensure may be met by the 20 hours required by this subsection.

The applicant for APN authorization who completed an advanced educational program on or after January 1, 1996 must submit to the board evidence of holding current certification in an advanced nursing role and specialty recognized by the board. This certification must be granted by a national certifying body recognized by the board. If an appropriate certification examination is not available and the board has not designated an alternate examination, the applicant may petition the board for waiver from the certification requirement (BON R & R § 221.4).

The Board of Nursing's Rules and Regulations §221.8 outlines requirements for APN licensure renewal. These requirements include:

1. Maintaining current national certification by the appropriate certifying body recognized by the board; this requirement applies to APNs who completed an advanced educational program on or after January 1, 1996, or were authorized as APNs based upon obtaining national certification
2. Having a minimum of 400 hours of current practice within the preceding 2 years
3. Obtaining 20 contact hours of continuing education in the advanced specialty area and role within the preceding 2 years; the 20 contact hours required for RN licensure may be met by the 20 hours required by this subsection

Starting in 2007, programs of study in this state for APNs must be at the master's level (22 TAC § 221.3 [2000]).

Privileges and Credentialing

In 1995, Sellards and Mills noted that some hospitals gave admitting privileges to selected APNs (usually nurse midwives) but only with direct supervision of a staff physician. Then only the District of Columbia and the state of Washington had laws prohibiting the discrimination of admitting privileges. Although at the time many states had some form of privileging for APNs, the scope of authority (admitting vs. clinical) and the type of APN allowed privileges varied from state to state. Presently, the majority of states do not have laws either promoting or prohibiting the granting of privileges to APNs.

PRIVILEGES VS. CREDENTIALING: WHAT'S THE DIFFERENCE?

Credentialing is the process by which the professional provides evidence he or she is qualified to perform designated clinical activities (Rustia, 1997). The focus is on education facts, practice experiences, licensure, certification, and professional liability (Hodson, 1998). Privileging is the process through which the employing organization grants a professional specific authority to perform the designated clinical activities (Rustia, 1997). Clinical privileging is a form of credentialing used by hospitals and other facilities to authorize selected health care providers to provide specific patient care services. Having such privileges enables the health care provider to practice within that facility under the conditions specified in the privileges. Clinical privileging requirements are usually developed by the medical staff through bylaws (AANA, 2000). Credentialing is an administrative process that collects and verifies information on a practitioner's training and experience. For nurses this process involves graduation from nursing school, advanced degrees, prior practice experience including references and speciality certification, licensure and certification history, teaching appointments and references, professional associations, and professional liability history including insurance carriers and judgments or settlements naming the applicant as a defendant in a malpractice suit (Rustia, 1997).

Privileging, however, involves a decision made by professional peers who judge the clinical competence of an applicant based on the documentation provided in the credentialing process. Criteria are developed to grant specific areas of privilege and to evaluate whether or not the practitioner has maintained clinical competence over time. This will ultimately require nurses to collect, document, and analyze data on the outcomes of care they have provided (Rustia, 1997). Employers must maintain confidentiality of privileging information and place it in a separate file from the credentialing information to provide a statutory protection from discovery (Rustia, 1997).

WHY DO FACILITIES PERFORM PRIVILEGING/CREDENTIALING?

Hopkins and Kadzielski (1998) note that there are four primary reasons to credential or evaluate the qualifications and competence of providers: (1.) to comply with legal requirements as many states have incorporated credentialing requirements into managed care laws or laws regulating managed care organizations; (2.) to achieve accreditation from one of the organizations involved in accrediting managed care organizations (MCOs); (3.) for the MCO to obtain a marketing and contracting advantage by being able to represent that the healthcare providers contracting with the MCO are a distinct group subject to ongoing review; (4.) to address liability concerns.

Two major reasons for developing a comprehensive credentialing and privileging system are to foresee and avoid potential legal problems and to provide evidence that the employer of the health provider's services has put forth considerable effort to obtain information on the competency of the applicant and that all statements regarding the individual's competence were verified. Once credentials have been verified, the nurse may be granted privileges as allowed by state and federal law to perform designated clinical activities or to exercise cognitive or evaluative management skills (Rustia, 1997). The privileging process should provide for ongoing evaluation of the competence of APNs in their credentialed practice areas, which will require a quality assurance program that can produce clinically relevant data to serve as minimum benchmarks of performance (Rustia, 1997).

ELEMENTS OF PRIVILEGING/CREDENTIALING PROGRAMS

Before an APN can be credentialed or privileged, the following parameters must be established: documentation of job descriptions and qualifications; development of physician and nurse practice agreements; definition of reporting mechanism; budgetary considerations; policy and procedure updates to reflect advanced practice; liability concerns; development of patient care protocols; and definition of skill procedures to be performed by APNs (Hodson, 1998).

To reduce the possibility of litigation, Rustia, 1997, recommends that nurses in group and individual practices as well as institutions employing faculty to teach advanced clinical practice should have a credentialing policy that (1.) details the existence and scope of the process and the requirement that nurses adhere to it as a condition of affiliation or employment; (2.) stipulates the format of reference requests and tracking procedures that will be used to assure files are complete and current, and (3.) provides releases from liability for those involved in the decision-making process as well as for those providing information on the performance of the applicant nurse. Any employment contracts must contain clear standards for performance that serve as a basis for termination, suspension, or revocation of privileges.

Other essential elements of a credentialing program are a corrective action policy for identified problems including potential contract termination, restriction of privileges, suspension from clinical practice, and other actions as appropriate. A fair process for reviewing negative decisions, clearly articulated in the employment contract or the bylaws, should also be in place (Rustia, 1997). Hopkins, 1998, suggests that all entities performing credentialing should document and verify a provider's current credentials including the license to practice within the state, controlled substances registration, professional liability insurance, references, board certification, and other appropriate credentials. According to the standards of the NCQA (National Committee for Quality Assurance), which accredits MCOs, the credentialing process must include primary source verification and provide for initial visits to the offices of primary care practitioners and OB/GYNs to assess the quality of the health care delivery site (Hopkins, 1998). MCO recredentialing must take place at least every 2 years and must include primary source verification and consideration of member complaints, results of quality reviews, utilization management, member satisfaction surverys, medical records review, and onsite visits to a practitioners office (Hopkins, 1998).

STATE AND FEDERAL RULES REGARDING PRIVILEGING AND CREDENTIALING

Hopkins et al., 1998, note that federal and state law as well as accreditation requirements establish procedures and limitations on the selection and deselection process in credentialing. Under JCAHO standards, NPs can qualify as affiliate professional staff in the same way as podiatrists and oral surgeons (Sellards, 1995). JCAHO requires physician members of the medical staff to be credentialed and privileged. According to JCAHO, NPs and CRNAs may be credentialed and privileged through the hospital's medical staff bylaw process or the institution's human resource credentialing process. It is the health care facility's choice to determine which credentialing and or privileging process should be utilized for APNs (AANA, 2000). JCAHO has standards requiring that all providers permitted by law and the network to practice independently be appointed or reappointed to the network's practitioner panel through defined processes (Hopkins, 1998). JCAHO requires that the network evaluate the clinical records and office practices of each practitioner being considered for appointment to the network's practitioner panel. At reappointment, which must occur at least every 2 years, practitioner specific information from performance improvement activities is compared to aggregate information. The network must have a defined, documented process for terminating the appointment of licensed independent practitioners and for considering provider appeals of decisions to terminate appointment (Hopkins, 1998). Many states have peer review statutes protecting the entity as well as the participants and members of committees who conduct peer review and those individuals who assist the committees; peer review protection is also afforded under the federal Healthcare Quality Improvement Act for certain professional review actions. Hopkins, 1998, indicates that generally MCOs must provide their members or contracting providers with certain procedural rights, such as notice and an opportunity to be heard prior to restricting or terminating members' or contracting providers' rights. Private organizations are legally required to refrain from arbitrary action and their actions must be both substantively rational and procedurally fair; a decision to expel or exclude an individual is arbitrary if the reason underlying the rejection is irrational or if the organization has proceeded in an unfair manner. For example, in Texas, health maintenance organizations (HMOs) must make available and disclose to physicians and providers upon request written application procedures and qualification requirements for contracting with HMOs. If there is a denial, the HMO must provide written notice of the reason the initial application was denied. Before terminating a contract with a physician or provider, the HMO must provide a written explanation of the reasons for the termination; insurer-sponsored preferred provider organizations (PPOs) must provide a "fair reasonable and equivalent opportunity" to physicians, practitioners, and other healthcare providers to become preferred providers; designation as a preferred provider may not be unreasonably withheld and the insurer must give the provider who is being denied initial designation as a preferred provider with a written reason for the denial (Hopkins, 1998). The Association of Nurse Anesthetists (AANA) has published a document entitled The AANA Guidelines for Clinical Privileges, which contains guidelines for granting clinical privileges to the CRNA and a prototype of an application for clinical privileges. These guidelines are available from the AANA at 222 South Prospect Avenue, Park Ridge Illinois (AANA, 2000).

LEGAL IMPLICATIONS OF HOSPITAL ACTIONS REGARDING DENIAL OF STAFF PRIVILEGES TO APNS

Antitrust Lawsuits

Occasionally, hospitals deny staff privileges to APNs for reasons that appear to be arbitrary and unfair. Unfortunately, APNs who feel they are wrongly denied these privileges have few legal options in challenging privileging decisions. One of these options is to bring an antitrust law-suit against the hospital. If the APN is successful in this suit, treble damages, costs of the suit, and reasonable attorney fees are available under Section 4 of the Clayton Act (15 U.S.C. §15 [1988]). Still, antitrust cases are difficult to prove. If the APN hopes to be successful in bringing such a lawsuit, the first point that must be proven is that there is a relationship between the challenged action and interstate commerce. Section 1 of the Sherman Act prohibits every contract, combination or conspiracy "in restraint of trade or commerce among the several States . . ." (15 U.S.C. § 1 [1988]). However, this act prohibits only unreasonable restraints of trade (*Business Elecs. Corp. v. Sharp Electronics Corp.*, 1988). Section 2 of the Sherman Act prohibits establishment of monopolies, attempts to monopolize, and conspiracies to monopolize in interstate commerce (15 U.S.C. §2 [1988]). Federal courts have interpreted this prohibition two ways: (1.) under a *per se* rule, where certain activities are considered illegal, with no requirement to prove actual damage to competition, or (2.) under the "rule of reason." (*Odom v. Lee et al.*, 2000). The rule-of-reason test should be applied to cases of termination of staff privileges to determine whether the facility's conduct was unreasonable (*Miller v. Indiana Hospital*, 1988; "In a hospital staff privilege case in which the hospital defends on lack of professional ability, the rule of reason test would apply."). Under the rule-of-reason test "after the claimant has proven that the conspiracy harmed competition, the fact finder must balance the restraint and any justifications or pro-competitive effects of the restraint in order to determine whether the restraint is unreasonable." (*Oltz v. St. Peter's Community Hospital*, 1988). To establish a prima facie case of unlawful trade restraint, the healthcare provider must initially prove three elements: (1.) an agreement or conspiracy among two or more persons or distinct business entities; (2.) by which the persons or entities intend to harm or restrain competition; and (3.) that actually injures competition (Oltz, 861 F.2d at 1445). Only after the plaintiff proves these three elements is it incumbent upon the fact finder to "balance the restraint and any justifications or pro-competitive effects of the restraint in order to determine whether the restraint is unreasonable." (Oltz, 861 F.2d at 1445). For a private litigant seeking treble damages to have standing, "[a] plaintiff must show not only the fact of injury from the alleged violation, but that the injury alleged is 'of the type the antitrust laws were intended to prevent and that flows from that which makes defendants' acts unlawful.'" Furthermore, the "plaintiff must demonstrate that the defendant's conduct was intended to or did have some anticompetitive effect beyond his own loss of business or the market's loss of a competitor." (*California Computer Products., Inc. v. International Business Machines Corp.*, 1979). When proving that the restraint on trade was unreasonable, the APN will first have to prove the threshold question of whether the defendant has sufficient market power to exert anticompetitive behaviour. Then the next question is whether there is a restraint of trade and, if so, whether it is unreasonable (Sfikas, 1991). Only if the claim involves price fixing or where the defendant has market power or unique access to a business element necessary for effective competition will the court not undertake the reasonability analysis; in these cases the restraint is determined to be so blatantly anticompetitive that it is considered to be per se illegal (Sfikas, 1991, *Northwest Wholesale Stationers v. Pacific Stationery and Printing*, 1985). An APN bringing such a lawsuit must therefore prove that the hospital has a significant effect on interstate activity including the proximity of the facility to other comparable facilities, treatment of a measurable number of out of state patients, purchase of equipment and supplies from other states, revenues generated from out of state insurance programs, and revenues obtained through payments from out of state patients (Sfikas, 1991).

Conspiracy Claims

Often the APN challenging privileging decisions will allege that privileges were denied due to a conspiracy. To satisfy the requirements of the Sherman Act, the APN must prove that the concerted conduct by more than one person or entity occurred as an unreasonable restraint of trade (*Oltz v. St. Peter's Community Hospital*, 1988). In evaluating a conspiracy claim for denial of staff privileges, the ninth circuit in Oltz, 1988, considered three elements: (1.) an agreement or conspiracy among two or more persons or distinct business entities, (2.) by which the persons or entities intend to harm or restrain competition, and (3.) an agreement or conspiracy that actually injures competition. Sometimes in bringing these cases, the person denied privileges alleges that the hospital and the medical staff conspired to wrongly deny the privileges. The federal courts are divided on whether a hospital is legally capable of conspiring with members of the medical staff. The third circuit (New York), under Section 1 of the Sherman Act (*Weiss v. New York Hospital*, 1984), does not accept the theory that a hospital is legally capable of conspiring with the medical staff. Neither does the sixth circuit (Georgia) (*Nurse Midwifery Associates v. Hibbett*, 1990). However the ninth and eleventh circuits have held, under Section 1 of the Sherman Act (*Bolt v. Halifax Hospital Medical Center*, 1990; Oltz, 1988), that hospitals are indeed capable of conspiring with the medical staff. If the APN seeks to prove that two or more hospitals have conspired to deny her or him privileges, she or he must show that (1.) the alleged conspirators' business activities constituted parallel conduct, (2.) the conspirators had a motivation to enter into a conspiracy, and (3.) the actions taken were contrary to the conspirators' individual economic interests (Nurse Midwifery Associates, supra). The APN must also establish that she was injured in her "business or property" by the antitrust violation (15 U.S.C. §4 [1988]).

Boycott Claims

APNs may also claim an illegal boycott or a concerted refusal to deal. Group boycotts constitute per se violations of the Sherman Act § 1 (Oltz, supra; "Group boycotts or concerted refusals to deal constitute per se categories . . . ."). The three characteristics "indicative of per se illegal boycotts [are]: (1.) the boycott cuts off access to a supply, facility, or market necessary to enable the victim firm to compete; (2.) the boycotting firm possesses a dominant market position; and (3.) the practices are not justified by plausible arguments that they enhanced overall efficiency or competition." (*Hahn v. Oregon Physicians' Serv.*, 1988; see also *Northwest Wholesale Stationers, Inc. v. Pacific Stationery & Printing Co.*, 1985). "[A] prima facie case of attempt to monopolize is made out by evidence of a specific intent to monopolize 'any part' of commerce, plus anti-competitive conduct directed to the accomplishment of that unlawful purpose." (*Greyhound Computer v. International Business Machines*, 1977). The court noted that "the more market power that exists, the more likely it is that a given course of questionable conduct will suggest the existence of intent to monopolize."(*Greyhound Computer v. International Business Machines*, 1977). In *Weiss v. York Hospital*, 1984, the jury found that the defendants had engaged in a policy of discrimination against the plaintiff and other osteopaths by applying unfair, unequal, and unreasonable procedures in reviewing their applications. The court of appeals decided that the hospital's actions were appropriately characterized as a boycott; because the facility offered no public service or ethical norm rationale for its actions, the court held that the actions were per se illegal.

Defense to Antitrust Cases

Even if the APN is able to prove all the elements required for an antitrust case, the facility may be able to win the case if it is able to prove immunity under the state action doctrine. Under this doctrine, a facility's actions are shielded from antitrust laws if (1.) the challenged restraint is clearly articulated and affirmatively expressed as state policy and (2.) the conduct in question is actively supervised by the state itself (Sfikas, 1991; *California Retail Liquor Dealers Assn. v. Midcal Aluminum*, 1980).

Legal Issues Surrounding the Revocation of Privileges

Sometimes practitioners claim defamation when their privileges are revoked. A prima facie case of defamation requires the plaintiff to establish "(1.) a false and defamatory statement; (2.) an unprivileged publication to a third party; (3.) fault amounting at least to negligence on the part of the publisher; and (4.) the existence of either 'per se' actionability or special harm." (*French v. Jadon, Inc.*, 1996). For a statement to be libel per se, "the words used must be so unambiguous as to be reasonably susceptible of only one interpretation — that is, one which has a natural tendency to injure another's reputation." (*Fairbanks Publishing Co. v. Pitka*,

1962). In the case of *Odom v. Fairbanks Memorial Hospital et al.* (2000), plaintiff claimed that Fairbanks Memorial Hospital (FMH) defamed him in its reporting of disciplinary action to the federally mandated National Practitioner Data Bank, a report FMH was required to make. The court noted that although a health care entity complying with the federal reporting requirement, pursuant to 42 U.S.C. § 11133(a)(1), is afforded a certain amount of immunity in reporting to the Data Bank, that immunity is limited. 42 U.S.C. § 11137(c) provides that "No person or entity . . . shall be held liable in any civil action with respect to any report made under this subchapter . . . without knowledge of the falsity of the information contained in the report." FMH, therefore, was immune from liability unless it had knowledge that the report was false. In the court's view, "falsity" in this statute refers to a false report of the nature of or the stated reasons for the actions of a health care entity. In *Brown v. Presbyterian Healthcare Services*, 1996, a report was made to the Data Bank that Brown's obstetrical privileges had been suspended for the coded reasons "Incompetence/Malpractice/Negligence." But the reason stated by the health care provider in the suspension order was that Brown had failed to abide by an agreement to consult in handling certain types of cases. Because the stated reason relied on by the health care provider did not necessarily match the stated reason reported to the Data Bank, the court concluded that a jury question was presented as to whether or not the report to the Data Bank was false and whether or not the defendant who had made the report knew it to be so.

Review of Selected State Laws Regarding Privileging/Credentialing

California
The granting of hospital privileges to the APN is at the discretion of the facility (Pearson, 1999).

Florida
Each facility must establish specific procedures for the appointment and reappointment of RNFAs and for granting, renewing, and revising their clinical privileges (NPA § 464.027).

Each licensed hospital facility must establish rules and procedures for consideration of an application for clinical privileges submitted by an ARNP licensed and certified in this state. No licensed facility may deny an application solely because the applicant is licensed as an ARNP or because the applicant is not a participant in the Florida Birth-Related Neurological Injury Compensation Plan. The applicant's eligibility for staff membership or clinical privileges must be determined by the applicant's background, experience, health, training, and demonstrated competency; the applicant's adherence to applicable professional ethics; the applicant's reputation; and the applicant's ability to work with others and by such other elements as determined by the governing board, consistent with state law. The governing board of each licensed facility must set standards and procedures to be applied by the facility and its medical staff in considering and acting upon applications for staff membership or clinical privileges.

These standards and procedures must be available for public inspection. Upon the written request of the applicant, any licensed facility that has denied staff membership or clinical privileges to any applicant must, within 30 days of the request, provide the applicant with the reasons for denial in writing. A denial of staff membership or clinical privileges to any applicant must be submitted, in writing, to the applicant's respective licensing board (Fla. Stats. § 395.0191 [1999]).

Section 455.557, Florida Statutes addresses standardized credentialing for health care practitioners. This law establishes a credentials collection program which provides that once a health care practitioner's core credentials data are collected, they need not be collected again except for corrections, updates, and modifications that must be made within 45 days. The core data collected includes current name, any former name, any alias, any professional education, professional training, licensure, current Drug Enforcement Administration certification, social security number, specialty board certification, Educational Commission for Foreign Medical Graduates certification, hospital or other institutional affiliations, evidence of professional liability coverage or evidence of financial responsibility, history of claims, suits, judgments, or settlements, final disciplinary action reported, and Medicare or Medicaid sanctions.

Illinois

All hospitals licensed in this state must comply with the following requirements:

1. No hospital policy, rule, regulation, or practice will be inconsistent with the provision of adequate collaboration, including medical direction of licensed APNs.
2. A licensed physician, dentist, or podiatrist may be assisted by a licensed APN granted clinical privileges to assist in surgery at the hospital.
3. CRNAs with clinical privileges may administer anesthesia (210 ILCS 85/10.7 [2000]).

All ambulatory surgical treatment centers licensed by the state must comply with the following requirements:

1. No policy, rule, regulation, or practice will be inconsistent with the provision of adequate collaboration, including medical direction of licensed APNs.

2. A licensed physician, dentist, or podiatrist may be assisted by a licensed APN granted clinical privileges to assist in surgery by the consulting committee of the ASTC.
3. CRNAs with clinical privileges may administer anesthesia (210 ILCS 5/6.5 [2000]).

Massachusetts

Each maternal/newborn service must develop and implement written administrative policies that include provisions for staff privileges granted to each MD, physician, certified nurse midwife, and each nurse practicing in an advanced practice role must specify those areas in which his or her practice is limited and or requires consultation before therapeutic intervention (105 CMR 130.616).

New York

Hospitals may give privileges to CRNAs to administer anesthesia. The director of the anesthesia service, in conjunction with the medical staff, is responsible for recommending to the governing body privileges to those persons qualified to administer anesthetics including the procedures each person is qualified to perform and the levels of required supervision as appropriate. CRNAs must work under the supervision of an anesthesiologist who is immediately available as needed or under the supervision of the operating physician who has been found qualified by the governing body and the medical staff to supervise the administration of anesthetics and who has accepted responsibility for the supervision of the CRNA (10 NYCRR § 405.13 [2000]).

In an upgraded diagnostic and treatment center, the governing body will determine which categories of health care practitioners are eligible candidates for appointment to the medical staff. The eligible categories may include NPs or CNSs (10 NYCRR § 752-2.1 [2000]). In primary care hospitals and critical accesss hospitals, the governing body will determine which categories of health care practitioners are eligible candidates for appointment to the medical staff. The eligible categories may include NPs or CNSs (10 NYCRR § 407.1 [2000]). Hospitals must have a governing body legally responsible for directing the operation of the hospital in accordance with its mission. The governing body must:

1. Determine, in accordance with state law, which categories of health care practitioners are eligible candidates for appointment to the medical staff
2. Ensure the implementation of written criteria for selection, appointment, and reappointment of medical staff members and for the delineation of their medical privileges; criteria must include standards for individual character, competence, training, experience, judgement, and physical and mental capabilities

3. Ensure that staff membership or professional privileges in the hospital are not dependent solely upon certification, fellowship, or membership in a specialty body or society
4. Appoint members of the medical staff after considering the recommendations of the existing members of the medical staff in accordance with written procedures, as established by hospital and medical staff bylaws
5. Ensure that actions taken on applications for medical staff appointments and reappointments including the delineation of privileges are put in writing
6. Require that members of the medical staff practice only within the scope of privileges granted by the governing body (10 NYCRR § 405.2 [2000]).

Texas
25 TAC § 133.41 indicates that hospital medical staff may be composed of podiatrists, dentists, and other practitioners appointed by the governing body.

ENHANCE YOUR LEARNING

1. Compare the requirements for licensure in your specialty area in your state and two other bordering states.
2. Read the text of any legislation introduced in your state this year regarding APN licensure.
3. Interview an APN who has been licensed in more than one state regarding differences in the licensure process.
4. Read the NCSBN's proposed uniform rules for APN licensure.

TEST YOUR COMPREHENSION

1. Discuss the difference between credentialing and privileging.
2. Identify two states that do not recognize the CNS.
3. Discuss the legal issues related to revocation of privileges.
4. Identify two facts that must be initially proven by an ANP bringing an antitrust lawsuit regarding privileges.

REFERENCES

Association of Nurse Anesthetists. (2000). *CRNA scope of practice*. Available online at http://www.aana.com/library/proscope.asp.
Hodson, D. (1998). The evolving role of advanced practice nurses in surgery. *Association of Operating Room Nurses (AORN) Journal, 67*(5) 998–1006.

Hopkins, J., & Kadzielski, M. (1998). Credentialing and "deselection" of providers in healthcare delivery systems. *Journal of Health Law, 31*(1) 1–17.

Pearson, L. (1999). Annual update of how each state stands on legislative issues affecting advanced nursing practice. *The Nurse Practitioner, 24*(1), 16–83.

Rustia, J., & Bartek, J. (1997). Managed care credentialing of advanced practice nurses. *The Nurse Practitioner, 22*(9), 90–103.

Sellards, S., & Mills, M. (1995). Administrative issues for use of nurse practitioners. *Journal of Nursing Administration, 25*(5), 64–70.

Sfikas, Peter M. (1991). Antitrust challenges by allied health care professionals involving hospital staff privileges. *Journal of Health Law, 24*(12), 361.

Spatz, D. (1996). Women's health: The role of advanced practice nurses in the 21st century. *Nursing Clinics of North America, 31*(2), 269–277.

Thornton, C. (1996). Nurse practitioner in a rural setting. *Nursing Clinics of North America, 31*(3), 495–505.

Cases

Bolt v. Halifax Hospital Medical Center, 891 F2d 810 (1990).

Brown v. Presbyterian Healthcare Services, 101 F.3d 1324, 1334 (10th Cir. 1996).

Business Electronics Corp. v. Sharp Electronics Corp., 485 U.S. 717, 723, 99 L. Ed. 2d 808, 108 S. Ct. 1515 (1988).

California Computer Products, Inc. v. International Business Machines Corp., 613 F.2d 727, 732 (9th Cir. 1979).

California Retail Liquor Dealers Assn. v. Midcal Aluminum, 445 U.S. 97 (1980).

Fairbanks Publishing Co. v. Pitka, 376 P.2d 190, 194 (Ala. 1962).

French v. Jadon, Inc., 911 P.2d 20, 32 (Ala. 1996).

Greyhound Computer v. International Business Machines, 559 F.2d 488, 504 (9th Cir. 1977).

Hahn v. Oregon Physicians' Serv., 860 F.2d 1501, 1509 (9th Cir. 1988).

Miller v. Indiana Hosp., 843 F.2d 139, 144 n.6 (3d Cir. 1988).

Northwest Wholesale Stationers v. Pacific Stationery and Printing, 472 U.S. 284 (1985).

Nurse Midwifery Associates v. Hibbett, 918 F2d 605 (1990).

Odom v. Fairbanks Memorial Hospital et al., 999 P2d 123, Ala. Supreme Court (2000).

Odom v. Lee et al., 999 P2d 755, Ala. Supreme Court (2000).

Oltz v. St. Peter's Community Hospital, 861 F.2d 1440, 1445 (9th Cir. 1988).

Weiss v. New York Hospital, 745 F2d 786 (3d Cir 1984).

Standardized Procedures, Protocols, and Guidelines

Most states that require advanced practice nurses (APNs) to practice under written protocols provide specific requirements for those protocols. Other states do not require the use of protocols by the APN. This chapter will outline the requirements in the selected states for these protocols and will discuss considerations to follow when developing protocols, procedures, and guidelines.

In a 1998 survey, 78% of respondents indicated that they were using published standards and guidelines in their practice setting (AWHONN, 1998). In creating evidence-based guidelines, one should do the following:

- Identify an area for which new or revised guidelines are necessary and appropriate.
- Define the problem to be resolved or the question to be answered by the guideline.
- Conduct a systematic, thorough literature search.
- Create an interdisciplinary team to evaluate the selected literature.
- Assess the selected literature.
- Establish clinical guidelines, policies, or protocols based on the recommendation of the team and evaluate the success of the guidelines after they have been in place for some time (Sams, 1998).

Stein, 1996, opines that protocols/practice guidelines should be revised every 2 years to remain current.

Tye, 1997, notes that even in Britain, while clinical protocols are perhaps an inevitable consequence of an increasingly litigation-conscious society, there is a danger that rigid, over-prescriptive policies may restrict professional judgment and may have a detrimental impact on the cost effectiveness of use of advanced practice nurses.

ARIZONA

This state does not require the use of protocols.

CALIFORNIA

Nurses in this state function under "standardized procedures" when performing medical functions. The procedures are agency-specific and must meet specified requirements, including collaborative development by nursing, medicine, and the administration within the agency. The level of supervision required is also specific to the practice setting and is specified in the standardized procedure. Standardized procedures are not required when functioning within the certified nurse midwife (CNM) scope of practice (Pearson, 1999). The Board of Nursing (BON) and Board of Medicine (BOM) jointly promulgate guidelines for the development of standardized procedures (Ca. Code of Regs. Tit. 16, Div. 14, Art. 7, § 1470). Standardized procedures must include a written description of the method used in developing and approving them as well as methods for revision. The procedures must also:

1. Be written, dated, and signed by personnel authorized for approval
2. Specify which standardized procedure functions nurses may perform and under what circumstances
3. State any specific requirements to be followed by the nurse in performing particular standardized procedure functions
4. Specify any experience, training, and or educational requirements for performance of standardized procedure functions
5. Establish a method for initial and continuing evaluation of the competence of those nurses authorized to perform standardized procedure functions
6. Provide for a method of maintaining a written record of those persons authorized to perform standardized procedure functions
7. Specify the scope of supervision required for performance of the functions
8. List circumstances under which the nurse must immediately communicate with the physician concerning the patient's condition
9. State the limitations, if any, on the setting in which the functions may be performed
10. Specify patient record-keeping requirements
11. Provide for a method of periodic review of the procedures (16 C.C.R. § 1474).

FLORIDA

When a physician enters into an established protocol with an ARNP that includes the performance of medical acts identified and approved by the state, the physician must submit notice to the medical board. The notice must contain a statement indicating the name and professional license number of the physician, address of the physician, and the number of ARNPs with whom the physician has entered into a protocol. This notice must be filed within 30 days of entering into the protocol. Notice also must be provided within 30 days after the physician has terminated the protocol (Fla. Stat. § 458.348).

An ARNP may only perform medical acts of diagnosis, treatment, and operation pursuant to a protocol between the ARNP and a Florida-licensed medical doctor, osteopathic physician, or dentist. The degree and method of supervision, determined by the ARNP and the physician or dentist, must be specifically identified in the written protocol and must be appropriate for prudent health care providers under similar circumstances. General supervision by the physician or dentist is required unless the rules set a different level of supervision for a particular act. The number of persons to be supervised will be limited to ensure that an acceptable standard of medical care is rendered in consideration of the following factors:

- Risk to patient
- Educational preparation, specialty, and experience of the parties to the protocol
- Complexity and risk of the procedures
- Practice-setting
- Availability of the physician or dentist (64B8-35.002, F.A.C.)
- A written protocol signed by all parties, representing the mutual agreement of the physician or dentist and the ARNP, must include the following, at a minimum.

General Data

1. Signatures of individual parties to the protocol, including (a.) name, address, ARNP certificate number of applicant and (b.) name, address, license number, and DEA number of the physician or dentist
2. Nature of practice and practice location, including primary and satellite sites
3. Date developed and dates amended with signatures of all parties

Collaborative Practice Agreement

1. Description of the duties of the ARNP
2. Description of the duties of the physician or dentist (must include consultant and supervisory arrangements in case the physician or dentist is unavailable)
3. Management areas for which the ARNP is responsible, including (a.) conditions for which therapies may be initiated; (b.) treatments that may be initiated by the ARNP, depending on patient

condition and judgment of the ARNP, and (c.) drug therapies that the ARNP may prescribe, initiate, monitor, alter, or order

4. A provision for annual review by the parties
5. Specific conditions and a procedure for identifying conditions that require direct evaluation or specific consultation by the physician or dentist (64B8-35.002, F.A.C.)

The parties to the protocol, to ensure an acceptable standard of supervision and medical care, will decide the detail and scope needed in the description of conditions and treatments and in doing so will consider the factors regarding limits on the number of persons to be supervised above. The original of the protocol and the original of the notice must be filed yearly with the state, and a copy of the protocol and a copy of the notice must be kept at the site of practice of each party to the protocol. Any alterations to the protocol or amendments should be signed by the ARNP and the medical doctor, osteopathic physician, or dentist and filed with the state within 30 days of the alteration. After termination of the relationship between the ARNP and the supervising professional, each party is responsible for ensuring that a copy of the protocol is maintained for future reference for a period of 4 years (64B8-35.002, F.A.C).

2000 FL H.B. 591, enacted in June of 2000, created Florida Statutes Section 458.348, subsection 3, which indicates that all protocols relating to electrolysis or electrology using laser or light-based hair removal or reduction by persons other than licensed physicians must require the person performing the service to be appropriately trained and to work only under the direct supervision and responsibility of a licensed physician.

ILLINOIS

Written collaborative agreements in Illinois must describe the working relationship between the APN and physician and must authorize the categories of care, treatment, or procedures to be performed by the APN (Regs Tit. 68, § 1305.3). The collaborative agreement must promote the exercise of professional judgment by the APN commensurate with his or her education and experience; the services the APN provides must be services that the physician generally provides to his or her patients in the normal course of his or her clinical medical practice (Regs Tit. 68, § 1305.3). The agreement does not have to describe the exact steps that the APN must take with respect to each specific condition, disease, or symptom but it must specify which authorized procedures require a physician's presence (Regs Tit. 68, § 1305.3). Methods of communication must be outlined in the agreement (Regs Tit. 68, § 1305.3). The agreement must be updated annually and be provided to the state upon request; the APN must inform each collaborating physician of all agreements the

APN has signed and provide a copy of these to any collaborating physician upon request (Regs Tit. 68, § 1305.3).

Certified registered nurse anesthetists (CRNAs) are not required to have a written agreement to provide anesthesia services ordered by a physician, dentist, or podiatrist but must have one to be delegated prescriptive authority (Regs Tit. 68, § 1305.3). CRNAs who provide anesthesia in a physician's office, dental office, or podiatric office must have a written practice agreement with either an anesthesiologist or the physician, dentist, or podiatrist performing the procedure (Regs Title 68 §1305.5). The agreement must describe the working relationship between the CRNA and physician and will authorize the categories of care, treatment, or procedures to be performed by the CRNA (Regs Tit. 68, § 1305.5). In a dental or podiatric office, the CRNA may only perform those procedures that the dentist or podiatrist is authorized to provide (Regs Tit. 68, § 1305.5). The physician, dentist, or podiatrist must participate through discussion of and agreement with the anesthesia plan and must remain physically present and be available on the premises for diagnosis, consultation, and treatment of emergency medical conditions (Regs Tit. 68, § 1305.5).

Written policies, protocols, and procedures under which physicians, nurse practitioners, and certified nurse midwives provide family planning services must be approved by the delegate agency's medical director. Written policies, protocols, and procedures must include:

- Intake procedures for new clients
- Patient education
- Obtaining written informed consent
- Schedule and content of visits including (a.) initial; (b.) annual; (c.) scheduled return visits specific to type of method of contraception; (d.) problem visits, specific to type of problem
- Counseling procedures
- Referral procedures
- Follow-up procedures for appointments, failed appointments, and referrals
- Maintenance of client records
- Approved medical orders
- Maintenance and distribution of pharmaceuticals
- Organizational structure of the unit and functional responsibilities of medical, nursing and ancillary personnel
- Medical procedures including (a.) Pap smears and gonorrhea cultures; (b.) intrauterine device (IUD) insertions; (c.) fitting diaphragms/cervical caps; (d.) treatment of sexually transmitted diseases (STD); (e.) initiating oral contraceptives; (f.) laboratory procedures; (g.) treatment of minor gynecologic problems; (h.) other medical procedures performed

- Release of patient records
- Emergency procedures (77 Ill. Adm. Code 635.80).

MASSACHUSETTS

All nurses practicing in an expanded role (physician's office, institution, or private practice) must practice in accordance with written guidelines developed in collaboration with and mutually acceptable to the nurse and to:

- A physician expert by virtue of training or experience in the nurse's area of practice in the case of the nurse in the physician's office and the nurse in private practice or
- The appropriate medical staff and nursing administration staff of the institution employing the nurse (244 CMR 4.22).

The written guidelines must designate a physician who will provide medical direction as is customarily accepted in the specialty area. Guidelines may authorize the nurse's performance of any professional activities included within her area of practice. The guidelines must:

- Specifically describe the nature and scope of the nurse's practice
- Describe the circumstances in which physician consultation or referral is required
- Describe the use of established procedures for the treatment of common medical conditions that the nurse may encounter
- Include provisions for managing emergencies (244 CMR 4.22).

In addition to the above requirements, the guidelines pertaining to prescriptive practice must:

- Include a defined mechanism to monitor prescribing practices, including documentation of review with a supervising physician at least every 3 months
- Include protocols for the initiation of intravenous therapies and Schedule II drugs
- Specify the frequency of review of initial prescription of controlled substances; the initial prescription of Schedule II drugs must be reviewed within 96 hours
- Conform to M.G.L. c. 94C, regulations of the Department of Public Health at 105 CMR 700.000 et seq., and M.G.L. c. 112, § § 80E or 80G, as applicable (244 CMR 4.22).

A nurse practicing in an institution may not practice in an expanded role until (1.) the governing body, including the medical staff and nursing administrative staff of the institution, formally reviews and approves of the guidelines under which she proposes to practice and (2.) a physician is designated who will provide such medical direction as is customarily accepted in the specialty area. If there is no professional staff of nurses and physicians, the guidelines must be reviewed by the board. Such formal approval must be in writing and otherwise in accord with the governing body's by-laws. Once formally approved, guidelines may remain in effect for 2 calendar years. Prior to the end of the 2-year period, a nurse who wishes to continue to practice in an expanded role under the guidelines after their expiration must review them in collaboration with the appropriate persons authorized to develop them and the governing body must review and formally approve of them (244 CMR 4.22).

The BON may request at any time an opportunity to review the guidelines under which a nurse is practicing or proposes to practice in an expanded role. Failure to provide guidelines to the board is basis for and may result in disciplinary action. The board may require changes in the guidelines if it determines that they authorize a nurse to perform professional activities without adequate supervision or collaboration or to perform professional activities that exceed the bounds of the nurse's area of practice or her or his education or experience. The board may also disapprove guidelines in their entirety if it determines that the institution that approved them is incapable of assuring that professional activities performed under them will be in accordance with the board's standards of professional nursing (244 CMR 4.22).

The board may at any time review, either directly or indirectly, the activities of a nurse practicing in an expanded role to determine whether the activities conform to the applicable guidelines. Generally the board may indirectly review activities of nurses practicing in physicians' offices or institutions by requesting reports from supervising physicians or the nurse practicing in the expanded role or the medical staff or nursing administrative staff. Review may result in disciplinary action. Any nurse, physician, or institution aggrieved by a decision of the board is entitled to have the board reconsider its decision on the basis of a record compiled at an adjudicatory proceeding (244 CMR 4.22).

Guidelines authorizing a nurse to practice midwifery that includes obstetrical care must comply with the provisions of M.G.L.C. 112, § 80C, which requires that a nurse midwife function as a member of a health care team that includes a qualified physician licensed to practice medicine in the Commonwealth and who has obstetrics admitting privileges in a hospital licensed by the Department of Public Health for the operation of maternity and newborn services or has a consultative relationship with a physician who has these privileges. An NM whose practice does not include obstetrical care will function as a member of a health care team that includes a qualified physician licensed to practice medicine in the Commonwealth and who has hospital admitting privileges or has a consultative relationship with a physician who has these privileges (244 CMR 4.25).

Psychiatric nurse mental health clinical specialist's practice guidelines must include the points noted below. Guidelines that do not include prescriptive practice must be established in consultation with a fully qualified collaborating professional, ie, psychiatrist, psychologist, licensed independent clinical social worker, or registered nurse, authorized to practice in the expanded role as a clinical specialist in psychiatric-mental health nursing. Areas of the guidelines that address the indications for referral to or consultation with a psychiatrist must be developed in consultation with a psychiatrist whose name must appear on the guidelines.

Psychiatric nurse mental health clinical specialist's practice guidelines must include:

- The scope of continued collaboration and the frequency of periodic reviews with a fully qualified professional, ie, psychiatrist, psychologist, licensed independent clinical social worker, or registered nurse, authorized to practice in the expanded role as a clinical specialist in psychiatric-mental health
- Periodic detailed reviews of the nurse's practice with a collaborating professional
- Procedures for physical examination and medical clearance of patients
- Procedures to be followed for managing psychiatric emergencies including the source of medical coverage
- Procedures to be followed for the care of patients requiring medication
- Indications for referral to or consultation with a psychiatrist (244 CMR 4.25).

Guidelines under which a nurse practices as a nurse anesthetist may authorize her or him to provide anesthesia only under the medical direction of a qualified physician expert by virtue of training or experience as a member of an anesthesia care team. The guidelines must provide that a nurse anesthetist's activities are under the overall direction of the physician director of anesthesia services or his qualified anesthetist designee when a full time anesthesiologist heads the service. In an institution without a physician director of anesthesia services, the guidelines must provide that a nurse anesthetist's activities are under the overall direction of the surgeon or obstetrician responsible for a patient's care. If the physician primarily responsible for a patient's care is not a surgeon, the guidelines must provide that a nurse anesthetist obtains approval from the director of anesthesia services before administering elective anesthesia to a patient. If an institution has no director of anesthesia services, the guidelines must provide that a nurse anesthetist obtains the approval of a designated surgeon on the institution's staff before administering elective anesthesia to a patient. The guidelines under which a nurse practices as a nurse anesthetist must also provide that a physician is immediately available to assist the nurse anesthetist in case of an emergency such as cardiac standstill or cardiac arrhythmia (244 CMR 4.25).

243 CMR 2.10 provides detailed rules regarding physician supervision of nurses engaged in prescriptive practice. Supervising physician means a physician holding an unrestricted full license in the Commonwealth who:

- Has completed training in the United States approved by the Accreditation Council for Graduate Medical Education (ACGME) or in Canada approved by the Royal College of Physicians and Surgeons in Canada (RCPSC) in a specialty area appropriately related to the nurse's area of practice, is board-certified in a specialty area appropriately related to the nurse's area of practice or has hospital admitting privileges in a specialty area appropriately related to the nurse's area of practice; physician who supervises a psychiatric nurse mental health clinical specialist must have completed training in psychiatry approved by the ACGME or the RCPSC, or be board-certified in psychiatry
- Holds valid registration(s) to issue written or oral prescriptions or medication orders for controlled substances from the Massachusetts Department of Public Health and the U.S. Drug Enforcement Administration
- Signs mutually developed and agreed-upon guidelines with the nurse engaged in prescriptive practice and
- Reviews the nurse's prescriptive practice at least every 3 months and provides ongoing direction to the nurse regarding prescriptive practice or delegates such review and direction to another physician who meets the requirements of valid registration and mutually agreed-upon guidelines as noted above

A supervising physician must review and provide ongoing direction for the nurse's prescriptive practice in accordance with written guidelines mutually developed and agreed upon with the nurse. This supervision will be provided as necessary, taking into account the education, training, and experience of the nurse, the nature of the nurse's practice, and the availability to the nurse of clinical back-up by physicians, to ensure that the nurse is providing patient care services in accordance with accepted standards of practice (243 CMR 2.10).

A supervising physician must sign prescriptive practice guidelines only when able to provide supervision consistent with the rules outlined above, taking into account factors including but not limited to geographical proximity, practice-setting, volume and complexity of the patient population, and the experience, training, and availability of the supervising physician and the nurse(s) (243 CMR 2.10). A supervising physician may not enter into guidelines unless the nurse has professional malpractice liability insurance with coverage of at least $100,000.00 per claim, with a minimum annual aggregate of not less than $300,000.00, unless the guidelines limit the nurse to engage in prescriptive practice in or on behalf of federal, state, county or municipal health care facilities (243 CMR 2.10).

In all cases, the written guidelines must:

1. Identify the supervising physician
2. Include a defined mechanism for the delegation of supervision to another physician including, but not limited to, duration and scope of the delegation
3. Specifically describe the nature and scope of the nurse's practice
4. Identify the types of medication(s) to be prescribed, specify any limitations on medications to be prescribed, and describe the circumstances in which physician consultation or referral is required
5. Describe the use of established procedures for the treatment of common medical conditions the nurse may encounter
6. Include provisions for managing emergencies
7. Include a defined mechanism to monitor prescribing practices, including documentation of review by the supervising physician at least every 3 months
8. Include protocols for the initiation of intravenous therapies and Schedule II drugs
9. Specify the frequency of review of initial prescription of controlled substances; the initial prescription of Schedule II drugs must be reviewed within 96 hours
10. Conform to M.G.L. c. 94C, the regulations of the Department of Public Health at 105 CMR 700.000 et seq., M.G.L. c. 112, § 80E or 80G, and 244 CMR 4.00 et seq., as applicable

Written guidelines governing the practice of a nurse midwife engaged in prescriptive practice must also comply with the requirements of M.G.L. c. 112, § 80C and 244 CMR 4.25(1).

The BON may request at any time an opportunity to review the guidelines under which a physician is supervising a nurse or nurses engaged in prescriptive practice. Failure to provide guidelines to the board is a basis for and may result in disciplinary action. The board may require changes in the guidelines if it determines that they do not comply with 243 CMR 2.10 and accepted standards of medical practice. The board may also disapprove guidelines in their entirety if it determines that the supervising physician is incapable of providing adequate supervision to the nurse(s) engaged in prescriptive practice (243 CMR 2.10). The board may request at any time documentation of review by the supervising physician of the nurse engaged in prescriptive practice. Failure to provide documentation to the board is a basis for and may result in disciplinary action (243 CMR 2.10).

MISSOURI

This state only requires protocols for prescriptive authority.

NEW YORK

Practice agreements and practice protocols must be maintained in the practice setting of the nurse practitioner (NP) and collaborating physician and be available to the state for inspection. Practice agreements must include provisions for referral and consultation; coverage for emergency absences of either the NP or collaborating physician; resolution of disagreements between the NP and collaborating physician regarding matters of diagnosis and treatment; the review of patient records at least every 3 months by the collaborating physician; and may include such other provisions as determined by the NP and collaborating physician to be appropriate. Protocols must identify the area of practice to be performed by the NP in collaboration with the physician and must reflect accepted standards of nursing and medical practice. Protocols must include provisions for case management including diagnosis, treatment, and appropriate record keeping by the NP and may include such other provisions as are determined by the NP and collaborating physician to be appropriate. Protocols should be updated periodically (8 NYCRR § 64.5).

The state in its discretion or upon request of a NP or collaborating physician may review practice protocols for the purpose of insuring that they are in conformance with accepted medical and nursing practice and with the statutes and regulations governing the practice of medicine, nursing, and the prescribing of drugs and may render an opinion that will be binding upon the parties to the protocol. A practice and protocol committee designated by the Deputy Commissioner for the Professions will review practice protocols and recommend findings as to their adequacy and conformity with current accepted medical and nursing practice. If the state determines that a protocol is inadequate or contrary to current accepted medical and nursing practice, it will communicate in writing that determination and the reasons for this determination to the NP and the collaborating physician. The NP and collaborating physician must conform to accepted medical and nursing practice immediately and must submit a revised protocol within 30 days of receipt of the state's determination unless an extension of time is requested and granted. Continuation of practice in violation of the determination constitutes unprofessional conduct by either or both licensees (8 NYCRR § 64.5). An appeal from a determination that a practice protocol is inadequate or contrary to current accepted medical and nursing practice may be filed within 30 days after receipt of the notice of determination by a petition setting forth the reasons for the appeal and must be signed by both the nurse practitioner and the collaborating physician. The appeal must be filed with the Division of Professional Licensing Services and will be determined by the Committee on the Professions whose determination will be final (8 NYCRR § 64.5).

TENNESSEE

Tennessee Rules 0880-6-.02 (2000) indicates that for APN practice, protocols are required and must:

1. Be jointly developed and approved by the supervising physician and APN
2. Outline and cover the applicable standard of care
3. Be reviewed and updated biennially
4. Be maintained at the practice site
5. Account for all protocol drugs by appropriate formulary
6. Be specific to the population seen
7. Be dated and signed
8. Be maintained at the practice site and made available upon request for inspection by the respective boards.

The supervising physician must develop clinical guidelines in collaboration with the APN to include a method for documenting consultation and referral (Tennessee Rules 0880-6-.02).

TEXAS

BON Rules and Regulations §221.1 defines protocols as a written authorization to provide medical aspects of patient care that are agreed upon and signed by the APN and the physician, reviewed and signed at least annually, and maintained in the practice setting of the APN. Protocols or other written authorization must be developed to promote the exercise of professional judgment by the advanced practice nurse commensurate with his or her education and experience. Protocols need not describe the exact steps that the APN must take with respect to each specific condition, disease, or symptom and may state types or categories of drugs that may be prescribed rather than just list specific drugs.

BON Rules and Regulations §221.13 indicates that when providing medical aspects of care, APNs must utilize mechanisms that provide authority for that care. These mechanisms may include but are not limited to protocols or other written authorization. Protocols or other written authorization must promote the exercise of professional judgment by the APN commensurate with his or her education and experience. The degree of detail within protocols, policies, practice guidelines, and clinical practice privileges will vary in relation to the complexity of the situations covered by the protocols, the advanced specialty area of practice, the advanced educational preparation of the individual, and the experience level of the individual APN. Protocols or other written authorization

1. Should be jointly developed by the APN and the appropriate physician(s)
2. Must be signed by both the APN and the physician(s)
3. Must be reviewed and re-signed at least annually
4. Must be maintained in the practice setting of the APN
5. Must be made available as necessary to verify authority to provide medical aspects of care

BON Rules and Regulations §221.16 regarding provision of anesthesia services by CRNAs in outpatient settings requires that CRNAs practicing in certain outpatient settings verify that the appropriate policies or procedures are in place. Policies, procedures, or protocols must be evaluated and reviewed at least annually and must be kept on file in the setting where procedures are performed and be made available upon request.

Policies or procedures must include, but are not limited to:

1. Management of outpatient anesthesia. At a minimum, these must address patient selection criteria; patients/providers with latex allergy; pediatric drug dosage calculations, where applicable; ACLS algorithms; infection control; documentation and tracking use of pharmaceuticals including controlled substances, expired drugs, and wasting of drugs; discharge criteria;
2. Management of emergencies to include but not be limited to cardiopulmonary emergency, fire, bomb threat, chemical spill, natural disaster, power outage
3. EMS response and transport including delineation of responsibilities of the certified registered nurse anesthetist and person performing the procedure upon arrival of EMS personnel. This policy should be developed jointly with EMS personnel to allow for greater accuracy.
4. Adverse reactions/events, including but not limited to those resulting in a patient's death intraoperatively or within the immediate postoperative period, must be reported in writing to the board and other applicable agencies within 15 days. Immediate postoperative period is defined as 72 hours.

ENHANCE YOUR LEARNING

1. Develop a written protocol in compliance with the laws of your state. If your state does not require written protocols, choose another state that does.
2. Look up protocol requirements for one state that requires protocols not covered in this chapter.
3. Compare and contrast the requirements for protocols in your state and one neighboring state.
4. Interview an APN who has practiced in different states regarding the differences in protocols and how those differences impacted his or her practice.

TEST YOUR COMPREHENSION

1. Identify two states that do not require protocols for any category of APN.
2. List at least one requirement for protocols that is common to all the states covered in this chapter.
3. List two states that only require protocols for prescriptive authority.
4. Identify one state with specific protocol requirements for CRNAs.

REFERENCES

Association of Women's Health Obstetric Neonatal Nursing. (1998). Are you using standards and guidelines in your practice? *Lifelines, 2*(1), 25.
Pearson, L. (1999). Annual update of how each state stands on legislative issues affecting advanced nursing practice. *The Nurse Practitioner, 24*(1), 16–83.
Sams, L. (1998). Seize the evidence and the opportunity. *Lifelines, 2*(3), 15.
Stein, E. (1996). Peer review in a New York chapter of the ACNM 1987–1994. *Journal of Nurse Midwifery, 41*(5), 401–404.
Tye, C. (1997). The emergency nurse practitioner role in major accident and emergency departments: Professional issues and the research agenda. *Journal of Advanced Nursing, 26,* 364–370.

Professional Liability Issues

Introduction

Reported malpractice payments for nurses are rare. As of 1998 such payments accounted for only 1.7% of all payments reported since the establishment of the National Practitioner Data Bank in 1986. Twenty-four percent of the nurse payments were for nurse anesthetists, 5.9% for certified nurse midwives (CNMs), and 3.8% for nurse practitioners (NPDB, 1998). Advanced practice nurses (APNs) are fortunate in that, compared to physicians, they are infrequently sued. This is generally believed to be due to the increased satisfaction that patients tend to have with their relationships with APNs over physicians.

Nevertheless, it is important for all APNs to have a working knowledge of how the courts define malpractice as it applies to them and to be aware of cases in which APNs have been found legally liable for patient injuries. A 1994 survey indicated that of nurse practitioners (NPs) who were sued, 50% of claims involved allegations of failure to diagnose, and 42% involved claims of negligent treatment; more than half of the missed diagnosis cases were female cancers of the reproductive system, one third of the improper treatment cases were medication-related (Pearson and Birkholz, 1995).

WHAT IS MALPRACTICE?

Malpractice is typically defined as failing to do that which a reasonable prudent practitioner with similar experience and background would do in a given situation or, conversely, doing that which a reasonable prudent practitioner with similar experience and background would not do in a given situation. Most states do not have laws that apply this concept directly to the advanced practice nurse. Rather, the courts fashion rules for the APN based upon those traditionally applied to physicians and other nurses. Another term for malpractice is professional negligence.

Regardless of the state involved, there are always four elements to any claim by a patient for professional negligence: duty, breach, causation, and harm.

Duty

Duty means that the health care provider must have been obligated to act on the patient's behalf. This duty usually arises out of the patient/provider relationship and lasts until this relationship has been formally ended by either the patient or the provider. A health care provider has a duty to exercise that degree of care, skill, and learning possessed, rather than actually practiced, by a reasonably prudent practitioner of the same profession under the same or similar circumstances (*Harris v. Groth*, 1983). Duty can arise from statutory codes, regulatory law, case law and professional standards.

Breach

Breach means that the provider did not act in accordance with the duty owed to the patient. This can take the form of affirmative actions as well as failures to act. Some states define breach through statutes. As an example, Idaho Code § 6-1012 indicates that in a case where the plaintiff is claiming negligence against a health care provider, including APNs, the plaintiff must prove by direct expert testimony and by a preponderance of the evidence that the defendant negligently failed to meet the applicable standard of health care practice of the community in which the care was provided as the standard existed at the time and place of the alleged negligence and as the standard existed regarding the type of healthcare provider the defendant was and in which capacity the provider was functioning. Individual providers are judged in comparison with similarly trained and qualified providers of the same class in the same community, taking into account training, experience, and fields of medical specialization if any. If there is no other similar provider in the community, evidence of the standard in similar communities at the time may be considered. Breach is usually obvious but must be established by expert testimony. In *Planned Parenthood v. Vines* (1989), the standard of care for a nurse practitioner inserting an IUD was established to be the same standard as that applicable to physicians performing the same task.

Causation

Causation means that the breach in duty has to have some effect on the patient, ie, it has to cause something to happen to the patient. The legal standard is that the plaintiff must prove proximate cause, which is defined as a cause "which in natural and continuous sequence, unbroken by any controlling, intervening cause, produces injury, and without which it would not have occurred" (*Johnson v. Minneapolis St. Paul & SSM Ry. Co*, 1926).

Harm

Harm means that the effect caused by the breach must be harmful to the patient. When there is a duty and a breach of that duty and that breach causes some effect, the effect must be injurious to be actionable (Prosser, 1941).

Unless the patient can prove all four elements to the jury, the patient cannot be awarded compensation regardless of his or her condition. Almost all cases require the testimony of expert witnesses to establish each of the four elements. Most states require that the expert witness be a health care provider engaged in a similar or related area of practice as the defendant health care provider (*Tompkins v. Bise*, 1996).

In some very rare circumstances, a legal rule called *res ipsa loquitor* applies in malpractice cases. This rule means "the thing speaks for itself" and is used in those cases in which the patient's injury is one that never occurs absent malpractice such as leaving a surgical sponge inside a patient. This doctrine is a rule of evidence peculiar to the law of negligence and is a qualification of the general rule that negligence is not to be presumed but must be affirmatively proved. By virtue of the doctrine, the law recognizes that an accident or injurious occurrence may be of such nature or may happen under such circumstances; that the occurrence is of itself sufficient to establish the fact of negligence on the part of the defendant, without further or direct proof, thus placing upon the defendant the duty to come forward with an exculpatory explanation, rebutting, or otherwise overcoming the presumption or inference of negligence on his part (Morner v. Union Pacific Railway Company). There are, however, specific requirements that must be met before a patient can use this special rule. Box 6-1 lists the three elements necessary for the application of *res ipsa loquitor*.

There are three situations when the first element is established: (1.) when the act causing the injury is so palpably negligent that it may be

---

BOX 6-1	*Res Ipsa Loquitor*

Elements required for the application of *res ipsa loquitor*:

- The occurrence producing the injury must be of a kind that ordinarily does not occur in the absence of negligence;
- The injury is caused by an agency or instrumentality within the exclusive control of the defendant; and
- The injury-causing occurrence must not be due to any contribution on the part of the plaintiff.

(*Zukowsky v. Brown*, 1971; *Horner v. Northern Pacific Beneficial Association Hospitals, Inc.*, 1963).

inferred as a matter of law, ie, leaving foreign objects, sponges, scissors, and so forth, in the body, or amputation of a wrong body part; (2.) when the general experience and observation of mankind teaches that the result would not be expected without negligence; and (3.) when proof by experts in an esoteric field creates an inference that negligence caused the injuries (*ZeBarth v. Swedish Hospital Medical Center*, 1972; *Horner v. Northern Pacific Beneficial Association Hospitals, Inc.* 1963).

When each of the elements of *res ipsa loquitur* are supported by substantial evidence, including an inference from expert medical testimony that negligence caused the injury to the patient, plaintiffs are entitled to a *res ipsa loquitur* instruction (*Miller v. Kennedy*, 1974). A plaintiff emerging from abdominal surgery with a paralyzed arm is such an extraordinary occurrence within the general observations of mankind as to raise an inference of negligence requiring an explanation and proof of non-negligence; and where no explanation of the occurrence was given by the defendant, and there was also medical testimony raising an inference of negligence, a jury was warranted in inferring that the plaintiff's injury was the result of someone's negligence (*Horner v. Northern Pacific Beneficial Association Hospitals, Inc.*, 1963).

STATUTES OF LIMITATIONS

Most states allow patients to file professional negligence claims within 1 year of the time the patient discovered or should have discovered that their injury was caused by an act or omission of a health care provider or within 3 years of the act or omission that is claimed to have caused the injury. For example, Washington State's ARCW § 4.16.350 outlines the statute of limitations for health care providers including nurses and nurse practitioners in that state. Like other states, Washington's statute of limitations for these lawsuits stops or tolls the time to file a lawsuit if the patient can prove fraud, intentional concealment, or the presence of a foreign body not intended to have a therapeutic or diagnostic purpose or effect, until the date the patient or the patient's representative has actual knowledge of the act of fraud or concealment, or of the presence of the foreign body; once the patient has actual knowledge of these facts, the lawsuit must be filed within one year. South Dakota, however, provides a 2-year statute of limitations for malpractice cases (SDCL 15-2-14.1).

Some states allow minors to sue for injuries up to the age of 21 when the suit involves claims of injuries sustained at birth. California allows minors to sue up to 3 years from the date of the malpractice or up to the minor's eighth birthday, whichever provides the longer period (CCP § 340.5). Washington, however, transfers knowledge of an injury from a parent to a minor, which means that if the parents are aware of the injury, the child himself has only 1 year from the time the parents become aware of the injury in which to file a lawsuit (ARCW §4.16.350). Likewise, Louisiana does not provide a special statute of limitations for minors (LSA-RS 9:5628).

STATUTORY IMMUNITY

Some states provide immunity from malpractice claims to providers who provide charitable care. For example, Mississippi Code Annotated § 73-25-38 states that any NP who provides charitable medical care is immune from liability for any civil action if the NP and patient execute a written waiver in advance of services rendered. Iowa Code § 147A.10 (1999) provides immunity from civil liability for nurse practitioners who give orders from another physical location to other care providers at the scene of an emergency unless their conduct amounts to reckless behavior. NPs are also not civilly liable for failure to obtain consent before giving emergency care to a patient when the patient is unable to give consent and there is no other person reasonably available who is legally authorized to give such consent.

OTHER TYPES OF ACTIONS BROUGHT AGAINST HEALTH CARE PROVIDERS

Sometimes lawsuits against health care providers contain claims other than those for general professional negligence. The most frequently used claims will be discussed here.

Lack of Informed Consent

Some states allow patients to make separate claims alleging lack of informed consent; others consider this to be part of a claim for professional negligence. This claim states that the APN failed to disclose the risks, benefits, and alternatives of the proposed treatment. The patient must prove that the APN didn't disclose facts material to the patient's decision to accept the proposed treatment, that the patient consented without knowing the facts, and that a reasonable, prudent patient would not have consented if informed. Box 6-2 discusses the case of *Snow v. A.H. Robbins*, 1985.

It is important to note that the law also requires health care providers to disclose the risks of refusing tests. In *Truman v. Thomas*, 1980, the court found that the defendant was negligent for failing to disclose the risk of refusing to have a Pap smear performed.

Negligent Infliction of Emotional Distress (NIED)

This claim basically means that while negligently caring for the patient, the health care provider negligently caused emotional distress. In most states this claim as to the patient is not an independent cause of action

BOX 6-2	Informed Consent

In the case of *Snow v. A.H. Robbins* (1985), a NP inserted a Dalkon Shield IUD after representing to the patient that it was as effective as the birth control pill. The patient became pregnant and the NP advised termination of the pregnancy. A physician, nevertheless, advised her she could leave in the IUD and continue with the pregnancy. She opted to terminate and the same physician performed the procedure. The patient later saw a "60 Minutes" show about the manufacturer's misleading information about the pregnancy rate and sued the NP for understating the risks of pregnancy with the IUD.

but is included in the general tort of professional negligence and involves the same elements of duty, breach, causation and harm. Box 6-3 discusses the case of *Perry et al. v. Magee et al.*, 1992. Box 6-4 discusses the case of *Scott et al. v. Capital Area Community Health Plan et al.*, 1993.

A person other than the patient can also claim negligent infliction of emotional distress under certain circumstances. There are two legal theories under which someone who isn't the patient can sue a health care provider for NIED: the direct victim theory and the bystander theory. Under the direct victim theory, the non-patient plaintiff must have had a pre-existing consensual relationship with the offending health care

BOX 6-3	Negligent Infliction of Emotional Distress Denied

In the case of *Perry et al. v. Magee et al.* (1992), the court denied the mother's claim for negligent infliction of emotional distress as a result of the stillbirth of her infant. In reaching this decision, the court found that the mother's theories of liability against the obstetrician and CNM were based upon certain alleged actions or failures to act in the course of the mother's treatment, namely; (1) the obstetrician's failure to induce labor earlier; (2) the CNM's failure to adequately communicate the extent of the fetal distress to the obstetrician; (3) the obstetrician's inadequate response to the child's distress when informed of the fetal condition by the CNM during a phone conversation, and (4) the CNM's failure to prepare the mother for a cesarean deliveryin a timely fashion. Here, it was impossible for the plaintiff to identify and comprehend any of these alleged negligent acts or omissions by the defendants. This cause of action requires that the plaintiff witness or comprehend the negligent acts bringing about the harm as they were being committed. The court found that a parents' pain and suffering caused by their child's negligent death have never been recoverable *unless* the pain and suffering were *accompanied* by or as a result of a physical *injury to the parent.*

BOX 6-4	Negligent Infliction of Emotional Distress Denied

In the case of *Scott et al. v. Capital Area Community Health Plan et al.* (1993), plaintiffs alleged medical malpractice committed by defendants in their pre-natal care of plaintiff, and particularly the failure of defendant Trish Bagley, a nurse practitioner employed by defendant Capital Area Community Health Plan Inc., to properly diagnose fetal cardiac and pulmonary distress that resulted in the stillbirth of their term infant. Their only injury was the emotional distress brought on by the death of the fetus. The court dismissed the case, indicating that it is well settled that a mother may not recover for emotional and psychic harm as the result of a stillbirth absent physical injuries distinct from the injury to the fetus. Even accepting for the sake of argument that the temporary symptoms alleged by plaintiff may be properly characterized as an "injury," the court still believed that they were not distinct or independent from the cardiac distress suffered by the fetus, but that they were the direct result and, in fact, the very manifestation of the fetal impairment. This was not a case where the fetal demise was a proximate result of the injury to the mother. Rather, it was one where the injuries alleged by the mother were caused by the breach of a claimed duty to the fetus.

provider, and the health care provider's conduct must have been outrageous. This direct victim theory is rarely proven. The bystander theory requires that the non-patient plaintiff prove that he or she:

- Is closely related to the injured party
- Was present at the time of the injury-producing event and was contemporaneously aware that an injury was being caused to the injured party (ie, was aware of the injury at the time it was occurring; this is the hard part to prove)
- As a result, suffered serious emotional distress

Wrongful Death

This claim asserts that the health care provider negligently caused the patient's death. Some states now allow this claim if a viable fetus dies in utero due to negligence.

Wrongful Birth/Life

Wrongful birth is the parents' claim; wrongful life is the child's claim. The elements of this claim are:

- The health care provider negligently counseled, tested, and treated the mother of the child regarding genetic defects and disabilities.
- The negligent counseling, testing, and treating caused the parents to be unaware of the possibility of the child's having a hereditary condition, thus depriving them of the opportunity to choose not to

conceive a child with a genetic defect or of the opportunity to make an informed decision about aborting the pregnancy.

- The health care provider's negligence was a cause of the child's being born.
- The child was born with a congenital or genetic defect or ailment.
- The parents/child sustained special damages consisting of money spent to compensate for the extraordinary additional medical care and training necessitated by the child's ailment or defect.

Box 6-5 discusses the case of *Azzolina et al. v. Dingfelder et al.*, 1985.

Loss of Consortium

This claim asserts that the patient, because of the health care provider's negligence, was unable to perform his or her usual marital and household duties. The plaintiff for this claim is always the patient's spouse. When the patient is injured in such a way that substantially affects his or her capacity to participate in the marriage, the other spouse has an independent cause of action for loss of consortium.

Intentional Torts

The most frequently pled intentional torts against health care providers are spoliation of evidence, battery, fraud, and intentional infliction of emotional distress. There are three important things about these claims that may have a great impact on the defendants:

1. They are not covered by professional liability insurance. The insurance company will usually pay to defend these claims if they are part of a professional negligence case, but if damages are awarded based on one of these claims, the insurance company will not pay the damages and may seek reimbursement from the insured for the costs of defense.
2. They are subject to punitive damages awards that can reach staggering amounts that will not be paid by insurance.
3. The plaintiff may also be awarded costs and fees, which means that the losing defendant will be forced to reimburse the plaintiff for their costs of litigation on top of any other damages awarded.

Spoliation of evidence requires plaintiff to prove that:

- The health care provider intentionally acted in such a way that records pertaining to the patient were destroyed, damaged, lost or concealed.
- The provider knew of the existence of a claim by the patient.
- The patient's opportunity to prove her claim was substantially disrupted.

BOX 6-5	Wrongful Birth/Life

In *Azzolino et al. v. Dingfelder et al.* (1985), a medical malpractice action was brought by a child and his parents and siblings alleging that the defendant family nurse practitioner's and obstetrician's negligent failure to advise the parents properly of the availability of amniocentesis and genetic counseling and negligent prenatal care of the mother prevented the termination of the mother's pregnancy by abortion, thereby resulted in the child's birth. The child had Down syndrome. The court concluded that neither the parents' claim for relief for "wrongful birth," the child's claim for "wrongful life," nor the siblings' claim presented a claim upon which relief could be granted. The court noted that the terms "wrongful birth" and "wrongful life" are descriptive titles used in those jurisdictions that have recognized claims for relief of parents and children for negligent medical treatment or advice which deprives parents of the opportunity to abort a fetus in order to avoid the birth of a defective child, that "wrongful life" refers to a claim for relief by or on behalf of a defective child who alleges that but for the defendant's negligent treatment or advice to its parents, the child would not have been born, and that "wrongful birth" refers to the claim for relief of parents who allege that the negligent treatment or advice deprived them of the choice of terminating pregnancy by abortion and preventing the birth of the defective child. The essence of the claims in this case was that but for the negligence of the defendants, the child would never have been born and he, his parents, and his siblings would not have suffered from his affliction with Down syndrome.

The court concluded that life, even life with severe defects, cannot be an injury in the legal sense, and noted that the overwhelming majority of jurisdictions that have been called upon to consider the issue have rejected claims for relief for wrongful life by children born with defects. Among the reasons the court ruled this way were: (1.) they felt there was no legal basis to recognize these claims without a clear legislative mandate, (2.) the plaintiffs did not allege that the defendants in any way directly caused the genetic defect, (3.) the only damages the plaintiffs allege they have suffered arose from the failure of the defendants to take steps which would have led to abortion of the already existing and defective fetus, (4.) damages in this type of case are hard to analyze and there is no clear rule for what should be allowed.

This court also noted that courts that have recognized claims for wrongful birth have failed to establish a clear trend or any real trend at all with regard to the measure of damages to be allowed. Under traditional theories of tort law, defendants are liable for all reasonably foreseeable results of their negligent acts or omissions, but few if any jurisdictions appear ready to apply this traditional rule of damages with full vigor in wrongful birth cases. Some courts have allowed the parents to recover the extraordinary expenses resulting from the child's impairment but not the expenses they would normally

(continued)

BOX 6-5	Wrongful Birth/Life (Continued)

incur in rearing the child. Others have permitted damages only for the parents' pain, suffering, and mental anguish resulting from the birth of the defective child. Still others have allowed both the extraordinary expenses and recovery for mental anguish. At least one court has allowed parents to recover all expenses involved in rearing the child with no reduction of the damages awarded by the cost of rearing a normal child.

Courts allowing parents' wrongful birth claims have also been unable to resolve issues concerning the extent to which traditional tort concepts requiring plaintiffs to take reasonable steps to mitigate or reduce damages are to be applied in wrongful birth cases. They have, for example, been unable to reach anything resembling a consensus as to whether damages in wrongful birth cases should be reduced or offset by any emotional or other benefits accruing to the parents by reason of the life, love, and affection of the defective child. Likewise, they have been unable to reach any consensus on the issue of whether there is a duty on the part of the parents to place the child for adoption in order to reduce their damages.

Perhaps most important to this court was the fact that the wrongful birth claim will almost always hinge on testimony given by the parents after the birth concerning their desire prior to the birth to terminate the fetus should it be defective. The temptation will be great for parents, if not to invent such a prior desire to abort, to at least deny the possibility that they might have changed their minds and allowed the child to be born even if they had known of the defects it would suffer.

Battery

Battery is a tort as well as a crime. It is an intentional, unprivileged, and nonconsensual offensive contact. This is usually claimed when a patient has been treated without informed consent.

Fraud

Fraud can be claimed as either intentional/affirmative misrepresentation or as concealment. For a patient to prove affirmative misrepresentation, he or she must prove that:

- The defendant made a representation as to a past or existing material fact.
- The representation was false.
- Defendant knew it was false when made or defendant made it recklessly without knowing if it was true or false.
- Defendant made the representation with the intent to defraud.
- Plaintiff was unaware of the falsity, acted in reliance on the truth of the representation, and was justified in so relying.

- Plaintiff sustained damage as a result of her reliance on the truth of the representation.

An example of when a patient might assert this claim is when a health care provider is accused of lying to the patient about his or her qualifications or experience with a certain procedure.

Concealment requires that:

- Defendant concealed or suppressed a material fact.
- Defendant was under a duty to disclose the fact to the patient.
- Defendant intentionally concealed or suppressed the fact with the intent to defraud the patient.
- Patient was not aware of the fact and would not have acted as she did if she had known of it.
- Concealment/suppression of the fact caused damage to the patient.

This claim may arise if the health care provider makes an error and doesn't tell the patient.

Intentional infliction of emotional distress requires that:

- The provider intentionally caused emotional distress to the patient /family.
- The provider's conduct was outrageous and done with the intent to cause emotional distress.
- The outrageous and unprivileged conduct caused the patient's emotional distress.

This claim is obviously not proven very often and requires more than just negligence. An example would be the case that occurred a few years ago where a surgeon carved his initials into the abdomen of a patient during a cesarean delivery.

Criminal Charges

In a stunning recent case, three Denver nurses, including a neonatal/pediatric nurse practitioner, were charged with criminally negligent homicide in the death of a healthy full term infant. The infant's mother had had positive RPR tests at the first visit, at 18 weeks, and at 29 weeks, however, a fourth test at 38 weeks was negative but was not documented on the prenatal records sent to the delivering facility. The mother had a NSVD at 40 weeks. Following CDC recommendations, but without knowing that the last test was negative, the neonatologist ordered 150,000 units of benzathine penicillin G IM. The hospital pharmacist filled the order with 10 times the ordered dose. The NP became involved when the maternal infant nurse turned over the administration of this unfamiliar drug because she realized that the dose sent up by the pharmacist would require five injections. The NP did not recognize that the dose was 10 times that ordered nor did she call the pharmacy to verify the volume sent. Instead she decided to investigate a different route for administration. The NP ordered that the medication be given IV after consulting with the Neofax 95, which described the alternative treatment as aqueous penicillin G slow IV push. The NP erroneously believed that "aqueous" and "benzathine" penicillin were the same drug and that benzathine was the brand name for the aqueous penicillin instead of realizing that it indicates the type of solution in which the penicillin is suspended. The NP and a Level 2 nursery nurse proceeded to administer the IM preparation by IV push. After 1.8 ml of the drug was administered, the infant went into cardiac arrest. Attempts at resuscitation lasted 3 hours but the infant could not be revived. The NP was fired by the hospital. Because the errors resulted in the unexplained death of an infant, the case was investigated, a coroner's autopsy was ordered by the district attorney's office, and a grand jury found probable cause for the death of the infant. Several months later, the nurses were indicted in criminal court for criminally negligent homicide. This charge means they were accused of gross deviation from the standard of care that a reasonable nurse would exercise and failure to perceive a substantial and unjustifiable risk. Shortly before the trial was to start, the NP accepted a plea bargain that required her to plead guilty and for which she received a deferred sentence of 2 years' probation and 24 hours of community service teaching nursing students the danger of improper drug administration. Her record will be expunged of the conviction if she avoids additional criminal litigation for 2 years and adheres to the state board of nursing review of her license (Plum, 1997, Hagedorn,1999).

Respondeat Superior—Liability for the Acts of Others
Obviously, the individual APN is legally responsible for his or her own actions. There are also times when the APN may be legally responsible for the actions of others. This responsibility arises from any legal relationships the APN has entered into. Henry, 1996, reminds us that legal relationships are created when the APN enters into an employment agreement or a collaborative agreement. If the APN is an employee, then the employer will traditionally be liable for the APN's actions. The employer will not be liable if the APN's actions were performed outside of the scope of employment, such as when the APN renders care beyond or in deviation of the established protocols for the practice (Henry, 1996). A collaborative practice can also create additional liability for the people involved. Each member of a joint practice is liable for his or her own actions as well as potential liability for the actions of the other members. This potential liability is defined by the collaborative arrangement: if the practice is established as a formal partnership then each partner is liable for the acts of the other partner; if there is no formal (legal) partnership, then the terms of the collaborative agreement would govern whether each party assumes legal liability for the acts of the others (Henry, 1996).

In situations involving consultations and referrals, liability issues can also arise. When an APN seeks a consultation from another provider, the APN retains responsibility for the patient's care and all final treatment decisions rest with the APN (Henry, 1996). It is important to document acceptance or rejection of the consultant's recommendations, as failing to do so could lead to a finding that the APN ratified the recommendations and could require explanation as to why the recommendations were not followed (Henry, 1996). APNs are held legally responsible for selection of a proper, qualified consultant and can be held liable for negligent selection should the patient receive negligent care from a consultant (Henry, 1996). The same principle applies when APNs are making referrals. Box 6-6 discusses the case of *Baird v. Sickler*, 1982.

Selected Liability Cases Against Advanced Practice Nurses

CRNAs

In the early morning of January 25, 1991, Kathy and Butch LaCroix went to the Women's Pavilion of Denton Regional Medical Center for the birth of their first child. Kathy was admitted to the hospital under the care of her obstetrician, who ordered an anesthesia consult for a labor epidural. Because Nurse Blankenship, the CRNA on duty in the Women's Pavilion, was involved in another procedure at that time, she told the requesting nurse to call someone else with the anesthesia group. Nurse Hill, who was off-duty, was called and he came to the Women's Pavilion. Around 9:30 a.m., Nurse Hill placed a catheter in Kathy's epidural space and began her on the anesthetic Marcaine using an epidural pump. No physician ever ordered the Marcaine. After starting the epidural, Nurse Hill reported to Nurse Blankenship what he had done. Nurse Hill then left the Women's Pavilion, and Nurse Blankenship assumed Kathy's anesthesia care. Around 11:00 a.m., Nurse Blankenship was called to Kathy's labor room because her blood pressure had dropped. Nurse Blankenship turned off the epidural pump and gave Kathy ephedrine. No physician ever ordered the ephedrine. When Kathy's blood pressure responded, Nurse Blankenship turned the epidural pump back on. Around 1:30 p.m., the obstetrician decided that a cesarean delivery was warranted because of an occasionally low fetal pulse and slow cervical dilation. While the cesarean section was an emergency in that it was unscheduled, it was not a "stat" emergency cesarean delivery that had to be done immediately. On her own and without a physician's order, Nurse Blankenship discontinued the Marcaine and began Nesacaine, a cesarean epidural anesthetic, in the labor room. Nurse Blankenship gave a total of 20 mL of Nesacaine. Nurse Blankenship testified that she cannot administer anesthesia without the medical direction of a physician and that she administered anesthesia and other drugs to Kathy under the obstetrician's medical direction and supervision. The obstetrician testified that he did not give Nurse Blankenship medical direction for her anesthesia care of

BOX 6-6   Respondeat Superior

In the case of *Baird et al. v. Sickler* (1982), the plaintiff sued the surgeon who performed a laminectomy and who helped position the patient and otherwise assist the CRNA with the patient's intubation. Plaintiff was rendered permanently a paraplegic from C-6 level down as a result of faulty intubation and positioning. The court found that a chief surgeon's immunity for the negligent acts of an assisting nurse-anesthetist is not a matter of law. The court felt that the physician may, under the doctrine of *respondeat superior,* indeed be liable for the alleged negligence of the nurse-anesthetist who assisted him during the operation. Under the doctrine of *respondeat superior,* the "master" is liable for the negligence of his "servant" when the latter is engaged in performing the work of the former (*Mider v. United States,* 1963; *Van Meter v. Publication Utility Commission,* 1956). However, a master–servant relationship exists only when one party exercises the right of control over the actions of another and those actions are directed toward the attainment of an objective which the former seeks (*Bobik v. Industry Commission,* 1946; *Duke v. Sanymetal Products Co.,* 1972). For the relationship to exist, it is unnecessary that the right of control be exercised; it is sufficient that the right merely exists (*Pickens & Plummer v. Diecker & Brother,* 1871).

All requisite indices of the master–servant diad were found to be present in the relationship between appellant Dr. Sickler and J. A. Nichol, the nurse-anesthetist who assisted him. Dr. Sickler admitted that, before the intubation, he instructed Nichol as to the procedures he wished to follow because of Baird's special condition. He stated that, during the intubation, he watched to ensure that Nichol did not hyperflex or hyperextend the neck and admitted that had he observed any misfeasance in the conduct of the intubation, he would have possessed the right and duty to halt the procedure. The doctor testified that, following the intubation, he held the patient's head as she was turned and placed on the operating table and monitored her positioning to ensure that neither her airway nor eyes were compromised. The doctor, clearly, not only controlled but also participated in administering the anesthetic. Moreover, even if he had failed to exercise control over the intubation, he clearly, as he himself admitted, had the right to control it.

The doctor contended that the doctrine of *respondeat superior* was inapplicable because Nichol, the nurse-anesthetist, was an employee and servant of Anesthesia Associates, not of Dr. Sickler. The court rejected this argument because of the "loaned servant" rule, which indicates that one who borrows another's employee may be considered a temporary master liable in *respondeat superior* for the borrowed employee's negligent acts if acquiring the same right of control over the employee as originally possessed by the lending employer (*Weaver v. Bennett,* 1963). Whether a surgeon may be held vicariously liable for the negligence of one assisting in the operation depends on whether, in particular case, the surgeon had the right to control the manner in which the assistant performed.

Kathy, that he did not supervise Nurse Blankenship, and that he would never supervise a CRNA because he is not qualified to do so. Before the cesarean delivery began, Kathy complained several times of breathing difficulty. When the pediatrician who was going to treat the baby after delivery arrived in the operating room, he noticed that Kathy appeared to be in respiratory distress and heard her say, "I can't breathe." He asked Nurse Blankenship if Kathy was okay; the nurse responded that Kathy was just nervous so he went about preparing his pediatric equipment. Soon after that Kathy's eyes "got big" and she whispered again to her husband that she could not breathe. Her husband, who was alarmed, stood up and shouted, "She can't breathe. Somebody please help my wife."

Nurse Blankenship asked that he be removed from the operating room because Kathy was having what appeared to her to be a seizure and Nurse Blankenship knew that she might have to put Kathy to sleep and intubate her. Nurse Blankenship, who could not establish an airway with an airbag and mask because Kathy's teeth were clenched shut from the seizure, told the obstetrician, in response to his asking her whether he should continue, to take the baby rather than stop the cesarean delivery. She also told one of the nurses: "Get one of the anesthesiologists here now!" Dr. Green, who was in his car, was paged. When he received the page, he immediately drove to the Women's Pavilion. The obstetrician was already making the cesarean incision when the seizure occurred, and he told Nurse Blankenship that Kathy's blood was dark, as opposed to oxygenated blood, which is bright red. When the baby was delivered, she was not breathing and the pediatrician had to resuscitate her. Meanwhile, to intubate Kathy to establish an airway for her, Nurse Blankenship had to paralyze her, using the drug Anectine, and put her to sleep, using Sodium Pentothal, a general anesthetic. She was then able to intubate Kathy, but it was an esophageal intubation, rather than tracheal. At that time, a nurse in the Women's Pavilion sounded a "Code 99" throughout the entire hospital. After the obstetrician, who was still working inside Kathy's abdomen, pointed out that he thought that the intubation was esophageal, Nurse Blankenship removed the tube and successfully intubated Kathy. While the obstetrician was closing the cesarean delivery incisions, Kathy's blood pressure and pulse dropped, and Nurse Blankenship gave her ephedrine to try to raise her blood pressure. Kathy then went into full cardiac arrest and her heart stopped beating. A physician and nurse from the hospital's emergency room had responded to the code and came into the operating room. The pediatrician testified that the emergency room physician said that he did not know how to resuscitate pregnant women and left without providing any medical care. The obstetrician and a nurse began CPR on Kathy, and the pediatrician, once he was finished treating the infant, took control of the code and directed nurses to give Kathy atropine and epinephrine to resuscitate her. Kathy's heart resumed beating after one dose of epinephrine. Although Kathy was resuscitated, she had suffered an irreversible brain injury caused by hypoxia. She was comatose for 3 days and was hospitalized for a total of 13 days. Kathy was then transferred to a rehabilitation hospital, where she stayed for 50 days. Because of her brain injury, Kathy has a full scale IQ of 76, which places her on the borderline of intellectual functioning, and she is totally and permanently disabled from independent living. Nurse Blankenship and Dr. Hafiz settled with the LaCroixs by paying $500,000 and $750,000, respectively, for a total settlement of $1.25 million. Dr. Hafiz was the DAA anesthesiologist on call for the Women's Pavilion on the day of Kathy's incident (*Denton Regional Medical Center and Epic Healthcare Group, INC. v. Lawrence Lacriox*, 1997).

In *Overton v. Fairfax Anesthesiology*, the plaintiff, a 33-year-old unemployed black man suffered a stab wound to his upper chest. The wound was successfully repaired in surgery. Two to three days thereafter the plaintiff developed bleeding around the lung that required a second surgery. Post-operatively, defendant nurse anesthetist took plaintiff off the monitors and subsequently failed to note that plaintiff's respiratory condition deteriorated rapidly. Plaintiff was discovered in a respiratory code. He was resuscitated but showed signs of profound anoxic encephalopathy, for which he will require institutional care for the remainder of his life. Plaintiff alleged that the CRNA was negligent in removing him from his monitors too soon and in failing to observe him for signs of respiratory compromise, resulting in profound brain damage. This case was settled for $700,000.

Another plaintiff, a 15-year-old girl, was admitted to Prince George's County Hospital for delivery of her baby. Fetal distress was noted and she was prepped for an emergency cesarean delivery. She was put under general anesthesia and the baby was delivered. Defendant nurse anesthetist, who was responsible for monitoring plaintiff's breathing, was addicted to Sublimaze. He did not notice that a kink had developed in the oxygen hose. Plaintiff was denied oxygen for approximately 5 minutes, causing severe brain damage. Plaintiff alleged that defendant was negligent in failing to properly monitor her during the surgery. A jury deliberated 7 hours prior to awarding plaintiff $4 million (Metro Verdicts Monthly, Case CAL87-11172).

In another case, a 40-year-old design engineer earning $50,000 a year, had been married for 3 years when he began experiencing pain in his right shoulder. He selected an orthopedic surgeon from his employer's preferred provider organization (PPO) list who recommended a conservative course of treatment that failed to give relief. He then recommended arthroscopic day surgery. On the day of surgery, a physician introduced herself to the patient for the first time, said that she was an anesthesiologist and that she would be giving him his general anesthetic.

According to the wife, the visit was a brief one, and there was no mention of a nurse anesthetist participating in the administration of anesthesia. At 9:30 a.m. a CRNA intubated him. The anesthesiologist remained for the intubation and positioning of the patient. She claimed that she listened for and confirmed the presence of bilateral breath sounds indicating that the endotracheal tube was inserted to a proper depth. She then left the operating room. A few minutes later, the CRNA called for the assistance to shut off an alarm on the anesthesia monitoring machine. The anesthesiologist then left again, not to return until she was summoned at 10:42 a.m. The surgeon was approximately two-thirds through the procedure when he saw the nurse anesthetist "fiddling" up under the surgical drapes. He asked if there was a problem. She replied she couldn't hear air in one lung. They discontinued the procedure. The patient was markedly cyanotic. The anesthesiologist returned to the OR and was followed by another anesthesiologist. The two anesthesiologists and four nurses began resuscitation efforts. At 10:45 a.m., the patient's heart was electroshocked back into a normal sinus rhythm. No one heard any alarms sound on the anesthesia monitors either before or after the arrest was discovered. The patient remained in a coma and died on October 3, 1997. The pathology department performed an autopsy and reported that his heart was normal on gross and microscopic examination. The autopsy confirmed the existence of severe anoxic brain damage. The CRNA's anesthesia record contained no vital sign documentation after 10:25 a.m. Plaintiffs' experts concluded that decedent was in arrest for over 10 minutes before any resuscitation efforts began. The family settled with the CRNA for $975,000.00 before trial (*Alexander et al. v. Battaglia et al.*, 1999).

Another defendant, a certified nurse anesthetist, placed a central line in plaintiff during a 12:30 p.m. surgery for diverticulitis. He placed it in the carotid artery rather than the jugular vein. The placement of the line was not noticed until 7 a.m. the next morning. By that time, plaintiff had suffered two or three strokes that left him permanently disabled from extensive brain damage. The parties agreed to damages of $350,000 and the case proceeded on the issue of liability only. Plaintiff alleged that: (1.) the central line was misplaced; (2.) the misplaced line went unnoticed for 19 hours, during which time emboli formed, broke off, and caused the strokes; (3.) the line was unnecessary; and (4.) plaintiff suffered a permanent disability as a result of this incident. The jury, after a 10-minute deliberation, found the CRNA liable (*Duell v. Anesthesia Associates et al.*, 2000).

In *Doe v. Roe*, the minor plaintiff was born in excellent health and developed normally. At age 9 months, he was admitted to the defendant hospital for elective surgical repair of a right inguinal hernia. Surgery was performed by the defendant general practitioner; anesthesia was supplied by a nurse anesthetist. When anesthesia was begun, the minor child was noted to be alert, responsive, communicative, and in good health. No blood pressure monitor was used. Approximately 25 minutes later, the child became bradycardic. The nurse anesthetist failed to institute treatment to reverse the condition in a timely manner, and the child suffered 2 minutes of arrest. There were two nurse anesthetists who provided the only anesthesia services available to the hospital. They comprised the entire anesthesia department and established and implemented all hospital anesthesia protocol. State law required that anesthesia by a nurse anesthetist be given under the direct supervision of a physician; but it was the custom and practice at the hospital that anesthesia given by either of the nurse anesthetists was completely unsupervised. The two nurse anesthetists were a partnership of professional corporations; though only one saw the patient, both were joined as defendants. Plaintiff claimed that both partner nurse anesthetists were negligent in having a business that agreed to undertake anesthesia of an infant without medical supervision and without routine blood pressure monitoring of any sort. Plaintiff also claimed that the anesthetist who administered the anesthesia administered an excessive dose of anesthetic, failed to recognize and respond to changes in the child's vital signs until cardiac arrest occurred, and failed to promptly administer resuscitative medications in a prompt fashion. Plaintiffs further claimed the nurse anesthetists were negligent in failing to establish and follow proper anesthesia protocols for the hospital, being aware that blood pressure monitoring on infants was not used by the anesthesia department and negligently failing to remedy the situation, and participating in and establishing protocols for an anesthesia program in violation of state law. It was claimed that the non-participating nurse anesthetist was liable because of her participation in the business that allowed these poor procedures. (The nurse anesthetist who performed the surgery was inadequately insured.) Plaintiffs claimed that the defendant physician was negligent in undertaking to perform surgery on an infant without medically supervised anesthesia in contravention of state law, failing to properly supervise the nurse-anesthetists and thus being directly responsible for the negligent failure to monitor and the negligent administration of anesthesia to the child, and failing to transfer the child to an appropriate medical facility. Plaintiffs claimed that the defendant hospital was negligent in establishing inadequate anesthesia protocols and regulations for the administration of anesthesia to infants, permitting the existing protocols to be violated in that medically unsupervised anesthesia was administered in contravention of state law, permitting anesthesia to be administered on infants without proper blood pressure monitoring devices, and failing to provide the anesthesia department with adequate and safe equipment for monitoring anesthesia. The child suffered anoxic brain damage resulting in multiple partial physical and mental disabilities. The case was settled for $3,060,506 (*Doe v. Roe*, 1987).

Nurse Practitioners

In the case of *Jenkins v. Payne*, 1996, the jury returned a verdict for the plaintiff, awarding $1.3 million in damages against the defendants, a family practice physician, and his nurse. The trial court amended the verdict to $1 million, pursuant to state law, then reduced that amount by $450,000 based on the settlement with the co-defendant gynecologist. In December 1992, Payne was diagnosed with terminal breast cancer. At that time, she had palpable masses in her left breast and had been experiencing continual soreness and discharge from her left nipple for 2 years. She died in April 1994. Payne had first sought treatment for her breast abnormalities on January 7, 1991, when she was examined by York, a nurse practitioner working under the supervision of Dr. Jenkins. She informed York that, for a period of several months, she had been experiencing a discharge and constant scabbing of her left nipple. York ordered a mammogram and prescribed oral and topical antibiotics as treatment for infection of the nipple. The mammogram showed no signs of tumors in the breast.

On July 18, 1991, Payne returned to York complaining of continuing pain and discharge from her left breast. York referred her to a dermatologist for treatment of the continuing irritation. York testified that she believed the dermatologist would perform a biopsy on the abnormal tissue. The medical records do not indicate that York discussed with Payne the need for a biopsy or the possibility of cancer. York did not determine whether Payne was treated by a specialist but assumed that Payne had followed her instructions. On October 21, 1991, and November 8, 1991, Payne sought treatment from Dr. Rothman, a gynecologist. Dr. Rothman recorded Payne's history and noted that for a period of 1½ years she had suffered from an inflamed and bleeding left nipple. Dr. Rothman prescribed oral antibiotics and a topical steroid cream to treat the condition. Dr. Rothman reassured her that she was only suffering from eczema. Payne expressed relief to Dr. Rothman, stating that she was afraid she had cancer. Payne made several additional visits to both York and Dr. Rothman. She was treated by York on January 29, February 27, and March 12, 1992. Payne's medical records for January 1992 indicate that she was concerned about "sores that have been slow to heal." York testified that she could not recall whether she had discussed with Payne any problems about Payne's breast after the July 1991 visit. Payne's medical records do not indicate that York and Dr. Jenkins made any other examination of Payne's breast or that they pursued the question of her need to see a specialist. York testified that she was unaware until September 1992 that Dr. Rothman had examined Payne. Dr. Rothman treated Payne for a urinary tract infection on April 2, 1992. At that visit, Dr. Rothman did not examine Payne's breast nor did he question her about whether the scabbing and discharge were still occurring. On September 23, 1992, York examined Payne and discovered the presence of multiple masses in

Payne's breast. In December 1992, Payne began receiving treatment from Dr. Morton C. Wilhelm, a surgical oncologist. He determined that the cancer had spread to her lymph nodes and was particularly aggressive, rendering her prognosis poor and the terminal nature of the cancer certain.

Plaintiff's experts testified that Payne died as the result of misdiagnosed breast cancer; that Payne would have had a 10-year survival probability of nearly 90% if her cancer had been diagnosed when it was still non-invasive; that Payne's cancer became invasive 3 to 6 months prior to her December 1992 diagnosis; that beginning in January 1991 York and Dr. Jenkins breached the standard of care by failing to recognize symptoms of breast cancer, by over-emphasizing the possibility of infection rather than cancer, by failing to refer Payne to a surgeon for a biopsy, and by failing to determine whether the surgeon had diagnosed the breast abnormality. They testified that Dr. Jenkins and York breached this standard of care on Payne's 1991 visits, as well as on her January, February, and March 1992 visits. Yvonne G. Newberry, an expert on the standard of care for family nurse practitioners, testified that, given Payne's history of breast problems, York should have performed a breast examination and discussed the possibility of cancer with Payne during the January, February, and March 1992 office visits. Newberry testified that York had an obligation to ask Payne about the progress of the breast treatment even when Payne did not specifically complain about it.

In a different case, a 14-year-old boy was being treated by defendants for Ewing's sarcoma. Shortly after his first dose of chemotherapy, the boy developed abdominal pain. Repeated telephone calls were made to defendant hospital describing the pain. Defendant nurse practitioner examined him, diagnosed constipation, treated him with stool softener, and released him. The pain continued. A few days thereafter, the boy went into full arrest at home and died due to sepsis and peritonitis secondary to appendicitis. Plaintiff alleged that defendants were negligent in failing to diagnose and treat decedent's appendicitis and that defendant hospital was negligent in having a nurse practitioner examine decedent when he presented to their clinic. The case was settled on the fifth day of trial for $200,000 (*Lusher v. Childrens Hospital Medical Center et al.*, 1992).

In January 1992, a 28-year-old woman was taken to defendant hospital with complaints of pain in the right lower abdomen, nausea, and vomiting that had awakened her in the morning. She was examined by an emergency room physician and released, although her white count was elevated. She returned several hours later with the same complaints and was re-examined by another emergency room physician who called in defendant surgeon. He examined the patient and released her from the hospital with a diagnosis of abdominal pain, etiology unknown, despite an even higher white count. She was given medication for a possible urinary tract infection. Thereafter went to a medical group on two occasions where she was examined by nurse practitioners and diagnosed with a bladder infection. The primary treating physician there did not see her personally. On March 31, she was in a great deal of pain and returned to the medical group where blood tests showed a drastically elevated white count and infection. No one told the physician about the results until the following day, almost 24 hours after the blood was drawn. The medical group attempted to immediately contact decedent by telephone but was unsuccessful. The decedent collapsed and went into cardiac arrest later that day, April 1, 1992, and died that evening at the defendant hospital of acute peritonitis due to a ruptured, gangrenous appendix. The Plaintiff asserted that the defendants were negligent for not diagnosing and treating the condition earlier when decedent presented to them on several occasions. The medical group claimed they only saw the patient on one occasion in January, 1992 and that she did not return until March 31; that there was evidence then that she had white cells in her urine and a bladder infection, for which she was treated; that by March 31, when she returned to the medical group, it was too late to have done anything even if they had advised her of the level of infection discovered by the blood tests. The medical group paid $200,000 in settlement of the case (*Jenkins v. Quini et al.*, 1993).

Twenty-seven days post-delivery, a nurse practitioner inserted an IUD in plaintiff, a 29-year-old homemaker. Although the IUD remained in plaintiff, she missed a period and went to the clinic on July 23, 1980, where she tested positive for pregnancy. Due to difficulties in removing the IUD, she was forced to undergo laparotomy to remove the device. Plaintiff sued, alleging that the IUD was placed too soon after delivery, at a time when she was susceptible to perforation by a foreign object such as IUD. She also claimed that the nurse practitioner negligently and improperly inserted the IUD, resulting in perforation of the uterus, subsequent pregnancy, and the need for the abortion and subsequent surgery. A jury awarded plaintiff $87,000 (*Garcia v. County of Los Angeles*, 1986).

In another case, plaintiff's mother went to her obstetrician's office at approximately 30 to 32 weeks gestation, complaining of leakage of clear fluid from her vagina. She was seen on the first occasion by the obstetrician, cultured, and reassured. When the symptoms continued, she was seen in the office by the obstetrician's NP. No tests such as nitrazine or ferning were done. The NP sent the patient home with reassurance that there was no premature rupture of membranes; she did not consult the doctor. Four days later the patient presented with chills, cramps, and chorioamnionitis. The baby was born septic and suffered from periventricular leukomalacia. Attorneys for the child claimed that the NP was negligent in failing to diagnose premature rupture of the membranes and/or in failing to at least warn the patient to be on the lookout for further leakage or fever or chills; that the nurse practitioner should have consulted with the doctor who would likely have admitted the patient to the hospital in order to minimize the risk of chorioamnionitis and premature labor; and that the doctor would have delivered her prior to the baby getting septic. The case was settled for $1 million (*Plaintiff Baby v. Nurse Practitioner*, 1994).

A malpractice action brought against a defendant physician and defendant nurse practitioner alleged that as a result of the defendants' negligent failure to properly examine, diagnose, and treat the minor plaintiff's respiratory problem, the child fell into respiratory arrest and sustained permanent brain damage. The case involved a healthy, 18-month-old baby girl who awoke one morning unable to catch her breath. The mother contacted a nearby hospital, detailed her baby's symptoms to the defendant nurse practitioner, and was informed that the child did not need to be seen. The child continued to suffer respiratory distress and her mother placed a second call to the hospital, insisting that her daughter be examined. At the hospital, the defendant NP noted that the child had a history of inspiratory stridor, ie, difficulty in breathing, which prompted the nurse to consult with the defendant physician on duty at the time the plaintiff was brought in. Despite knowledge of the child's respiratory history and her current condition, the defendant physician failed to examine her. The physician also failed to suggest re-evaluation of the child or to advise the mother to observe the child for a worsening of her condition. The defendant NP diagnosed the child's condition as croup and sent her home, assuring the mother that her daughter's condition was not serious. The child's episodes of severe respiratory distress continued, climaxing with her collapse from respiratory arrest in the early morning. She was rushed to the hospital where she was resuscitated and transferred to a metropolitan hospital. The child suffered severe brain damage due to a lack of oxygen. The plaintiffs alleged that the failure of the defendant physician and the defendant NP to properly examine, evaluate, and treat the child resulted in the severe and permanent brain damage sustained. The action was settled on the parents' claim only for $500,000 (Case No. 84-7433, 1990).

In the case of *JE vs. LC*, a death action was brought by the estate of the 57-year-old decedent against the defendant treating physician and his nurse practitioner alleging negligence in failing to properly monitor the plaintiff while on Coumadin therapy. As a result, the decedent became overly anticoagulated, ultimately resulting in a massive retroperitoneal hemorrhage that took his life. The evidence indicated that the decedent initially consulted with the defendant physician, whose specialty was neurology and internal medicine, for evaluation of dark spots in his eye. A diagnostic echocardiogram revealed a blood clot in the decedent's heart. The defendant physician prescribed Coumadin. It is essential that patient's receiving Coumadin therapy be closely monitored to assess anticoagulation. This assessment is performed by a blood test called a pro time test. A normal prothrombin time (PT) value should range between 15 to 20, and a value lower or higher can have serious life threatening consequences. The decedent was told to continue his Coumadin therapy after discharge but was never advised by either the defendant physician or his NP of the importance of returning for blood work to determine how he was responding to the Coumadin. Nor was he given clear instructions as to when he should return for a follow-up visit with the defendant doctor. Nine days after his discharge, the decedent's wife contacted the defendant physician to report that her husband was experiencing a nosebleed and to inquire why he had not been scheduled for blood testing or a follow-up with the defendant physician. The nurse practitioner instructed the plaintiff to come in the following day. At this visit, a PT test performed upon the decedent indicated a result of 64, a grossly elevated value. Despite the decedent's nosebleed and elevated PT reading, both clear signs of over anticoagulation, the defendant physician did not treat or hospitalize the decedent. Rather, he instructed the decedent to stop the drug for 3 days, resume therapy with 5 mg. per day for 2 days, and then return for a blood test. Two days later, the decedent's wife again contacted the defendant's office to report that the plaintiff was complaining of pains in his groin and leg, classic symptoms of over anticoagulation. The NP diagnosed the decedent's pain as a result of his having walked too much and she prescribed bedrest. The following day, the decedent began to experience back pain, a symptom commonly associated with retroperitoneal bleeding that can occur with over-anticoagulation. The decedent's wife contacted the defendant NP, who assured her that the decedent did not need to be evaluated by the physician. One day later, the decedent lost consciousness and was rushed to the hospital with a ruptured abdominal aortic aneurysm. The decedent suffered a massive hemorrhage that led to multi-organ failure and, ultimately, his premature death. The plaintiffs contended that the defendants' failure to adequately monitor the decedent's Coumadin dosage and failure to properly respond to tests and symptoms revealing a dangerous elevated PT level, led to the massive retroperitoneal hemorrhage that caused his death. The jury awarded the plaintiff $499,845 (*JE v. LC*, 1992).

CNM

In November 1989 minor plaintiff's mother presented for pre-natal care at an HMO facility. She had given birth to two children previously. The first child was born at 6 months gestation and was diagnosed as suffering from a congenital syndrome with multiple physical and cognitive problems. Her second child was born at the same facility in December 1988. That delivery was complicated by tight shoulders and necessitated application of suprapubic pressure and the McRoberts maneuver. The health care providers who saw the minor plaintiff's mother in connection with the pregnancy giving rise to this case were aware of her prior obstetrical history. However, she remained in the pool of women considered to have "uncomplicated" prior obstetrical histories, such that her baby was to be delivered by a nurse midwife rather than a physician. On April 19, 1990 minor plaintiff's mother was admitted to the HMO's hospital. Her obstetrical care was managed by a nurse midwife employed by defendant. The CNM was not aware of the prior history of a tight shoulder delivery and did not speak with any obstetrician regarding the mother prior to delivery. The midwife delivered the minor plaintiff, who weighed 9 lbs., 5 ounces. The delivery record notes that tight shoulders were present and that suprapubic pressure was applied. The record indicated that a problem with the minor plaintiff's left arm was noted immediately at the time of birth. Plaintiff claimed that defendants were negligent in allowing this delivery to be performed by a nurse midwife in view of the mother's prior obstetrical history; and that the nurse midwife placed excessive traction on the baby's head in delivering his left shoulder, thereby causing injury. The child's father recalled that, shortly after the baby's head popped out, the nurse midwife became panicked and concerned and began yelling for a doctor. She told the nurse to get the baby out quick. The nurse jumped on top of the mother and applied pressure to her lower abdomen while the nurse midwife pulled the baby out. No doctor arrived prior to delivery. The case was settled for $250,000 to compensate the child for a left brachial plexus palsy with permanent abnormal arm position, limited motion, weakness and muscle atrophy (*McCaffrey v. Kaiser*, 1994).

Amanda Sargood was born by cesarean delivery on February 5, 1993, with severe perinatal asphyxia. Amanda's brain injury included a static encephalopathy with cerebral palsy and spastic quadriplegia, accompanied by severe developmental delays. This suit for birth-related neurological injury alleged a delay in performing a cesarean delivery. When Amanda's mother was 16 years old, she fractured her pelvis in an auto accident. The multiple fractures of her pelvis required hospitalization and extensive follow-up care by orthopedic surgeons. When the surgeons released her from further care, they advised her to keep a set of her pelvic x-rays to show to her obstetrician if she ever became pregnant. The orthopedic surgeons warned her that the pelvic fractures, although healed, could have compromised the shape of her pelvis so that she might have to deliver by cesarean delivery. She married, and in June 1992, became pregnant. She selected an obstetrician to deliver her baby from her employer HMO's list of participating physicians. On her first prenatal appointment, she brought the pelvic x-rays for the obstetrician's review (as she had been instructed by her orthopedic surgeons 8 years earlier). However, her selected physician did not see her on this visit. Instead, she was seen by his partner, who looked at the x-rays and noted the previous auto accident in the "problems" section of the mother's chart. The partner agreed that because of her previous pelvic fractures she might need a cesarean section. However, he told the mother that the other physician was her obstetrician and she should discuss the matter with him on her next prenatal visit. Her selected obstetrician eventually examined her and assured her that if vaginal delivery created a problem, he would be there and would be ready to do a cesarean delivery. When the mother's labor pains began on February 5, she checked into the hospital and her obstetrician ordered pitocin to stimulate the contractions. At 12:55 p.m., her obstetrician examined her and found her almost completely dilated. Her obstetrician testified in his deposition that, at the time of this examination, he knew that she would be ready to start pushing within the next 30 minutes to 1 hour. The mother and her husband were therefore stunned when her obstetrician notified them that, although it was only one o'clock in the afternoon and although the mother was about to have her baby, he was leaving to attend one of his son's soccer games. Her obstetrician told the couple that the mother was going to be put into the hands of a midwife. (According to the obstetrician, he gave the mother the "choice" of selecting midwife delivery at this stage of her labor, a claim denied by the plaintiffs). After the obstetrician left the hospital for the soccer game, the pitocin infusion continued and over the next 2 hours the contractions became even stronger and more frequent. During this time, the baby's heart rate began to exhibit various abnormalities including decelerations in the fetal heart rate. However, the midwife and nurse who were managing the labor did not appreciate these abnormalities. By 2:45 p.m., the nurse began administering oxygen by mask to the mother. Although the nurse does not now remember why she started the oxygen, according to the midwife, it was probably due to the persistent decelerations in the baby's heart rate. Nevertheless (in violation of the hospital's own policies), the nurse continued the pitocin infusion, continued to have the mother push, and failed to request physician assistance. At about 3:25 p.m., the obstetrician who was serving as backup support for the midwife, happened to stop by the labor room. When he reviewed the electronic fetal heart monitor strip, he immediately saw that the baby was in trouble. He also learned (for the first time) that the mother had a history of severe pelvic fractures. Nevertheless, he did not order a cesarean delivery. Instead, he asked the midwife to attempt a vacuum extraction delivery. According to the hospital's chief of staff, the midwife did not even have privileges to perform vacuum extraction deliveries. After repeated attempts failed, the backup physician finally gave the order to take the mother to the cesarean delivery room, where, in her obstetrician's absence, he performed the procedure. By the time the baby was delivered at 3:58 p.m., she had no heart rate, no respiration, no muscle tone, and was blue. Her Apgar scores were 1/3/5 at 1, 5, and 10 minutes. Evidence of a compressed umbilical cord was found at the time of cesarean delivery. Subsequent review of her neonatal brain scans showed that she suffered a fracture of her skull during labor and delivery. The baby was resuscitated by the neonatal unit but continued to experience signs of severe brain injury. The case was settled. The defendant CNM's liability carrier tendered its policy limits of $750,000; defendant obstetrician's liability carrier tendered its policy limits of $1,000,000; defendant backup physician's liability carrier tendered its policy limits of $1,000,000; defendant OB medical group's liability carrier tendered its policy limits of $1,000,000; and the defendant hospital and its liability carrier contributed $2,000,000. The settlement was paid in lump sum (*Sargood v. Clements & Ashmore et al.*, 1995).

PROFESSIONAL LIABILITY INSURANCE

In almost every case where an APN is an employee of a facility or of a practice, the employer will provide the APN with professional liability insurance. Some APNs like to maintain their own coverage in addition to that provided by their employer. This decision should be based on a variety of considerations. First, you need to be aware of what your employment contract (if you have one) says about this issue. If the contract requires you to indemnify your employer in the case of your own negligence, then you should strongly consider getting your own policy. If you do not have an employment contract, or your contract does not address liability or indemnity issues, then this decision is much less clear. In general, your employer is legally responsible for any of your actions undertaken within the scope of your job (*Perez v. Van Groninger & Sons, Inc.*, 1986). In order for your employer to be responsible for your actions, you must be at work and/or carrying out duties by and for the employer. Your employer is also liable for any intentional or malicious acts committed by you while you are functioning within the scope of your employment. However, if personal malice is involved, the employer will not be held liable (*Martinez v. Hagopian*, 1986). Thus, while the facility would be liable if you submitted false documentation to the federal government for Medicare reimbursement, it would not be liable if, during your work day, you murdered the person having an affair with your spouse while that person was a patient at the facility. The employer's legal responsibility is separate from your own personal responsibility. In the case of an employee who does an intentional or malicious act that results in liability for the employer, it would be possible for the employer to seek indemnity from the employee, even in the absence of an express provision regarding indemnity in the employment contract. It is important to note that nobody can purchase insurance that will protect them against intentional criminal acts. If you are an independent contractor, you must have your own insurance, as the employer will not be liable for your defense no matter what.

Some states have laws regarding professional liability insurance for APNs. 2000 Florida H.B. 1067 indicates that CNMs and APNs must maintain medical malpractice insurance or provide proof of financial responsibility in an amount and in a manner determined by the board or department to be sufficient to cover claims arising out of the rendering of or failure to render professional care and services in this state. Exemptions may be granted to certain government employees or to those who have inactive or limited licenses and those who practice only in a teaching capacity. 64B9-4.002, F.A.C. defines the amounts required for APNs as liability coverage of at least $100,000 per claim with a minimum annual aggregate of at least $300,000.

Midwives in California who do not have liability insurance coverage for the practice of midwifery must disclose that fact to the client on the first visit or examination, whichever comes first. The disclosure, whether oral or written, must be noted and dated in the client's file by the midwife (CCR Tit. 16, Div. 13, Ch. 4, Art. 3 § 1379.20).

Each person licensed in Connecticut as an APN who provides direct patient care services must maintain professional liability insurance or other indemnity against liability for professional malpractice. The amount of insurance must not be less than $500,000 for one person, per occurrence, with an aggregate of not less than $1.5 million (Statutes §20-94a). 2000 Connecticut H.B. 5792 requires that each person licensed as an advanced practice registered nurse who provides direct patient care services must maintain professional liability insurance or other indemnity against liability for professional malpractice. The amount of insurance that each such person must carry as insurance or indemnity against claims for injury or death for professional malpractice must be at least $500,000 for one person, per occurrence, with an aggregate of at least $1,500,000. This requirement does not apply to CRNAs who provide services under the direction of a licensed physician.

The Massachusetts Board of Nursing is authorized to promulgate regulations requiring APNs to have professional malpractice liability insurance or a suitable bond or other indemnity against liability for professional malpractice in such amounts as may be determined by the board (Mass. Ann. Laws, Ch. 112, § 80B (2000)).

Wisconsin Statute § 655.23 (1999) indicates that every health care provider either must insure and keep insured the health care providers liability by a policy of health care liability insurance issued by an insurer authorized to do business in this state or must qualify as a self-insurer. Health care liability insurance may provide either occurrence or claims-made coverage. The limits of liability must be as follows: for occurrence coverage, at least $1,000,000 for each occurrence and $3,000,000 for all occurrences in any 1 policy year for occurrences on or after July 1, 1997. For claims-made coverage, limits are at least $1,000,000 for each claim arising from an occurrence on or after July 1, 1997 and $3,000,000 for all claims in any one reporting year for claims made on or after July 1, 1997.

R.R.S. Nebraska § 71-1723.04 (2000) requires that advanced practice registered nurses maintain in effect professional liability insurance with such coverage and limits as may be established by the board.

In evaluating a policy, you should determine whether it is an occurrence policy or a claims-made policy. An occurrence policy covers any incident that occurred while the APN was insured; claims-made policy only covers claims made when the policy is active regardless of when the incident occurred. Other aspects of the policy that should be evaluated include declarations, coverage agreement, supplementary payments, limits of liability, defense and settlement, policy territory, exclusions/restrictions, and conditions. In selecting a policy, you should discuss the facility/group's coverage with your employer and get a copy of that policy; evaluate the available options in the commercial market; compare premiums; identify your risk of exposure; insure for your biggest exposure with the broadest coverage; check the insurer's rating; ask whether they give a premium reduction for educational attendance; and investigate the availability of additional services.

It is extremely important that the APN notify his or her carrier promptly when becoming aware of a potential claim. If this is not done then the insurance company may refuse coverage for the incident. Box 6-7 discusses the case of *Draeger v. Travelers, et al.*, 1980.

It can be very important to have your own policy if a conflict with the facility/employer arises. The case of *Gregorino v. The Charlotte-Mecklenburg Hospital Authority*, 1996, illustrates how a conflict of interest can arise between an APN employee and a facility. Ms. Gregorino worked at the Hospital Authority's University Hospital as a nurse anesthetist. On August 16, 1991, while Ms. Gregorino was performing her duties, complications arose during a tonsillectomy and adenoidectomy surgery, leaving a minor child with severe and permanent brain injury. Early investigation into the incident focused on the placement of the endotracheal tube, which directly involved Ms. Gregorino's duties as a nurse anesthetist. She contacted Robert King, Vice President and Director of Legal Services for the Hospital Authority, inquiring about whether she would be afforded counsel to represent her in connection with any legal proceedings arising from the incident. In response to this inquiry, Mr. King sent two letters to her stating that the hospital would provide her with counsel and that her interests and those of the Hospital Authority were the same. Ms. Gregorino, however, concluded that her interests and the interests of the Hospital Authority were not identical. On or about 20 August 1992, she consulted Attorney John Golding about retaining him to represent her interests in connection with the incident. However, Ms. Gregorino soon learned that Mr. Golding had been retained by the Hospital Authority to represent it and the interests of its insurance carrier, St. Paul Fire and Marine. She requested a complete copy of Mr. Golding's file relating to the incident so that she could keep informed about the

BOX 6-7	Refusal of Coverage

In the case of *Draeger v. Travelers, et. al.* (1980), a CRNA's insurance company claimed that the CRNA did not provide it with sufficient notice of an occurrence covered by the policy and sought to deny coverage. The dispute arose from the alleged malpractice by the insured CRNA. On December 4, 1972, surgery was performed on the deceased plaintiff. The CRNA was employed by the hospital and was the nurse anesthetist for the surgery. During surgery respiratory problems developed, forming the basis for the malpractice claims. At that time, the CRNA had been issued nurse's malpractice liability insurance by Continental through its agents, Maginnis & Associates. Continental did not question the policy was in full force and effect on the date of the surgery. The CRNA was also insured as a hospital employee by Travelers Indemnity Company.

The CRNA's policy with Continental contained the following provision:

> 2. NOTICE OF OCCURRENCE. Upon the insured becoming aware of any alleged injury or occurrence covered hereby, written notice shall be given by or on behalf of the insured to the company or any of its authorized agents as soon as practicable. Such notice shall contain particulars sufficient to identify the insured and also reasonably obtainable information respecting the time, place and circumstances of the alleged injury or occurrence, the names and addresses of the injured and of available witnesses.

In late October 1973, the surgeon told the CRNA that attorneys for the patient's family had requested the hospital records, and he thought a lawsuit might be filed. On other occasions, the surgeon expressed his concern to the CRNA that anyone connected with the surgery might be sued. On or about May 11, 1974, the CRNA sent a first-class latter to Maginnis, the issuing agent, supplying the information about the surgery required under the policy. Maginnis never received the letter. On June 28, 1974, Travelers, the hospital's insurer, advised the CRNA by letter to notify her insurance carrier of the matter. She disregarded the letter since she had already sent the May 11 letter to Maginnis. A malpractice action was commenced November 18, 1975, naming the surgeon and the hospital as defendants. The CRNA was deposed shortly thereafter and become aware of the formal allegations of negligence on her part. The CRNA was not named as a party-defendant until October 1977. Upon service, she forwarded the suit papers to Continental, who denied coverage alleging noncompliance with the notice of occurrence condition in the policy.

As the appeals court noted, the notice of occurrence requirement serves several functions. It gives an insurance company the opportunity to investigate possible claims against a policy while witnesses are available and their memories fresh. A company's investigation cannot begin until it receives notice of the claim. An early determination of policy defenses is also facilitated. Compliance by the insured with the notice of occurrence provision is

(continued)

| BOX 6-7 | Refusal of Coverage (Continued) |

a condition precedent to the company's contractual duties of defense and coverage. The court held that a reasonable person could infer that mail was considered an acceptable method of communication and that absent express language in the policy to the contrary, an insured's duty to give notice of occurrence is met upon mailing the required information. The insurance company also contended that the CRNA should have notified the company in October 1973, after the surgeon told her that the family's attorneys were examining the hospital records. The duty to give notice arises when an insured has reasonable grounds to believe he or she is a participant in an accident. An insured should not rely on his or her subjective evaluation of potential liability. Rather, the controlling test is objective. The court found that unsubstantiated rumors of litigation would not cause a reasonable person to notify his or her insurer. Although they did not hold that an insured need not give notice until a complaint has been filed, they felt there must be more than rumors to impose a duty on the insured to notify the company.

case. Mr. Golding refused to deliver copies of the file to Ms. Gregorino. Consequently, Ms. Gregorino retained Attorney R. Marie Sides to represent her and obtain the requested files. Ms. Sides requested an opinion from the North Carolina State Bar on this issue. The Ethics Committee decided that Ms. Gregorino was entitled to a copy of the joint file from either the Hospital Authority or from Mr. Golding. Thereafter, Ms. Gregorino received a file from Mr. Golding. Ms. Gregorino considered the file to be incomplete and filed a complaint with the North Carolina State Bar. In April 1993, all potential claims regarding the surgical incident were fully settled with full release to the Hospital Authority and all its employees. On February 17, 1994, Ms. Gregorino instituted the instant action against the Hospital Authority to recover attorney's fees she incurred in connection with the incident. The trial court dismissed the case, so the CRNA appealed. The CRNA argued that she should be indemnified for attorney's fees incurred in retaining separate counsel in connection with this incident.

The Hospital Authority argued that Ms. Gregorino was not entitled to indemnification because no action was ever threatened or pending against her. The appeals court found that a genuine issue of material fact existed as to whether the attorney's fees had been actually and necessarily incurred in connection with a threatened action seeking to hold Ms. Gregorino liable. The record indicated that Ms. Gregorino, a nurse anesthetist, had been involved in a surgical procedure that left a minor child with severe and permanent brain damage. The initial investigation into the incident focused on the placement of the endotracheal tube that directly involved Ms. Gregorino's duties as a nurse anesthetist. She immediately became concerned because as a nurse anesthetist, the misplacement of the tube could affect her future licensing and insurability if she were found "at fault" for the injuries sustained by the child.

Furthermore, the Hospital Authority's Risk Management Department obtained from Ms. Gregorino a statement about the incident and required her to submit to a drug-screening test. No other surgical team member was required to undergo a drug-screening test. The evidence also showed that certain medical records regarding the incident were missing or had been altered by a Hospital Authority employee. Additionally, certain items used during the surgery that would normally have been present in the operating room immediately following a surgical procedure were missing. Statements of the anesthesiologist and of the surgical team member also differed from Ms. Gregorino's recollection of events. Furthermore, Ms. Gregorino was denied access to documents by Mr. Golding, who represented both the Hospital Authority and its employees including Ms. Gregorino. Based on these actions, Ms. Gregorino retained Attorney Sides to represent her in this matter. After Ms. Gregorino retained Ms. Sides, the victim's attorney, Mr. Sitton, sent Ms. Sides a letter stating that "if a lawsuit was filed, Jane Gregorino would be a Defendant." The letter also stated, "I did relate to you that I had an expert's report, which concluded that Jane Gregorino did not meet the standard of care for CRNA practicing in Charlotte in August of 1991. It appears to me that that fact is beyond dispute." Moreover, in a draft of the lawsuit prepared by Mr. Sitton, the named defendants were Jane Gregorino and the Hospital Authority. The court felt that a genuine issue of material fact existed as to whether Ms. Gregorino's attorney's fees were actually and necessarily incurred in connection with any threatened action seeking to hold her liable, so it was wrong for the trial court to dismiss the case.

Documentation

In order to successfully defend a negligence case, the documentation must reflect the APN's compliance with applicable standards. In my experience there tend to be four major problems with records: missing records, altered records, failure to correct and failure to document.

In the case of *Brewer v. Dowling*, the plaintiffs, parents of a child who suffered birth related neurologic injury, asked the court to instruct the jury that the hospital's loss of the fetal monitor strip created a rebuttable presumption that the information on the strip would have been unfavorable to the hospital. The court refused to do so because the hospital provided the testimony of several providers who had reviewed the strips as well as the labor nurse's notes in other parts of the hospital chart that referenced findings present on the strips, and because the plaintiffs were unable to present evidence that the strips were intentionally destroyed.

Charting dos and don'ts:

- Follow facility's guidelines for charting.
- Chart legibly, spell correctly, and use only institutionally approved abbreviations.
- Use clear, objective language.
- Correct any errors according to institutional policy, never erase or use correction fluid.
- Chart only your own observations and actions.
- Make an entry for every observation.
- Every entry must be dated, timed, and signed.
- Make use of late entries when appropriate.
- Chart all physician consultations, examinations, results, review of printouts and lab work, etc.
- Chart all communication with other providers including the information relayed and the response.
- If the patient needs physician care and the physician does not respond in a timely fashion or responds in an inappropriate fashion, document the use of the chain of command if one exists in your facility.
- Chart all changes in patient status that are indicative of deterioration and actions taken in response to the changes.
- Chart all assessments, interventions, treatments, responses, and evaluations.
- Document all teaching and evaluation of patient understanding.
- Chart medication administration, amount, route, time, site and response. For prescribed medications, chart drug, amount, route, frequency, number prescribed as well as a discussion with the patient regarding any side effects or special instructions regarding taking the medications.
- Sign every entry.
- Never document in advance.
- Never replace or falsify any information.

Some states have laws that outline acceptable documentation standards, usually in the context of state-funded healthcare programs. For example, N.J.A.C. § 10:58-1.9 indicates that the certified nurse midwife must keep legible, individual records as necessary to fully disclose the kind and extent of services provided, and the medical necessity for those services. Minimum documentation requirements for services performed by the certified nurse midwife include a clinical note or a progress note in the clinical record for each visit that supports the procedure code or codes to be claimed. At a minimum, documentation of services performed by the CNM must include:

Date of service
Name of the patient

Patient complaint, reason for visit
Subjective findings
Objective findings
An assessment
A plan of care including, but not limited to, any orders for laboratory
    work, prescriptions for medications
Signature of the practitioner rendering the service
Other documentation appropriate to the procedure code being billed

The CNM's involvement must be clearly demonstrated in notes reflecting the practitioner's personal involvement with, or participation in, the service rendered.

N.J.A.C. § 10:58A-1.4 outlines similar rules for the NP and CNS.

Telephone Triage

Briggs, 1997, describes telephone triage as a "systematic process that screens a caller's symptoms for urgency and advises the caller when to seek medical attention based on the severity of the problem described. The process also helps to direct callers to the most appropriate health care setting or advises home care" (pp.1-2). Frequently APNs who work in office practice settings are being called upon to handle telephone triage calls. Legally speaking, the APN's duty to the patient begins when he or she starts to give advice to a caller (Robinson, et al., 1997). Unfortunately, these calls can lead to liability problems as the result of several potential pitfalls:

- Failure to correctly evaluate the nature or urgency of the situation prompting the call: The caller may not give you enough information to allow you to accurately evaluate the situation. This may be because the caller does not correctly perceive or evaluate the urgency of the situation. It is important to ask nonleading questions to elicit adequate data to allow you to appropriately deal with the call and to avoid dismissing the caller's subjective evaluations of symptoms such as pain and weakness.
- Failure to speak directly with the patient: Unless the patient is a child (younger than an adolescent) you should insist on speaking directly with the patient. In the case of a minor, you can also get information from the parent, but it is important to speak with the patient directly. Much important information can be lost in translation between the patient and the person making the call, and many times the caller will summarize the problem and will not be able to give you the detailed information needed to handle the call appropriately. If the patient is too ill to speak, the caller should be told to bring the patient immediately to the office or take the patient to the emergency room.
- Failure to document the call: Careful documentation is essential so that other staff can be aware of the interaction should the patient

call again, so that the physician can review the record of the call, and so that if a legal case arises, there will not be any questions about what information the caller provided and what advice was given.

The importance of avoiding these pitfalls is illustrated by the case of *Descheness v. Anonymous*, 1992. A gravida 3 para 1 female delivered following a prolonged second stage of labor. The obstetrician performed a Scanzoni maneuver, which involved the rotation of the baby's head with mid forceps. The delivery was then accomplished with the assistance of low forceps. The mother experienced abdominal pain and difficulty urinating during the postpartum period. During the next several days she reported by phone to the doctor's office that she had severe pain, hardening of the abdomen, cramps, nausea, vomiting, fever, fatigue, and seepage from the vagina. These symptoms were attributed to the flu and constipation but the patient was never seen for an examination. Nine days after the birth as her symptoms became worse, she was taken to the hospital. She was diagnosed with sepsis, ARDS, and a perforated bladder. She died several days later. Few records of the telephone calls to the office were produced, with only one health care provider admitting to having spoken with the patient. The family was awarded $1.3 million.

Avoiding the legal problems that can arise from telephone triage involves three actions: developing and following triage protocols, careful documentation, and timely follow-up. Henry, 1994, reminds us that in a negligence action, the APN must establish that providing telephone advice is an action within the scope of the APN's practice and that the advice given was provided from established and approved practice protocols; failing to have and follow a written protocol may result in a presumption of negligence. Robinson et al., 1997, suggest that a descriptive, prospective study be conducted to reveal the peak call periods as well as the number of calls received and the types of calls received prior to developing protocols. Protocols should exist to identify at a minimum which calls involve life-threatening situations. In an emergency the provider must either give appropriate advice or referral since termination of the call may be considered to be patient abandonment (Robinson et al., 1997).

There are several important things to remember when developing protocols. First, the protocol must not set out goals that are unrealistic for the practice setting or the patient population, as unrealistic goals will be difficult to follow. There is a great liability risk in having protocols that are routinely ignored or only partially followed. The assumption is that if a protocol has been developed, it is acknowledged that the protocol sets out the standard of care for a given situation; so failing to follow the protocol is automatically below the standard of care. The second important thing about protocols is that they must be reviewed and updated on a regular basis (usually yearly) to keep pace with any changes in medical consensus regarding the conditions involved. Third, old protocols should be kept for at least 10 years in the event that a lawsuit is filed that involves questions about a protocol in existence several years prior. This allows you to be able to refer to the protocols as they existed at the time of the advice given to the patient.

As for documentation, the use of standardized, carbonless copy triage documentation is highly recommended. At a minimum the form should provide space to document the patient's name, age, current medications, complaints, primary physician, and a brief medical history. The form should also provide space to record which protocol was used to triage the call, what advice was given to the patient, the plan for follow-up, and a space for co-signature by the physician. Robinson et al., 1997, remind us that it is important to warn the caller about the consequences of not complying with the advice given and to document this discussion. One copy of the completed form should be kept in a binder at the triage desk for reference should the patient call back, and one copy should be filed in the patient's chart.

Follow-up is one of the most important issues that arise in lawsuits over telephone triage care. At a minimum, the patient should be instructed to call back if things become worse or if there is no improvement within a reasonable period of time. The reasonable period of time will vary depending on the nature of the patient's complaint. It is also important from a liability standpoint that when a patient calls repeatedly with symptoms that appear vague, follow-up occurs. This could consist of the APN calling the patient back or having the patient come in for a visit. The importance of follow-up such as this was a major part of a case I was involved in several years ago involving a postpartum woman who died of sepsis. The woman and her husband made repeated calls to the physicians' office after being discharged from an uncomplicated vaginal delivery with vague complaints of lethargy, abdominal pain and distention, and ankle swelling. No notes were made regarding any of the calls despite the patient talking to several different providers at the office. Two weeks after the delivery, she presented to the emergency room in septic shock; she died soon thereafter. Due in large part to the lack of documentation and follow-up, the case had to be settled. Robinson et al., 1997, also recommend that an orientation program be developed to include a thorough review of written protocols, training sessions, call simulations, preceptor involvement, and a step-by-step procedure for handling each call. As with other clinical activities, telephone triage should be monitored through the practice's quality assurance committee in order to maintain consistent standards (Robinson et al., 1997).

APN/MD Communication

Breakdowns in communication between the APN and physicians can be a major source of liability for both providers. In the case of *Anonymous v. Anonymous*, 1998, plaintiff mother presented to defendant hospital for delivery of her child. She was monitored by defendant nurse midwife. During labor, the fetal monitor began to indicate fetal distress. At approximately the same time, plaintiff mother developed a fever. Defendant nurse midwife advised defendant obstetrician/gynecologist about the situation, but he did not immediately respond. Plaintiff infant allegedly suffered oxygen deprivation resulting in severe mental retardation and cerebral palsy. Plaintiffs alleged that defendants were negligent in failing to properly monitor plaintiff mother during labor and in failing to intervene in a timely manner when the fetal monitor indicated fetal distress. Further, plaintiff infant suffered brain asphyxia due to defendants' negligence. The case settled prior to trial for $4.25 million, $3.75 million of which was paid by the CNM and physician and $.5 million of which was paid by the hospital.

Other times, conflicts can arise that lead to lawsuits between the physician and the APN. In the case of *Deleon v. Slear* (616A2d 380, 1992), a surgeon sued an NP for statements she made to the chief of surgery regarding his work. During the surgeon's period of residency, Elaine Slear, the NP, relayed complaints about the surgeon's work to the chief of surgery at the hospital. Nurse Slear was the supervising NP at the hospital and it was her duty to act as the liaison between the NPs and the chief of surgery. She related to the chief of surgery that other hospital physicians had asked that the surgeon not be called to see their patients, that he had failed to respond to an emergency call, and that the surgeon was late for his scheduled surgeries causing patients to be anesthetized for an unnecessarily long time. The surgeon sued the facility when it denied his application for medical staff privileges, alleging defamation, but the court dismissed the case. He then sued Nurse Slear, but this case was dismissed as well, the court holding that a plaintiff cannot sue employees for defamation occurring within the scope of employment when plaintiff has already unsuccessfully sued the employer for defamation and when the alleged defamatory statements in both cases were part of the same transaction or transactions.

APNs can enhance their communications with physicians by remembering these strategies for negotiation:

- Avoid issues that can negatively affect negotiations (such as conflict, criticism, and controversy) to keep the interaction from becoming personal or emotional, which could reduce people's objectivity.
- Promote a positive process through communication, collaboration, and cooperation.

- Enhance problem-solving with creativity, concession, and commitment to reach a mutually agreeable solution (Kasnic et al., 1998).

Advanced Skills

As APN practice evolves, it is anticipated that the APN scope of practice will expand to allow performance of procedures that APNs do not currently perform. At least one professional organization, the American College of Nurse-Midwives (ACNM), has taken this into account and developed Guidelines for the Incorporation of New Procedures into Nurse-Midwifery Practice (1992). Some states, most notably Alabama, specifically address advanced skills of the APN through statements adopted by the Boards of Nursing. Examples will be discussed below.

Ultrasound

Limited ultrasound is becoming an accepted nursing role for many nurses in obstetric nursing practice. As early as 1992, responsibility for performing obstetric scans was being assumed by CNMs (Gegor, 1992). Menihan, 2000, defines limited sonography as a sonogram performed to ascertain specific information in clinical situations in which a more complete ultrasound examination cannot be performed. The limited scan is used to (1.) determine placental location, (2.) detect the presence or absence of cardiac activity, (3.) assess the amniotic fluid volume, (4.) determine the presenting part, (5.) guide the delivery of the second twin during twin delivery, (6.) assist with amniocentesis and cephalic versions, and (7.) assess fetal well-being (Menihan, 2000). It is important that APNs who take on the role of performing limited ultrasounds do so only after receiving appropriate education and training in order to avoid legal liability for negligent performance of this advanced skill. Menihan, 2000, notes that a minimum of 12 hours of didactic content is recommended by AWHONN. AWHONN has also published the guideline Clinical Competencies and Education Guide: Limited Ultrasound Examination in Obstetric and Gynecologic/Infertility Settings, 1998.

Punch Biopsies

Alabama's Board of Nursing has taken the position that performing this procedure is within the scope of practice of NPs, if this procedure is recognized as an appropriate function of the NP by the respective national certification organization and the NP has successfully completed an organized program of study that includes didactic instruction as well as supervised clinical practice (Alabama BON, 1994).

Removal of Chest Tubes

Alabama's BON has taken the position that it is within the scope of practice of NPs and CNSs to remove chest tubes as directed by a physician in accordance with guidelines that include:

- Successful completion of a formal program of study followed by supervised clinical practice
- Protocols that include:
  - proximity of the physician when the NP or CNS removes the tube
  - type of supervision provided by the physician
  - physician evaluation of patient condition indicating need to remove tube
  - guidelines for patient monitoring prior to and after removal
  - guidelines for dealing with potential complications or emergencies (Alabama BON, 1998).

Colposcopy

Alabama's BON has declared that it is within the scope of practice of the NP and CNM to perform colposcopy without additional training or guidelines (Alabama BON, 1994).

Endometrial Biopsies

Alabama's BON has adopted a statement indicating that it is within the scope of practice for CNMs and NPs in obstetrical/gynecological settings to perform endometrial sampling with the use of a flexible plastic Pipelle curette under the following conditions:

- The CNM or NP has completed an organized program of study on endometrial sampling with supervised clinical practice.
- A physician is on site to respond to complications. (Alabama BON, 1996).

Insertion and Removal of Norplant

Alabama's BON has adopted a statement indicating that it is within the scope of practice of CNMs and NPs to insert and remove the Norplant system as prescribed by a physician provided that:

- The NP or CNM must successfully complete an organized program of study and supervised clinical experience that should include classroom instruction on the system; patient selection, education, and management issues; practice on a model arm; and a sufficient number of physician supervised insertions and removals on actual patients to ensure competency.
- Only those NPs certified as reproductive NPs, family planning NPs, family NPs, adult NPs, or obstetric/gynecologic NPs may insert and or remove Norplant.
- Each patient must have a complete medical history and physical examination by a physician, CNM, or NP prior to the insertion or removal of the Norplant.

- If all capsules cannot be removed at the first attempt, the patient must be referred to the physician. (Alabama BON, 1994).

Lumbar Punctures

The Alabama BON has adopted a statement indicating it is within the scope of practice of NPs to perform lumbar punctures as directed by a physician if the procedure is recognized as an appropriate function of the NP by the respective national certification organization and if the NP has successfully completed a formal program of study followed by supervised clinical practice (Alabama BON, 1994).

ENHANCE YOUR LEARNING:

1. Interview your facility's risk manager regarding risk management practices related to APNs.
2. Design a research study to determine the incidence of charting errors in your facility.
3. Design a research study to determine the level of satisfaction among practitioners at your facility regarding APN/physician communication.
4. Design telephone triage protocols for your practice site.

TEST YOUR COMPREHENSION

1. List the four elements of a professional negligence claim.
2. Describe the circumstances under which a person who was not the patient can sue a health care provider.
3. List four of the do's and don'ts related to charting.
4. Discuss two of the potential pitfalls in providing telephone triage.

REFERENCES

American College of Nurse-Midwives. (1992). *Guidelines for the incorporation of new procedures into nurse-midwifery practice*. Available online at http://www.midwife.org/prof/guide.htm.

Alabama Board of Nursing. (1994). Statement regarding colposcopy by certified registered nurse practitioners and certified nurse midwives.

Alabama Board of Nursing. (1996). Statement regarding endometrial biopsies by advanced practice nurses.

Alabama Board of Nursing. (effective 1992, March 27; last revised 1994, September). Statement regarding insertion and removal of Norplant system by certified registered nurse practitioners and certified nurse midwives.

Alabama Board of Nursing. (effective 1984, July 27; last revised 1994, September). Statement regarding lumbar punctures by certified registered nurse practitioners.

Alabama Board of Nursing. (effective 1993, September 23; revised 1994, September). Statement regarding punch biopsies by certified registered nurse practitioners.

Alabama Board of Nursing. (adopted 1999, September 25; revised 1998, January 29). Statement regarding removal of chest tubes by advanced practice nurses (NPs and CNSs).

Association of Women's Health, Obstetric, and Neonatal Nursing (AWHONN). (1998). Clinical competencies and education guide: Limited ultrasound examinations in obstetric and gynecologic/infertility settings. Washington, DC: Author.

Briggs, J. K. (2001). *Telephone triage protocols for nurses* (2nd ed.). Philadelphia: Lippincott.

Gegor, C. (1992). Obstetric ultrasound: Who should perform sonograms. *Birth, 19*(2), 92–99.

Hagedorn, M., & Gardner, S. (1999). Legal issues in neonatal nursing: Considerations for staff nurses and advanced practice nurses. *Journal of Obstetric, Gynecologic and Neonatal Nursing, 28* (3), 320–330.

Henry, P. (1996). Analysis of the nurse practitioner's legal relationships. *Nurse Practitioner Forum, 7* (1), 5–6.

Henry, P. (1994). Legal principles in providing telephone advice. *Nurse Practitioner Forum, 5*(3) 124–125.

Kasnic, T., Meyer, J., & Barriger, V., (1998, December). Negotiation skills every nurse needs. *Lifelines, 2*(6) 37–38.

Menihan, C. (2000). Limited obstetric ultrasound in nursing practice. *JOGNN, 29*(3) 325–330.

National Practitioner Data Bank. (1998). *1997 Annual Report*. Chantilly, VA: Author.

Pearson, L. & Birkholz, G. (1995, March). Report on the 1994 readership survey on NP experiences with malpractice issues. *The Nurse Practitioner, 20* (3), 18–30.

Plum, S. (1997). Nurses indicted: Three Denver nurses may face prison in case that bodes ill for the profession. *Nursing 97, 23* (7), 33.

Prosser, W. (1941). *Handbook on the law of torts* (2nd ed.) St. Paul, MN: West Publishing.

Robinson, D., Anderson, M., & Erpenbeck, P. (1997). Telephone advice: New solutions for old problems. *The Nurse Practitioner, 22*(3), 179–192.

Cases

Alexander et al. v. Battaglia et al., Case 98-05567, Texas Reporter-Soele's Trial Report (December 1999).

Anonymous v. Anonymous, *The Ohio Trial Reporter, 12*(5), 1 (1998).

Azzolino et al. v. Dingfelder et al., 337 SE2d 528 (1985).

Baird et al. v. Sickler, 433 NE2d 593 (1982).

Bobik v. Indus. Comm., 146 Ohio St. 187 (1946).

Brewer v. Dowling, 862 SW2d 156.

Case 84-7433, *New England Jury Verdict Review & Analysis, 5*, (12) (June 1990).

Case CAL87-11172, *Metro Verdicts Monthly, 2*(10), 413.

Doe v. Roe, Case 001, *Verdictum Juris Press* (12), DOE 001 (1987).

Deleon v. Slear, 616A2d 380 (1992).

Denton Regional Medical Center and Epic Healthcare Group, INC. v. Lawrence Lacriox, individually and as next friend of Katherine Lacroix, and as next friend and parent of Lawryn Lacroix, Tex. Court of Appeals 947 S.W.2d 941 (1997).

Descheness v. Anonymous, No. 89-2002, Worcester County Superior Court, Mass. February 13, 1992.

Draeger v. Travelers, et al., 300 N.W.2d 79 (1980).

Duke v. Sanymetal Products Co., 31 Ohio App. 2d 78 (1972).

Duell v. Anesthesia Associates et al. Case 98-CV-0462, *The Ohio Trial Reporter, 14*(6), 34 (February 2000).

Garcia v. County of Los Angeles, Case SCC04972, *Confidential Report for Attorneys* (15), 7 (1986).

Gregorino v. The Charlotte-Mecklenburg Hospital Authority, 468 SE2d 432 (1996).

Harris v. Groth, 99 Wn.2d 438, 443-47, 663 P.2d 113 (1983).

Horner v. Northern Pacific Beneficial Association Hospitals Inc., 62 Wn.2d 351, 382 P.2d 518 (1963).

Jenkins v. Payne, 465 SE2d 795 (1996).

Jenkins v. Quini et al., Case 659 193, Confidential Report For Attorneys: Issue-Pg: 19-29 (August 16, 1993).

Johnson v. Minneapolis St. Paul & SSM Railway Company. 209 NW 786 (1926).

Lusher v. Childrens Hospital Medical Center et al., Case A-8904717, *Ohio Trial Reporter, 7*(1), 23 (January 17, 1992).

McCaffrey v. Kaiser, Case LC 005 6865, Confidential Report For Attorneys: Issue, 19-11, 1994.

Martinez v. Hagopian, 182 Cal. App. 3d 1223 (1986).

Mider v. United States, 322 F.2d 193 (C.A. 6, 1963)

Miller v. Kennedy, 11 Wn. App. 272, 279, 522 P.2d 852 (1974), *aff'd per curiam*, 85 Wn.2d 151, 530 P.2d 334 (1975).

Morner v. Union Pacific Railway Company, 31 Wn. (2d) 282, 196 P. (2d) 744.

New England Jury Verdict Review & Analysis, 8(3), JE v. LC, Case No. 88-6761A, September 1992.

Overton v. Fairfax Anesthesiology, Metro Verdicts Monthly, 10(10), 39, Case 162682.

Perez v. Van Groninger & Sons, Inc., 41 Cal. 3d 1223 (1986).

Perry et al. v. Magee et al., No. 1723 Common Pleas Court of Philadelphia County, 23 Phila. 513 (1992).

Pickens & Plummer v. Diecker & Brother, 21 Ohio St. 212 (1871).

Plaintiff Baby v. Nurse Practitioner, CRA No. 5380 Confidential Report For Attorneys: Issue, 19-21 (1994).

Planned Parenthood v. Vines, 543 N.E. 2d 654 (1989).

Sargood v. Clements & Ashmore et al., Docket No 94-2890, FJVR Reference No. 95:11-53, *Florida Jury Verdict Reporter*, November 1995.

Scott et al. v. Capital Area Community Health Plan et al., 191 AD2d 772 (1993).

Snow v. A.H. Robbins (1985).

Tompkins v. Bise 910 P2d 185, Kansas (1996).

Truman v. Thomas (1980).

Van Meter v. Pub. Util. Comm., 165 Ohio St. 391 (1956).

Weaver v. Bennett, 259 N.C. 16, 129 S.E.2d 610 (1963).

ZeBarth v. Swedish Hospital Medical Center, 499 P2d1 (1972).
Zukowsky v. Brown, 488P2d 269 (1971).

Further Reading: Telephone Triage

Briggs, J. K. (2001). *Telephone triage protocols for nurses* (2nd ed.). Philadelphia: Lippincott.

Brown, J. L. (1994). *Pediatric telephone medicine: Principles, triage and advice* (2nd ed.). Philadelphia: Lippincott.

Katz, H. P. (1990). *Telephone medicine triage and training.* Philadelphia: FA Davis Co.

McGear, R., & Price-Simms, J. (1988). *Telephone triage and management : A nursing process approach.* Philadelphia: W.B. Saunders Co.

Simonsen, S. (1996). *Telephone health assessment: Guidelines for practice.* St Louis: Mosby-Yearbook Inc.

Wheeler, S. (1993). *Telephone triage, theory and protocol development.* Clifton Park, NY: Delmar Publishers.

Trial and Discovery Process

This chapter outlines the legal process regarding trials of malpractice cases and discusses important steps to take in the event of a lawsuit. As indicated in the last chapter, advanced practice nurses (APNs) are infrequently sued; nevertheless, this information is important to know as a matter of professional development and risk management.

Filing and Service of Complaint

Some jurisdictions require that the plaintiff give notice to the health care providers of the intent to file a lawsuit prior to actually filing one. If you are served with a complaint, you must notify your insurance carrier immediately and request counsel. Be prepared to fax a copy of the paperwork you received to your insurance carrier as there is a time limit within which you must respond to the complaint. Failure to do so may result in a default judgment being entered against you by the court. Once you are assigned an attorney, the attorney will contact you and you will need to meet with the attorney to discuss the case. The attorney will evaluate your case by meeting with you, reviewing all pertinent medical records, and obtaining review of the records by an expert.

RESPONSIVE PLEADINGS

Two different responses can be made to a complaint: (1.) a general denial of the allegations in the complaint with affirmative defenses or (2.) a demurrer stating that even if everything in the plaintiff's complaint is true, the plaintiff still has no legal claim. Common affirmative defenses include:

- Statute of limitations: This is the time frame during which a case must be filed or the patient loses the right to bring the claim. It begins to run when the act occurred or when the injured patient discovered or should have discovered the wrong. It may be tolled (ie, stopped) if the patient was reasonably unaware of the existence of the wrong. The time frame is usually 1–3 years but for minors it may last until age 21.

- Good Samaritan Doctrine: The law relieves providers from liability for care rendered in an emergency situation unless the care is grossly negligent or the provider charges for the services rendered.
- Statutory immunity: Most states provide other types of statutory immunity for certain health care providers. Florida Statutes § 766.1115 (1999) provides sovereign immunity against medical malpractice to health care providers who contract to provide indigent medical care as agents of the state. District of Columbia Code § 2-1345 (2000) provides immunity from civil damages for registered nurses and certified nurse midwives practicing obstetrics/gynecology who provide health care or treatment at or on behalf of a free health clinic operating lawfully in the District of Columbia without the expectation of receiving or intending to receive compensation, unless the act or omission is an intentional wrong or manifests a willful or wanton disregard for the health or safety of others. To take advantage of this immunity, the provider must require his or her prospective client to sign under witness by two persons a written statement in which the parties agree to the rendering of the health care or treatment.
- Contributory negligence: This is based on the premise that a wrongdoer cannot benefit from the wrongdoing of others. If the defendant can show a causal connection between the patient's negligent conduct and the patient's injury, the patient may be barred from recovery of damages even when the defendant was also negligent.
- Assumption of risk: The patient assumes the risk of injury or harm inherent in a given situation when she or he knows of and understands the risks and voluntarily selects the course of behavior that can lead to harm.

DISCOVERY

The purpose of discovery is severalfold: to obtain factual information, to identify and gather additional evidence, to narrow and define the legal issues, and to preserve testimony for trial. There are several methods for conducting discovery:

- Oral deposition: This involves a face-to-face session in which questions are asked of the witness under oath to tell the truth. If the witness is a defendant, he or she will be accompanied by counsel, who will protect the witness from answering inappropriate questions. A deposition can last from an hour to several days depending on the witness' involvement with the case and the facts of the case.

- Written deposition: This is a rarely used discovery technique and simply involves the submission of written questions that the witness must answer in writing and under oath.
- Interrogatories: These are written questions sent to a defendant's attorney for the defendant to answer in writing under oath. Typically, interrogatories ask about the education and background of the witness as well as about facts pertaining to the case and about documents and witnesses to the circumstances that resulted in the lawsuit being filed.
- Requests for admissions: These are written questions phrased in the form of "admit that" certain facts are true. The defendant must answer these in writing under oath. Usually, these requests are only used to narrow or clarify certain specific facts.
- Requests for production: These are written requests for a defendant to produce copies of documents that may be relevant to the case. The defendant responds in writing under oath and provides copies of the documents requested if they are in the defendant's possession, custody, or control. Usually the documents produced consist of medical records and items related to the defendant's background such as professional licenses, proof of continuing education, and a resume.
- Physical/mental examination: Usually the defendant asks this of the plaintiff. It involves the plaintiff submitting to a medical examination by a physician hired by the defendant to determine the true nature and extent of the plaintiff's injuries. Typically, the attorneys for the parties both attend this examination unless it involves the plaintiff having to disrobe.

Deposition Dos and Don'ts

- Do review the medical record before the deposition and during the deposition if needed; never attempt to answer questions from memory.
- Answer only the question asked.
- Do not volunteer information.
- Request clarification of the question when needed.
- Remain calm.
- Unless instructed otherwise, do not answer questions to which your attorney has raised an objection.
- Answer all questions honestly and truthfully; never try to conceal or disguise information.
- Do not reveal any conversations with your attorney during the deposition.

- Do not discuss the case with anyone other than the risk manager and your attorney.
- Ask to speak with your attorney at any time you feel it is necessary.
- Avoid reviewing the entire chart; review only your own entries.
- Avoid forming opinions about the care rendered by any other providers.

SETTLEMENT

Often what the patient really wants from the health care provider is an expression of apology. While apologies should never be given to a patient once a lawsuit has been filed without speaking with your attorney, there may be some benefit to apologies given around the time of the event itself. Even if the patient later decides to sue, it may be difficult for the patient to prove liability based upon an apology. In Vermont, the state supreme court ruled in two medical malpractice cases that an apology by a physician for an "inadequate" operation is not an admission of liability (*Phinney v. Vinson*,1992). The court also held that an apology for a serious mistake made during surgery does not establish an element of a malpractice claim (*Senesac v. Associates in Obstetrics and Gynecology*, 1982). At least two states have laws that encourage so called "benevolent gestures." Massachusetts describes them as "actions which convey a sense of compassion or commiseration emanating from humane impulses" and excludes them as evidence of admission of liability in civil cases. Georgia also excludes actions "made on the impulse of benevolence or sympathy" (Keeva, 1999).

Settlement is often a business decision for the insurance company and the facility. If the facility is the only defendant and the nurse is not a named defendant, the nurse has no say in the decision and there are no direct consequences to the APN's license from a settlement by the facility. If the APN is a named defendant, settlement on his or her behalf cannot occur without written consent; settlement will be reported to the board of nursing and National Practitioner Data Bank and may have adverse consequences as to the APN's license and or hospital privileges.

It is important to be aware that almost every professional liability insurance policy contains what is known in the trade as a hammer clause. This clause basically says that you are legally bound to cooperate with the insurance company and your attorney in the defense of the lawsuit. Cooperation also means that if the attorney recommends that you settle the case, you must give consent or risk being personally responsible for the rest of the costs of the lawsuit as well as any judgment rendered against you if you lose.

Generally a settlement agreement includes the following terms: it is confidential; the defendant does not admit liability by agreeing to settle the case; it is a full and final resolution of the dispute; the money will be paid to the plaintiff in exchange for a dismissal of the case with prejudice (which means they can't ever refile the case); and it is subject to court approval, which is required if the plaintiff is a minor.

Reporting Requirements:

The insurance company must report settlements on behalf of individual practitioners to various state and federal agencies. Most states have specific reporting requirements outlined in state laws. Tennessee has a statute specifically pertaining to nurse practitioners (NPs) that indicates that medical malpractice judgments, awards, or settlements at or above $10,000 must be reported to the state pursuant to the "Health Care Consumer Right to Know Act of 1998" (Tenn. Comp. Rules & Regs. R. 1000-4-.05 [2000]). Idaho Code § [54-4601] (2000) created a database of individual profiles of health care providers that the public may access. Information collected includes educational background and work history, disclosure of any final board disciplinary actions, criminal convictions, malpractice history, and other pertinent information on health care providers including NPs and certified registered nurse anesthetists (CRNAs).

Federally the Health Care Quality Improvement Act of 1986 (Title IV, Public Law 99-660) created the National Practitioner Data Bank to improve the quality of health care by encouraging hospitals, state licensing boards, and other health care entities (including professional societies) to identify and discipline those who engage in unprofessional behavior and to restrict the ability of incompetent health care practitioners to move from state to state without disclosure of previous incompetence. The data bank serves as an information clearinghouse to collect and release certain information related to the professional competence and conduct of health care practitioners. The data bank help line provides recordings on common topics 7 days a week, 24 hours a day, and also provides information specialists who can answer questions from 8:30 AM to 6:00 PM EST. The number is 1-800-767-6732.

As to APNs, only medical malpractice payments, whether in the form of settlement or awards, must be reported to the NPDB. However, hospitals and other health care entities may at their discretion report professional review actions that adversely affect an APN's clinical privileges for a period of more than 30 days. In addition, it is optional for state licensing boards to report adverse actions against an APN's license to the NPDB. A notification is sent to the practitioner whenever the NPDB processes a report, and practitioners can submit a request for information disclosure to see if you have been reported to the NPDB. While practitioners cannot submit changes to reports, if information is inaccurate, you may contact the reporting entity to request that a correction be filed and also add your own statement (up to 2000 characters in length) to a report. State licensing boards, hospitals, and other health care entities have access to the information in the data bank. Attorneys for plaintiffs may query the data bank under certain circumstances, but the data bank is prohibited from disclosing information on a specific practitioner to a medical malpractice insurer, defense attorney, or member of the general public.

TRIAL

What To Expect

Most malpractice cases take anywhere from 1 to 3 weeks to conduct the trial. The more complicated the case, the longer it will take. Several defendants, severe injuries, and birth injuries are examples of factors that could increase the complexity of the case. Unless the parties have agreed to a bench trial (where only a judge decides the outcome), the trial will be conducted in front of a jury of twelve, plus two alternates (in some jurisdictions). The first day or two of the trial are typically spent selecting a jury. Experienced attorneys believe that jury selection is one of the most important things the attorney will do in the defense of the case.

Attendance Requirements

It is very important that the individual defendant be present for jury selection, so that the potential jurors get the message that she or he cares about this case and about the process. If you are a named defendant, ideally you should be present for every day of the trial. Occasionally trial dates will unavoidably conflict with your work schedule. If at all possible, you should be there every day as you can be sure that the patient and his or her family will be present.

Attire and Deportment

It is important that anytime you are present in the courtroom, your attire and actions show proper respect for the court and the jury. Business attire is mandatory; the more conservative the better. For women, a dark-skirted suit (at or below knee length) and for men a dark two-piece business suit are sure to be appropriate regardless of the area of the country where the trial is taking place. While you are in the courtroom, it is imperative that your actions be very constrained. You must stand when the judge and the jury enter and exit the room. You must not under any circumstances make faces or audible exclamations in reaction to anything that happens during the trial. If you need to communicate with your attorney, you should make a note on a notepad and discretely show it to your attorney. You will be able to speak with your attorney during the breaks. It is important that you avoid speaking directly with any of the jurors (eg, if you ran into a juror in the bathroom) for this communication could cause a mistrial.

Plaintiff First, Then Defendant

Because the plaintiff has the burden of proof, the plaintiff's attorney always goes first and finishes last. After the jury is chosen, both sides will present their opening statements in which they lay out their theories of the case and the evidence they expect to provide to the jury. Then the plaintiff will present all of his or her witnesses. Each witness will undergo what are known as a direct examination and a cross examination. The direct examination is a series of questions elicited by the party presenting the witness. The cross examination is a series of questions elicited by the other party and usually attempts to discredit the witness's direct testimony or to call in to question the witness's capacity for truthful or unbiased testimony. Lastly, the party who presented the witness may "redirect" the witness by asking questions to limit the damage caused by the cross examination. After a witness has been excused, he or she cannot be called back to testify more except in very unusual circumstances. After all the plaintiff's witnesses have been presented, the plaintiff rests his or her case. Then the defendant(s) present their witnesses. Once the defense rests, then both sides give closing arguments, which are intended to wrap up all the evidence presented and to sway the jury into believing that one side should prevail.

Jury Deliberations/Receiving the Verdict

After closing arguments, the judge gives the jury instructions, which are the legal rules by which the jury must decide the case. Then the jury begins to deliberate. This can take anywhere from under an hour to several days to weeks. Most often when a jury reaches a verdict quickly, it is a sign that they have found for the defendant. Once a verdict has been reached, the jury notifies the judge who contacts the attorneys for all parties involved and requests that they come to the courtroom to receive the verdict. Usually once a verdict has been reached, the parties have about an hour to get to the courthouse. All the attorneys must be present to receive the verdict. It is not mandatory that the parties be present; however, it is highly recommended that you attend if possible. This is the most dramatic and nerve-racking portion of the whole trial experience; nevertheless it is an enormous relief to hear the jury verdict read.

After the verdict is read, the parties and their attorneys are usually permitted to freely discuss the case with any jurors who wish to stay and speak with them. This can be very gratifying for a defendant who is found not liable, but the discussion can also be important in finding out why a jury voted to find a defendant liable.

Trial Testimony Dos and Don'ts
- Do visit the courtroom prior to the day of your testimony so that you know where the room is located and are familiar with the room's layout.
- Do dress conservatively.
- Do meet with your attorney within the 1 to 2 days prior to testifying.

- Do maintain eye contact with the jury when answering questions.
- Do review the medical records during your testimony if needed.
- Do review your deposition thoroughly prior to testifying.
- Don't respond to attorney attempts to make you angry.
- Don't answer right away; pause a moment to allow your attorney to object to questions.

Post Trial Motions/Appeal

Occasionally there will be a legal argument that the jury made an incorrect decision in rendering a verdict. If your attorney believes this happened, there are several possible ways for the verdict to be attacked. First is a motion for a new trial. This is usually made because of some event that occurred during the trial or because of a ruling that the judge made during the trial. Sometimes a jury will reach a decision that is, legally speaking, out of step with the evidence actually presented. In that case a motion would be made for a judgment notwithstanding the verdict. Usually a motion for a new trial must be made before a party can appeal the outcome. If a case is appealed, this means that the attorney asks the appellate court for the area to reconsider the actions of the trial court.

Time Frames

From the time a case is filed until the trial occurs, the legal process can take from 1 year up to 5 years. Appeals can take up to 2 years to be heard by the appellate court.

The APN As an Expert Witness

The expert witness presents to the jury the nursing standards at the time the incident took place. In many jurisdictions, however, physicians are still allowed to testify as expert witnesses regarding nursing standards of care. The expert gives an opinion as to whether or not the nurse adhered to the standards and acted as a reasonable and prudent nurse would have in the same or similar circumstances. An expert is not needed when legal duty is established by law, *res ipsa loquitor* applies, or when it is not helpful to the jury.

The qualifications of expert witnesses are outlined in Rule 702 of the Federal Rules of Civil Procedure, which has been adopted by most state courts. The rule indicates "If scientific, technical or other specialized knowledge will assist the trier of fact to understand the evidence or determine a fact in issue, a witness qualified as an expert by knowledge, skill, experience, training or education may testify thereto in the form of an opinion or otherwise." It is up to the judge to determine whether or not a particular witness is qualified as an expert witness. It is then up to the jury to determine the credibility of each expert witness.

Characteristics of a good expert witness include (McElhaney, 1993):

- Willing to spend time to prepare
- Answers the question asked
- Is comfortable with not knowing all the answers
- Grasps the big picture
- Persuades the jury
- Possesses the right demeanor
- Is believable
- Is sincere

In addition to giving his or her opinion, the expert may also give a dissertation or exposition of scientific or other principles relevant to the case, leaving the jury to apply that information to the facts. Most experts rely not only on their own experience in assessing a case but also refer to various sources to develop their expert opinion. These sources may include:

- Facility policy and procedure manuals
- State nurse practice acts and regulations
- American Nurses' Association (ANA) code for nurses
- ANA standards of practice
- Joint Commission for Accreditation for Hospital Organizations (JCAHO) standards
- Other accreditation standards
- Licensing regulations
- Professional association standards
- Textbooks and journals
- Continuing education curriculum

Factors that will contribute to the nurse expert's credibility include competence or expertise, knowledge of the facts, and trustworthiness (Purver et al., 1990). Experts should be aware of a trend in the law to hold them accountable to the parties who hire them. In California, Connecticut, Missouri, Pennsylvania, and Texas, courts have permitted experts to be sued by the parties who hired them for negligent handling of the case as an expert witness (Hansen, 2000). In Louisiana and Washington, courts have held that so-called friendly experts are absolutely immune from liability (Hansen, 2000). New Jersey's Supreme Court has held that even a court-appointed expert is not immune from liability for deviating from the accepted standards applicable to his or her profession (Hansen, 2000; *Levine v. Wiss & Co.*). There are several rules experts can follow to avoid being sued for malpractice (Hansen, 2000):

- Do not claim degrees, experience, or expertise that cannot be substantiated.
- Do not exaggerate work experience.

- Be careful about making factual statements about your background that can't be documented.
- Make sure your conclusions do not exceed the bounds of your data or the limits of science.
- Never claim to have conducted examinations that were not done or those for which you do not possess the requisite qualifications, experience, or necessary instrumentation.
- Never change or falsify the results of an examination to fit your client's theory of the case.
- Insure yourself against errors and omissions with a reputable insurance company.

In the case of *Carolan v. Hill et al.* (1996), the court held that a CRNA was qualified to testify about the standard of care related to the administration of anesthesia even when the CRNA was testifying as an expert on behalf of a defendant who was a doctor of osteopathy.

In the case of *Cornfeldt v. Tongen et al* (1977), a CRNA was not disqualified from testifying solely because he was not a licensed physician or because he did not graduate from medical school and had received only the training of a registered nurse anesthetist. If the CRNA otherwise had sufficient scientific and practical experience about the matter to which he would have testified, he would have been a competent expert witness.

In a wrongful death action based upon defendant orthopedic surgeon's alleged negligent supervision of a nurse anesthetist during surgery, an expert in nurse anesthesia was competent to testify that (1.) the nurse anesthetist needed supervision in ascertaining there was a medical crisis and in deciding what remedial measures should be taken and (2.) the surgeon had a duty to provide such supervision where the expert witness testified that, in her 15 years of practice as a nurse anesthetist, she had participated in thousands of operations because the expert witness was as knowledgeable as surgeons about what a nurse anesthetist can competently do without supervision (*Harris v. Miller*,1994).

Most states have laws that specifically deal with the qualifications of experts. For example, North Carolina General Statutes § 8C-1, Rule 702 (1999) indicates that in a medical malpractice action a person cannot give expert testimony on the appropriate standard of health care unless the person is a licensed health care provider in this state or another state and meets the following criteria:

1. If the party against whom or on whose behalf the testimony is offered is a specialist, the expert witness must specialize in the same specialty as the party against whom or on whose behalf the testimony is offered or specialize in a similar specialty, which includes within its specialty the performance of the procedure

that is the subject of the complaint, and have prior experience treating similar patients.

2. During the year immediately preceding the date of the occurrence that is the basis for the action, the expert witness must have devoted a majority of his or her professional time to either or both of the following: (a.) the active clinical practice of the same health profession in which the party against whom or on whose behalf the testimony is offered, and if that party is a specialist, the active clinical practice of the same specialty or a similar specialty that includes within its specialty the performance of the procedure that is the subject of the complaint and have prior experience treating similar patients, and/or (b.) the instruction of students in an accredited health professional school or accredited residency or clinical research program in the same health profession in which the party against whom or on whose behalf the testimony is offered, and if that party is a specialist, an accredited health professional school or accredited residency or clinical research program in the same specialty.

3. If the party against whom or on whose behalf the testimony is offered is a general practitioner, the expert witness during the year immediately preceding the date of the occurrence that is the basis for the action must have devoted a majority of his or her professional time to either or both of the following: (a.) active clinical practice as a general practitioner, and/or (b.) instruction of students in an accredited health professional school or accredited residency or clinical research program in the general practice of medicine.

4. A physician who qualifies as an expert and who by reason of active clinical practice or instruction of students has knowledge of the applicable standard of care for nurses, nurse practitioners, certified registered nurse anesthetists, certified registered nurse midwives, physician assistants, or other medical support staff may give expert testimony in a medical malpractice action with respect to the standard of care of which he or she is knowledgeable of nurses, nurse practitioners, certified registered nurse anesthetists, certified registered nurse midwives, physician assistants, or other medical support staff.

In *State v. Davis* (1993), the appeals court found that the trial court did not abuse its discretion by allowing a witness to testify as an expert in the area of gynecological exams where she testified that she was a certified family nurse practitioner, had been licensed since 1985, and had performed in her practice several hundred post rape gynecological exams; she stated that her findings in doing a gynecological exam on the victim were not inconsistent with the victim's history of sexual assault.

ENHANCE YOUR LEARNING

1. Attend a malpractice trial in your jurisdiction, taking note of the jury's reaction to the various witnesses who testify.
2. Interview an attorney who represents defendants in malpractice cases regarding how they analyze malpractice cases.
3. Interview a nurse expert in your city regarding his or her experiences testifying at trials.
4. Read your city's legal newspaper for information regarding malpractice verdicts.

TEST YOUR COMPREHENSION

1. List the major steps in the trial and discovery process.
2. Discuss two types of discovery and how they differ.
3. List at least four deposition do's and don'ts.
4. Discuss the importance of trial attendance and deportment for the defendant in a malpractice case.

REFERENCES

Hansen, M. (2000, November). Experts are liable, too. *American Bar Association Journal*, 17–18.
Keeva, S. (1999, December). Does the law mean never having to say you're sorry? *American Bar Association Journal*, 64–68, 95.
McElhaney, J.W. (1993). A good witness. *Litigation: The Journal of the Section of Litigation, 19*(4), 65–66.
Purver, J.M., Young, D.R., Davis, J.J., & Kerper, J. (1990). *The trial lawyer's book: Preparing and winning cases.* Rochester, NY: Lawyers Cooperative.

Cases

Harris v. Miller, 438 S.E.2d 731 (1994).
Levine v. Wiss & Co., 97 NJ 242
Phinney v. Vinson, 605 A2d 849 (1992).
Senesac v. Associates in Obstetrics and Gynecology, 449 A2d 900 (1982).
State v. Davis, 872 S.W.2d 950 (Tenn. Crim. App. 1993).

Patient Rights

The issue of patient rights is a hot topic these days. This chapter explores the following areas related to patient rights: privacy, right to self-determination, access to medical records, informed consent, as well as the special considerations that apply to the HIV-positive patients, minors, infertility patients, and victims of domestic violence.

Privacy

GENERAL PRIVACY LAW

Generally, invasion of patients' rights to privacy will fall within one of four domains:

1. Use of the patient's likeness or name without his or her consent for the commercial benefit of the defendant
2. Unreasonable intrusion into the patient's private affairs and seclusions
3. Public disclosure of private facts about the patient
4. Placing the patient in a false light in the public eye

Most privacy issues related to medical care and treatment relate to the third domain, public disclosure of private facts. Patients' medical information is considered to be a private fact. Generally a health care provider may not disclose medical information acquired in treating a patient. All states recognize the importance of confidentiality between the patient and health care provider. Courts have generally recognized a patient's right to recover damages from a health care provider for unauthorized disclosure of medical information as an invasion of privacy, a breach of the confidential relationship between health care provider and patient, a violation of statute, or breach of the fiduciary relationship between a health care provider and a patient. The patient's privilege against disclosure of medical information generally extends to hospital records.

Patients clearly have certain rights to privacy, even though they may be admitted to a facility for medical care. Both state and federal laws protect all individuals' right in maintaining privacy.

Public vs. Private Institutions

The laws surrounding privacy apply primarily to public institutions. Private facilities are less constrained by these federal rules. However, in some states, laws provide the same privacy protections to all persons and apply to both governmental and non-governmental entities. As an example, California's state constitution creates a broad right to privacy.

In a landmark drug testing case, *Hill v. National Collegiate Athletic Association* (1994), the California Supreme Court

- Held that California's constitutional right to privacy applies to non-governmental as well as to governmental entities
- Rejected the argument that any invasion of that right can be justified only by showing that it furthers a compelling interest
- Established a balancing test for determining whether or not a particular invasion of the right of privacy may be justified
- Found that the burden of establishing that there was no less intrusive means of accomplishing a legitimate end should not be placed on a nongovernmental defendant

The Hill court also found that the right of privacy encompasses two kinds of interests:

1. Interests in precluding the dissemination or misuse of sensitive and confidential information (informational privacy)
2. Interests in making intimate personal decisions or conducting personal activities without observation, intrusion, or interference (autonomy privacy)

The Court specifically noted that the freedom to act without observation in a home, hospital room, or other private place is an interest vindicated by the privacy tort (*Hill v. National Collegiate Athletic Association*, 1994).

In considering claims of invasion of privacy, the three elements that the claimant must prove are:

1. A legally protected privacy interest
2. A reasonable expectation of privacy
3. A serious invasion of the privacy interest

(*Hill v. National Collegiate Athletic Association*, 1994).

When the claimant has proven these three elements and establishes that there is a significant privacy interest involved, then the defendant must show that the action furthered a compelling interest (*American Academy of Pediatrics v. Lungren*, 1994).

Box 8-1 discusses the case of *C.M. v. Tomball Regional Hospital* (1997). Although the court did not agree with this patient's claims, it is still important for health care providers to do what they can to protect the privacy of patients being treated. Even if a court does not ultimately side with the patient making a privacy claim, the lawsuit and its attending publicity will damage the provider's reputation in the community. Policies regarding patient privacy should be developed to maximize privacy in the context of the logistical needs of patient care.

Patient Searches as an Invasion of Privacy

Both state and federal laws protect against unreasonable searches and seizures by the government. The Fourth Amendment of the United States Constitution prohibits unreasonable searches. In determining whether or not a given search is illegal, courts generally first look at whether or not the person claiming invasion of privacy had a reasonable expectation of privacy under the circumstances. In considering whether or not the patient had a reasonable expectation of privacy, a court would consider whether or not the patient had consented either verbally or in writing to the search. After considering the issue of reasonable expectation of privacy, the court will then look at whether or not the facility or institution was reasonable under the circumstances in conducting the search. Lastly, courts do recognize that searches may be conducted without consent when an emergency exists and protection of the health and safety of others is at issue.

Other important considerations regarding patient searches are:

- What type of facility is involved? If a drug rehabilitation or psychiatric facility, it is more likely that the conditions of admission include a blanket consent to searches of the patient's room and belongings; in the event that this consent is not included, the patient in such a facility will probably be considered not to have a reasonable expectation of privacy as it relates to searches for illegal drugs.
- Why was the patient hospitalized? If the patient were hospitalized for drug/alcohol abuse-related treatment, the argument would be that he or she had no reasonable expectation of privacy as to searches for illicit substances.

Drug Testing

Sharon and Wilkinson, 1988, note that APNs involved in drug screening programs are obligated to assure both the employer and employee of accuracy and fairness in the testing procedure. Policies regarding drug testing should express the company's expectations, employee obligations with regard to testing, and any proposed disciplinary action and contingent employee assistance plan, and should be distributed to all employ-

BOX 8-1	Patient Sues Hospital for Invasion of Privacy

In the case of *C.M. v. Tomball Regional Hospital* (1997), a minor who presented for care to the emergency room following a rape sued the hospital for invasion of her right to privacy under federal law. The minor alleged that the emergency room nurse caused information about the rape to be broadcast among other patrons of the emergency room by interviewing the minor in the public waiting room. She also claimed that the hospital violated her right to privacy under federal law by maintaining emergency room policies, customs, and practices that were deliberately indifferent to the patient's right to privacy, causing public disclosure of private facts.

The facts showed that rather than taking the minor to a private room, the emergency room nurse conducted the entire screening in the emergency waiting room. During the screening, the nurse was informed that the minor had been raped and that she was in severe pain. The nurse asked questions concerning the rape and asked if the minor had bathed. Learning that the minor had bathed, the nurse stated that there was nothing the hospital could do for the minor and told the minor and her mother to go to their family doctor.

When the nurse interviewed the minor and her mother in the public waiting room, 10 to 15 people were in the room and easily overheard the entire discussion. One person present was a person who apparently knew the minor; this person told others about the rape. The minor claimed to be emotionally devastated about the loss of confidentiality to the extent that the family was forced to relocate. Based on these facts, the minor claimed a privacy right regarding her medical records, her identity, and her condition as a victim of sexual assault.

In rejecting the minor's claim, the court noted that guarantees of personal privacy are limited to those fundamental or implicit in the concept of ordered liberty. One type of privacy interest protected by the U.S. Constitution is the right to be "let alone," which protects an individual's interest in avoiding the disclosure of personal information. This privacy interest focuses on government action that is intrusive or invasive, thus an individual's medical records have been declared to be within a zone of privacy protected by the Federal Constitution. However, the court found that because the minor was not admitted, a medical exam was not conducted and no notes were made, no medical record was created. Therefore the minor's privacy right regarding her medical records was not violated.

The court also rejected the minor's assertion that because she was interviewed in the waiting room, the hospital caused the public disclosure of private facts, which caused damage to her reputation. The court noted that there are no cases recognizing a person's constitutionally protected privacy interest in the facts of a crime committed against the person. The court cited a Federal case that held that injury to reputation is not a liberty interest protected by the Fourteenth Amendment. The court also rejected the plaintiff's claim for intentional infliction of emotional distress, because the nurse's behavior—although rude, insensitive and uncaring—did not rise to the level of extreme and outrageous conduct required to be proven for this claim.

ees in writing. Prior to collecting a specimen, the APN should take a medical history and provide a thorough explanation of the procedure including the precautions taken to assure accuracy. The APN should make sure that the lab selected to perform urine analysis follows a strict chain of custody procedure and confirms positive screens.

Privacy and Medical Records

The issue of privacy about patients' medical records is a hot topic these days. These privacy rights are established by various state and federal laws as well as by case law. In general, doctors and hospitals have a duty to protect patients' records from unauthorized disclosure (*Cannell v. Medical & Surgical Clinic*, 1974).

Federal laws that protect patients' privacy apply only to federally funded programs and facilities. These laws include the Freedom of Information Act and the Privacy Act. In addition, the U.S. Department of Health and Human Services (HHS) has adopted regulations that apply to all records in that agency's possession including records of the Medicare program. When insurance carriers and their intermediaries are performing functions under the Medicare program, they are considered to be federal agencies subject to the HHS regulations regarding records (45 C.F.R. §5.5 and 42 C.F.R. §401.101 [a][1], [a] [3]). There are also rules that apply to health maintenance organizations (HMOs) (42 C.F.R. §401[J]). These HMO rules require compliance with the Privacy Act as well as the regulations adopted by HHS regarding records maintained to administer the Medicare program (42 C.F.R. §417.486[c]). Additionally, HMOs that enter into contracts with HHS are required to maintain record-keeping systems on Medicare beneficiaries (42 C.F.R. §417.416[e][2]). The federal rules also provide special protection for people who have received treatment for mental illness and alcohol and drug abuse (42 U.S.C. §§10805[a][4], 10806 [1998]; 42 U.S.C. §260[d] [1998]; 42 C.F.R. §§2, 2.2[b]). These rules grant state systems that administer programs for such persons the right to have access to the individual's medical records, but they also impose a duty of confidentiality with respect to the records and require the agencies to maintain the same level of confidentiality required of the original treatment provider.

State laws vary with respect to medical record privacy. Knepper, 1998, notes that while all states have adopted some type of statute controlling disclosure of records of public entities, not all states have adopted statutes that apply to the disclosure of medical records maintained by private hospitals and other health facilities. Among states that have, she notes, the protections are not equal. Knepper, 1998, also notes that while state agencies are directed to safeguard the use and disclosure of patients' medical information to ensure that disclosures are limited to those relating to program administration and to ensure that the names of applicants and recipients are protected from routine disclosure, the requirements are not enforceable by patients living in states that have not otherwise recognized such rights.

In most facilities, the admission documents include language that gives the facility permission to release information to the patient's insurance company so the charges can be processed and paid. In the case of *Parkson v. Central DuPage Hospital* (1982), the court ruled that the hospital was allowed to consider the patient authorization sufficient to waive the privilege of confidentiality as to insurers. Medicaid applicants are expected to consent to the disclosure of their records for reasons of program administration; this consent is a prerequisite to receiving Medicaid (Knepper, 1998).

Noonan and Roth, 1997, note that in California the law prohibits disclosure of genetic test results to third parties without written authorization, and that test results and personal information from hereditary disorders programs are considered confidential medical records and can only be released with informed consent. Reporting of communicable diseases varies by state but usually includes communicable diseases such as hepatitis, as well as certain sexually transmitted diseases such as gonorrhea, syphilis, and AIDS.

Right to Self-Determination

Self-determination involves the right of a patient to establish what care he or she will receive in the event of incapacity or incompetence. The law of California will be used as a general example to discuss the issues of living wills and durable powers of attorney for health care (DPAHCs).

Living wills in California are governed by that state's Natural Death Act (NDA). This act establishes a procedure for patients to direct in writing that life-sustaining procedures be withheld or withdrawn under certain circumstances. The law in California provides two mechanisms for patients to exercise their right to control decisions related to their health care. In California, a patient may either designate a person to act as her or his surrogate decision-maker via a durable power of attorney for health care (DPAHC) and/or he or she may execute a declaration that instructs his or her physician to withhold or withdraw life-sustaining procedures when the person has a terminal condition or is in a permanent unconscious condition (Calif. Health & Safety Code §§ 7185-7194.5, Calif. Probate Code §§ 4600-4779). If a patient has both a valid DPAHC and a Natural Death Act declaration, the NDA provides that the DPAHC prevails over a Natural Death Act declaration unless expressly provided otherwise in the DPAHC. It is recommended that if the two documents conflict or present conflicting expressions of a patient's desire, legal counsel should be consulted.

A declaration under the NDA goes into effect when:

1. It is communicated to the patient's attending physician
2. The patient is diagnosed and certified in writing by the attending physician and a second physician who has personally examined the patient to have a terminal condition or to be in a permanent unconscious condition
3. The patient is no longer able to make decisions regarding administration of life-sustaining treatment (Calif. Health & Safety Code § 7187.5).

The NDA has created several responsibilities for physicians. Failure to fulfill these responsibilities is a crime; if prosecuted, the physician can be found guilty of a misdemeanor. These responsibilities include:

- Once it is determined that the patient has a terminal condition or is in a permanent unconscious condition, the attending physician who knows of a patients' NDA declaration must record the determination and the terms of the declaration in the patient's medical record along with a copy of the declaration (Health & Safety Code § 7189). A physician who willfully fails to record a determination of terminal condition or permanent unconscious condition or the terms of a declaration is guilty of a misdemeanor (Health and Safety Code § 7191[b]).
- If the attending physician or other health care provider is unwilling to comply with a declaration, "all reasonable steps as promptly as practical" must be taken to transfer care of the patient to another physician or health care provider who is willing to do so (Health and Safety Code § 7190). A physician or health care provider who refuses to comply with a declaration and willfully fails to transfer the care of a patient is guilty of a misdemeanor (Health and Safety Code § 7191[a]). Although these laws refer to physicians, it is reasonable to assume that a court would apply them to APNs.

The NDA also indicates that written directives other than an NDA declaration are valid and must be respected by health care providers. Box 8-2 lists documents also valid under the NDA.

The NDA provides that no health care provider is subject to criminal prosecution, civil liability, professional discipline, administrative sanction, or any other sanction where the health care provider acts in accordance with reasonable medical standards and believes in good faith that his or her actions are consistent with the NDA and the desires of the patient as expressed in the patient's declaration. The act also provides that no health care provider is subject to civil or criminal liability or professional discipline for giving effect to a declaration in the absence of knowledge of the patient's revocation of the declaration (Health and Safety Code § 7190.5).

BOX 8-2	Documents Valid Under the NDA

Also valid under the NDA are:

1. An instrument executed before January 1, 1992 that contains essentially the same language as that contained in an NDA declaration
2. An instrument governing the withholding or withdrawal of life-sustaining treatment executed in another state in compliance with the law of that state or of California
3. An instrument governing the withholding or withdrawal of life-sustaining treatment executed in another state that does not comply with the law of that state but substantially complies with the California Natural Death Act.

(Health and Safety Code §7192.5 and §7193.5).

California Law Regarding DPAHCs

The DPAHC allows a patient to select a surrogate decision-maker to consent to affirmative medical treatment and, in limited situations, to authorize withholding or withdrawing of life-sustaining procedures "so as to permit the natural process of dying" (Probate Code § 4723). The surrogate decision-maker's power to act only becomes effective when the patient is unable to make his or her own health care decisions either because of incapacity or incompetence. A health care provider is not subject to criminal prosecution, civil liability, or professional disciplinary action for failing to withdraw health care necessary to keep the patient alive (Probate Code § 4750[c]). However, if the patient has both a DPAHC and an NDA declaration that is valid, then the health care provider must transfer responsibility for the patient's care to another physician who will comply with the declaration or face misdemeanor criminal charges as discussed above.

It is also important to note that under California law, health care providers are not subject to criminal prosecution, civil liability, or professional disciplinary action except to the extent they would be if the patient had had capacity to consent and did so, if the health care provider relies on the decision by the surrogate under a DPAHC and

1. The decision were made by a surrogate whom the health care provider believed in good faith was authorized by law to make the decision
2. The health care provider believed, in good faith, that the decision was consistent with the patient's desires
3. If the decision involved the withholding or withdrawal of life-sustaining procedures, the health care provider made a good faith effort to determine the patient's desires and documented his or her findings (Probate Code § 4750).

California law regarding DPAHCs also provides that a DPAHC or similar instrument executed in another state in compliance with the laws of that state or of California is also valid, and that a physician or other health care provider may presume that a DPAHC or similar instrument is valid regardless of where it was executed (Calif, Probate Code § 4752).

Sampling of Other States' Laws Regarding DPAHCs and Living Wills

Other states have similar laws to protect patients' rights to determine the level of care they will receive if they become incapacitated or incompetent. Delaware has a Death With Dignity Act (16 Delaware Code §2501 *et seq.*) that recognizes the right of a competent adult to refuse treatment and authorizes the execution of an advance written declaration by a competent adult directing the withholding or withdrawal of medical treatment and life support in certain circumstances after the patient becomes incompetent. Delaware's law refers to this declaration as a living will.

The U.S. Supreme Court has indicated that when a person has clearly expressed his or her prior intentions about a course of treatment, in the event of incompetence those intentions should be respected (*Cruzan v. Director, Mo. Dept. Health*, 1990; see also *Matter of Tavel*, 1995).

New Jersey has the New Jersey Advance Directives for Health Care Act (New Jersey Stat. Ann. 26:2H–53–78). This act authorizes a patient to execute an advance directive at any time while competent. Under this act, a directive can either be a proxy directive, which is like a DPAHC, or an instruction directive, which is like an NDA declaration, or both. In New Jersey, competent persons may choose to terminate any medical treatment, even that which is life sustaining (*In re MR*, 1994). In New Jersey competent persons are entitled to a free range of choices as to their medical care, and generally they may choose to terminate any medical treatment, even life-sustaining treatment.

The right to make decisions about medical treatment is embraced in the federal constitutional right of privacy first recognized in *Griswold v. CT* (381 U.S. 479, 1965) and the right of all people to refuse life-saving treatment is included in the common law right of self-determination. However, this right is limited by four state interests: (1.) preserving life, (2.) preventing suicide, (3.) safeguarding the integrity of the medical profession, and (4.) protecting innocent third parties (*Matter of Roche*, 1996). Incompetent persons also have a common law right of self-determination except that it must be balanced with concern for their best interests because an adjudicated incompetent is a ward of the state and the state's *parens patriae* power supports the authority of the courts to allow decisions to be made for an incompetent that serve his or her best interests (*Matter of Roche*, 1996). If a patient has a DPAHC, the decision-maker must determine and effectuate insofar as possible the decision that the patient would have made if competent (*Matter of Hughes*, 1992).

Illinois passed the Living Will Act in 1992, which recognized the patient's right to develop a living will that would control decisions related to health care in the case of terminal illness (755 Ill. Code 35/1 *et seq.*). Later that year, the Powers of Attorney for Health Care Law was passed that basically authorizes DPAHCs in Illinois (755 Ill. Code 45/4-1).

Pennsylvania has the Advance Directive for Health Care Act (20 Pa. Code 5401 *et seq.*) that provides for the creation of advance written directives and provides for implementation of the patient's wishes.

Civil Liability for Ignoring DPAHCs and Living Wills

Providers who ignore valid documents expressing patients' wishes regarding life-sustaining care may face civil lawsuits brought either by the surviving patients or by their families. These cases are usually called "wrongful living" cases and involve the patient's right to enforce an informed, competent decision to reject life-saving treatment. This claim arises from the right to die recognized in the Cruzan case in 1990. The reasoning is because a person has a right to die, a medical professional is relieved of the duty to preserve life and is required by a legal duty to accede to a patient's express refusal of medical treatment; interference with a person's legal right to die is a breach of that duty to honor the wishes of the patient (*Anderson v. St. Francis-St. George*, 1996).

Courts have noted that when a patient clearly delimits the medical measures he or she is willing to undergo and a health care provider disregards such instructions, the consequence for that breach of duty would include the damages arising from any battery inflicted on the patient as well as appropriate licensing sanctions (*Anderson v. St. Francis-St. George Hospital*, 1996). A patient may expressly refuse treatment; if so, even in an emergency, any medical treatment is a battery (*Leach v. Shapiro*, 1984). In New York, courts have held that a hospital must respect the patient's right to decline even lifesaving medical treatment if, while competent, the patient stated that he or she did not want certain procedures to be employed under specified circumstances (*Matter of Storar and Matter of Eichner v. Dillon*, 1981).

When a patient has both a DPAHC and a living will, the DPAHC will generally prevail unless otherwise stated in the DPAHC or unless the two documents contain conflicting expressions of the patient's wishes. In the case of a conflict, an attorney should be consulted preferably before instituting or discontinuing any treatment.

Ethical Issues Regarding Patient Self-Determination

APNs may become involved in various ethical conflicts related to a patient's right to hasten his or her own death. As laws about assisted suicide are developed, the APN may find himself or herself faced with the issue of deciding whether or not to provide this type of service. The American Nurses' Association opposes active euthanasia and assisted suicide because such actions violate the ethical standards of the nursing profession (Kjervik, 1996).

Certified registered nurse anesthetists (CRNAs) already face ethical dilemmas when caring for DNR patients undergoing surgery.

Clark et al., 1994, note that there is no single standard for how to handle these patients and pose the following questions to be considered when a DNR patient is to undergo surgery:

- Should the surgery be performed?
- What is the meaning of resuscitation during surgery?
- Are the patient's basic objectives compromised if resuscitation is withheld?
- Are the operating room professionals willing to retain the DNR status?
- Has everyone involved in the process clearly communicated his or her wishes, beliefs, and feelings?

If the DNR status is suspended during surgery, the CRNA needs to make sure to clarify how long the DNR order should be suspended and get guidelines to follow in the event that an arrest occurs during anesthesia or in the immediate post-anesthetic period (Clark et al., 1994). At least one author supports the suspension of DNR orders during anesthesia and gives three reasons for this position:

1. General anesthesia involves the deliberate depression or manipulation of vital systems, which sometimes leads to resuscitation. Separating the administration of anesthesia, manipulation of vital systems, and resuscitation is difficult and artificial.
2. Suspending the DNR order during anesthesia and surgery is important because the difference between cardiorespiratory arrest that occurs spontaneously and cardiorespiratory arrest that occurs as a result of therapeutic intervention is difficult to discern.
3. Administration of an anesthetic to a physiologically unstable patient involves a delicate balance between analgesia and or amnesia and cardiovascular collapse. Suspension of the DNR order allows the practitioner to use all of his or her skills by providing the best anesthetic for the patient including cardiopulmonary resuscitation (Clark et al., 1994).

Access to Medical Records

In every state, patients are entitled to have access to their own health records. For example in California, Health and Safety Code §§ 123100-123149 guarantee patients and certain patient representatives access to medical and other health records. California law indicates that upon written request by a patient or a patient's representative and within 5 days of the request, the requester is entitled to inspect all or part of the patient's record. The patient or the patient's representative must perform the inspection; in addition, one other person of her or his choosing may accompany the patient or her representative. However, the health care provider may choose instead to prepare a summary of the patient's record that complies with the statute's requirements. These requirements are very detailed and specific.

Other states permit a summary to be provided in lieu of the actual records only with the consent of the patient. Generally the patient is given access to any mental health or substance abuse treatment records unless the provider determines there is a substantial risk of significant adverse consequences to the patient by seeing these records. Henry, 1993, reminds us that the health care provider has an absolute right to possession of the original record, but the patient has the exclusive control over the information contained in the record including review by third parties. Rules about the patient's access to the medical record are not uniform from state to state. Henry, 1993, notes that access can vary from providing a complete copy of the records to only providing selected portions of the record or even a summary or report. Every state does address and define the patient's right to have an attorney receive a copy of her or his records for purposes of litigation but only with the patient's written authorization (Henry, 1993). The laws usually provide for denial of access to the patient only when such disclosure may be detrimental to the patient's well-being. All states have laws specifying a time period during which the provider must maintain a patient's records. In California, for example, the law requires providers to maintain a patient's records for at least 7 years after the final discharge from care (Calif. Health & Safety Code §1795.2).

Federal laws require that Medicare records be kept 5 years beyond the time period that a tort civil action may be filed; in the case of minors this time frame could be as long as 25 years (Henry, 1993). Henry, 1993, notes that there are four legally recognized requests for release of information:

1. Written authorization executed by the patient or his or her legal representative. The APN must verify that the person signing the release is the patient or legal representative. When presented with such an authorization, the APN must make the chart available for copying within a reasonable time and may request a reasonable fee for making this information available.
2. Subpoena *duces tecum*, issued by the court or a government board, ordering that a copy of the chart be produced to the requesting party who is usually an attorney. A copy service will usually come to copy the records.
3. Deposition subpoena that orders the provider to appear with the original record for a deposition at which time an inquiry will be

made under oath as to when and how the record was maintained

4. Trial subpoena ordering the custodian to produce the original record in court.

The subpoenas are usually served on the custodian in person or by mail and generally require a notice to the patient that the records are being sought. A certain number of days must pass before the provider must produce the chart to allow the patient to object; if no objection is lodged with the provider by the patient, the provider must comply with the subpoena, as failing to comply is punishable as contempt of court and may also result in a fine and or imprisonment (Henry, 1993).

Informed Consent

GENERAL LAW REGARDING INFORMED CONSENT

When Must Informed Consent Be Given?

This varies among the states: some only require informed consent for invasive procedures, others require it for bed rest. Many states legislate informed consent for procedures such as HIV tests, hysterectomy, sterilization, and infertility procedures. In general, written consent is required for surgically invasive procedures and those treatments for which state law requires written consent.

What Information Must Be Given To Constitute Informed Consent?

The alternatives, risks, and benefits of the proposed treatment: facts material to a patient's decision whether or not to accept treatment, facts that a reasonable, prudent patient would need to have to make an informed decision, and the risks of failing to acccpt the proposed treatment.

Documentation for informed consent must include

- The patient's signature
- The witnesses signature
- The date and time
- Documentation of the conversation with the patient regarding the fact that the APN has discussed with her or him the risks, benefits, and alternatives and that the patient understands and has no questions.

There are two exceptions to the requirement for informed consent: the emergency exception and incompetence. Incompetence is when the patient is incapable of understanding her or his condition, the nature and effect of the proposed treatment, and the risks of pursuing or not pursuing the treatment (*Miller v. Rhode Island Hospital*, 1993). If a mentally ill patient refuses treatment, involuntary admission is generally limited to situations when it is determined that the patient is dangerous to self or others. In the case of the incompetent patient, you shouldn't treat them unless

- There is an emergency.
- There is a court order.
- The legal guardian consents.

In the case of guardian consent, it would be wise to ask to see the paperwork from the court approving the person as the guardian. The emergency exception indicates that treatment may proceed without the patient's consent as long as no evidence exists to indicate that the patient or her legal representative would refuse the treatment. Most states have laws specifically defining a medical emergency for purposes of this exception.

In general, a medical emergency exists when immediate services are required for alleviation of severe pain or immediate diagnosis and treatment of unforeseeable medical conditions are required because such conditions, if not immediately diagnosed and treated, could or would lead to serious disability or death (Calif. B. & P. Code § 2397c[2]-[3]).

APNs need to remember that written consent is required of a rape victim for the examination, photographs, release of evidence to the police, and medical treatment (Heinrich, 1987).

Urbanski, 1997, reminds us that a signed consent form can still be challenged in court if there is evidence that the process of adequately informing the patient did not take place; these cases are lost when the witness to the signature can only testify that the form was signed and cannot testify that the patient understood the form or procedure or when the major risks were not explained and the importance of the form was not explained.

The law does not allow health care providers to force treatment upon a competent patient who refuses it. In fact, doing so would be equivalent to committing battery on the patient. Unless the patient is determined by a physician to be mentally incompetent for the purposes of giving informed consent, the patient's wishes must be respected unless the emergency exception applies. The test for mental capacity to consent to medical treatment has been held by the courts to be whether or not the patient is able to reasonably understand the condition, the nature and effect of the proposed treatment, and the risks of both pursuing and not pursuing the treatment (*Miller v. Rhode Island Hospital*, 1993).

Several courts have recognized that alcohol intoxication can legally impair a patient's capacity to refuse medical treatment (*Miller v. Rhode Island Hospital*, 1993). In the case of mental illness, involuntary admission is generally limited to situations where it is determined that the patient is dangerous to themselves or others; otherwise the patient has a right to leave the hospital against medical advice (*Paradies v. Benedictine*, 1980).

Before a patient is discharged prior to the completion of treatment or contrary to medical advice, the physician must first attempt to provide the patient with information about the potential consequences of so doing. This information should include the risks involved in leaving, the benefits of continued hospitalization, and any alternatives so that the patient can make an informed decision as to whether or not to leave against medical advice (AMA) (*Truman v. Thomas*, 1980). It is imperative that the provider makes a detailed note reflecting all of the above noted elements of this discussion. In addition, the patient should be asked to sign a standard Discharge Against Medical Advice form that acknowledges the elements of the discussion with the provider. If the patient refuses to sign, that fact and the time of refusal must be noted.

Certain situations present complicated legal issues and mandate that the facility's attorney be consulted immediately:

1. The patient has an emergency medical condition that has not been stabilized.
2. The patient's decision to leave the facility will result in the withdrawal of life-sustaining treatment.
3. There is a potential for life-threatening consequences if the patient leaves AMA and the patient is incompetent or is a minor with a legal representative.

If the competent patient persists in the desire to leave, the providers should allow the patient to do so. Any IVs etc., should be removed by personnel to avoid patient injury. Precautions should also be taken to ensure that the patient leaves the facility safely. If the patient has received medications or has a physical condition that makes driving unsafe, an alternate means of transportation should be arranged. If the patient leaves without notifying anyone, usually called an "elopement," the person who discovers that the patient has left the premises should write a detailed chart note regarding the time and manner of the discovery of the patient's absence. An attempt should be made to contact the patient at the phone number of record to determine the reason for leaving, to attempt to encourage them to return, and to make recommendations for self care and follow-up care.

In *Paradies v. Benedictine Hospital* (1980), the court found that a voluntary mental patient had a right to leave the hospital on demand; in the absence of the patient showing signs of dangerousness, defendant providers had no duty to seek emergency involuntary commitment. Generally, no need to disclose arises where no diagnostic testing or treatment is recommended (*Munro v. Regents*, 1989). If, in a provider's professional judgment, a diagnostic test is not medically indicated, the provider has no duty to inform the patient of the test (*Vandi v. Permanente Medical*

Group, 1992). Deceit as to the therapeutic purpose of an otherwise offensive contact vitiates consent (*Rains v. Superior Court*, 1984).

In *Cornfeldt v. Tongen, et al.* (262 NW 2d 684, 1977), the court noted that the therapeutic privilege is a well-recognized exception to the objective standard of disclosure, which excuses the withholding of information where disclosure would be unhealthful to the patient. This privilege is applicable only if disclosure of the information would complicate or hinder treatment, cause such emotional distress as to preclude a rational decision, or cause psychological harm to the patient (*Rains v. Superior Court*, 1984).

Some states have laws that set out consent requirements for certain procedures. For example, California Health & Safety Code § 1704.5 requires physicians to inform the patient of alternative treatments for breast cancer, and California Health & Safety Code § 1690 sets out specific requirements regarding informed consent for a hysterectomy. A battery theory of liability should be reserved for those circumstances when a patient gives consent to perform one type of treatment and the provider performs another, as in this situation the requisite element of deliberate intent to deviate from the consent given is present. However, when the patient consents to certain treatment and that treatment is performed but an undisclosed inherent complication with a low probability occurs, the provider has not deviated from the consent but rather may have failed to disclose all the pertinent information to obtain the consent, so the claim should be one of negligence and not battery (*Mathis v. Morrissey*, 1992).

The scope of a provider's duty to disclose choices regarding proposed therapies and the dangers involved in each is measured by the amount of information a patient needs to make an informed choice. All information material to a patient's decision should be given. Material information is information the provider knows or should know would be regarded as significant by a reasonable person in the patient's position when deciding to accept or reject the proposed treatment. To be material, a fact must also be one that is not commonly appreciated; for example, if a patient declines a risk-free test or treatment, the provider has an additional duty to advise about all material risks that a reasonable person would want to be told before deciding not to undergo the procedure or test (*Truman v. Thomas*, 1980).

Special Considerations

THE HIV-POSITIVE PATIENT

General Law Regarding HIV Patients' Privacy Rights

In the context of HIV/AIDS, the patient's right to privacy is in conflict with the public's interest in preventing the spread of this disease. California will be used as an example of the laws surrounding specific privacy rights of

HIV/AIDS patients, as it is one of the more progressive states as relates to these diseases.

California generally prohibits disclosure of HIV-related information. However, disclosure is permitted under several narrow circumstances: (1.) when expressly authorized in writing by the patient, (2.) to other members of a health care team responsible for the treatment of an HIV positive patient, (3.) to certain categories of persons thought to have been at risk for exposure such as sexual assault victims and firefighters. These select persons can request a court to require testing of the persons whose bodily fluids they have come into contact with and the test results will only be disclosed to the requestor, ie, the person thought to have been placed at risk, (4.) to fulfill the needs of various state public health functions including disclosure of individually identifiable HIV-related information to local, state, or federal health agencies for surveillance and disease control purposes (Doughty, 1994).

Several courts have found that the federal constitutional right to privacy encompasses protection against disclosure of HIV-related information and several have held that disclosure of such information violates a patient's right to privacy (Doughty, 1994). It is important to note, however, that the constitutional privacy protection applies only to state action and does not allow an individual to claim violation of the federal privacy right by an individual health care provider (Doughty, 1994). Under California law, however, disclosure of HIV-related information might result in personal liability on the part of the person making the disclosure (Doughty, 1994). In terms of partner notification, California law allows a physician possessing a patient's positive HIV results to disclose that information to a person reasonably believed to be the spouse or to a person reasonably believed to be a sexual partner or a person with whom the patient has shared the use of hypodermic needles. Before notifying those noted above, the physician must first attempt to obtain the patient's consent. In the course of disclosure, the physician may not reveal any identifying information about the individual believed to be infected (Doughty, 1994). The law also permits the county health department to perform systemic partner notification (Doughty, 1994).

Disclosure of HIV Status

In general, a patient's HIV status is protected by law from unauthorized disclosure. Most states have laws specifically requiring that HIV data be kept confidential (Gostin & Webber, 1998). Most states also allow disclosure under certain circumstances such as disclosure to members of a health care team responsible for the treatment of the HIV-positive patient or for purposes of reporting to governmental agencies for the purposes of surveillance and disease control. Other states limit disclosure to the treating physician (Brooke, 1997). Under these laws, health care providers may be held liable for both intentional and negligent disclosure of a patient's HIV status.

The Supreme Court recognized a federal right to privacy in 1965 (*Griswold v. Connecticut*, 381 U.S. 479). Several courts have found that this right encompasses protection against disclosure of HIV-related information. Several have held that the disclosure of this information violated a patient's right to privacy (Doughty, 1994). Some health care providers feel they have a right or need to know if their patients are HIV positive. Gostin and Webber, 1998, note that these "right to know" claims are difficult to maintain, especially because universal precautions require health care providers to treat all patients as though they had blood-borne illnesses. Thus there is really no legitimate reason for health care providers to have this information.

Providers need to beware of the potential for punitive damages in cases where HIV-related information is improperly disclosed. As of 1993, three states expressly authorized such damages (Mo. Rev. Stat. § 191.656.6[2][b][1991]; Okla. Stat. Ann. Tit.63 § 1-502.2[H][1992]; and Wis. Stat. § 146.025[8][a][1989-1990]). In the case of *Doe v. Roe* (1993) discussed in Box 8-3, an appeals court in New York State also held that punitive damages could be given in such a case.

In the case of *Urbaniak v. Newton* (1991), the plaintiff disclosed his HIV-positive status to a nurse for the purpose of protecting her during a procedure that involved blood then asked that his condition not be shared. The nurse informed the physician for whom she worked; he in turn included the information in a medical report to the insurance company. The patient sued for breach of his privacy. The court agreed, ruling

BOX 8-3	Punitive Damages for Disclosure of HIV-Related Information

In *Doe v. Roe* (1993), a patient sued a physician for releasing his medical records that contained notations regarding his HIV status to an attorney representing his employer in a workers compensation claim related to ear and sinus problems. The patient had signed authorizations for release of records *2 years* prior to the time he had disclosed to this physician his HIV status. When he disclosed his HIV status, the patient specifically requested that this information be kept confidential and the physician verbally promised to do so. The court determined that the patient had a private right to sue the physician for violating New York law by disclosing the confidential HIV-related information, that the disclosure of the patient's HIV status in fact violated New York law, and that the patient had a right to sue the physician for breaching the promise to keep this information confidential.

that the disclosures by the providers violated the patient's right to privacy under California law.

All states have required reporting of Centers for Disease Control (CDC) defined AIDS, but only 28 states require HIV reporting and 3 additional states conduct HIV surveillance for pediatric cases only. All HIV reporting states except Maryland and Texas are name-based (Gostin & Webber, 1998). Ten states prohibit nonreportable, anonymous testing (Gostin & Webber, 1998). Most states have HIV-specific statutes requiring confidentiality of HIV data (Gostin & Webber, 1998).

Many states allow disclosure by physicians to third parties known to be at significant future risk of HIV transmission from patients known to be infected. Under some laws, the physician is required first to counsel the patient to refrain from the risky behavior; in providing the third-party warning, the physician is prohibited from disclosing the patient's identity (Gostin & Webber, 1998).

This duty to warn may extend to nonpatient third parties based on the provider's primary duty to the patient. In a case reported by Gostin and Webber, 1998, a physician failed to inform a teen or her parents that she had been transfused with HIV-contaminated blood. When the teen's sexual partner tested positive for HIV, the court upheld the partner's claim against the physician based on his failure to inform the patient.

Documentation of HIV Status

With respect to documentation of the patient's HIV status on the medical record, one author suggests that this may be done discretely by using a certain code or sticker in the patient's chart, as long as it is a confidential code (ie, not a red sticker with HIV or AIDS written on it) and the chart is not readily available to anyone other than health care providers involved in the patient's care (Brooke, 1997). Systems such as this must be used only after careful consideration and with extreme caution because the risks presented by inadvertent disclosure are great, not only to the patient but also to the provider. The case of *Behringer v. The Medical Center at Princeton* (1991), discussed in Box 8-4, illustrates the need for caution in this area.

An important consideration regarding the documentation of HIV-related information is keeping that information confidential when the medical record is released to others, whether or not pursuant to a patient's records request to subsequent treating physicians, to insurance companies for purposes of payment, or pursuant to a records subpoena. Most states require that an authorization to release medical records specifically state that the patient authorizes release of HIV-related information before the provider may do so without penalty. In addition, many states require that any HIV-related information released pursuant to an authorization must be accompanied by a written statement prohibiting further disclosure of this information.

BOX 8-4   Disclosure of HIV Status

In the case of *Behringer v. The Medical Center at Princeton* (1991), a physician on staff at the hospital was admitted to the facility and found to be suffering from *Pneumocystis carinii* pneumonia and to be HIV positive. The patient and his treating physician recognized the risk of his diagnosis becoming public if he remained a patient there. It was determined that he would leave the hospital and be treated at home. Within hours of his discharge, he began to receive telephone calls of condolence from other members of the medical staff as well as social friends. It was never determined which persons disseminated this information; however, the court agreed with the plaintiff that the facility's failure to implement meaningful restrictions on access to his medical records was sufficient to establish liability.

In finding that the hospital had breached its duty to the plaintiff regarding maintaining the confidentiality of his medical information, the court noted the various ways in which the hospital failed to take reasonable steps to safeguard this information: (1.) despite hospital policy stating that charts were limited to those persons having patient care responsibility, as a practical matter, the charts were available to anyone working in the hospital; (2.) despite the Centers for Disease Control recommendation that access to HIV results be limited, the hospital had no policy that physically restricted access to HIV test results or the charts containing those results to those involved with the particular patient's care; (3.) failure to give employees instructions regarding the confidentiality of HIV test results; (4.) failure of the laboratory to take steps to ensure that HIV test results were kept confidential by other facility departments after being placed in patient charts and failure to run confidentiality training programs; (5.) keeping plaintiff's chart at the nurse's station on the floor on which he was a patient; (6.) charting the HIV result and the AIDS diagnosis at numerous locations in the medical record; (7.) failure to attempt to keep knowledge of plaintiff's diagnosis limited to persons involved in his care; (8.) failure to provide written or verbal restrictions against health care providers involved in plaintiff's care discussing his diagnosis with other hospital employees. The court noted that in the absence of these special procedures directed at ensuring patient confidentiality it was inevitable that this patient's confidentiality would be breached.

The court also noted that among the alternatives to unrestricted charting of an AIDS diagnosis are (1.) sequestering those portions of the chart dealing with the HIV result and or AIDS diagnosis and (2.) segregating and securing the entire chart with access only to those health care workers demonstrating a bona-fide need to know. In the case of a teaching hospital, the court recognized that physicians or students other than those directly involved in the patient's care must have access to the patient's records, but that in those situations, the hospital must impress upon these physicians and students the significance of maintaining the confidentiality of patient records.

The HIV-Positive Health Care Provider

Several courts have held that health care professionals have a duty to disclose their HIV status to patients or health authorities, assuming that their professional activities pose a risk of transmission to patients; courts justify orders to disclose based on a duty to protect patients and on the doctrine of informed consent (Brooke, 1997). Some states allow the professional to continue practicing with appropriate restrictions and supervision without disclosing their HIV status (Brooke, 1997). In the case of *Application of M.S. Hershey Medical Center* (1991), two hospitals were permitted to disclose a physician's identity and his HIV-positive status to certain colleagues and to disclose to certain patients that a resident physician who participated in their surgical procedure or obstetrical care was HIV positive. In reaching this decision, the court noted that the physician's medical problem was not merely his; it became a public concern when he picked up a surgical instrument and became part of a team involved in invasive procedures.

Refusal to Treat

Providers cannot refuse to treat patients just because they are HIV positive. Courts have consistently held that providers have a legal duty to treat HIV/AIDS patients unless the professional lacks the skill required to render competent care (Gostin & Webber, 1998). In the case of *School Board v. Arline* (1987), the U.S. Supreme Court held that persons with contagious diseases are handicapped within the meaning of federal disability rights law and that the risk HIV poses to others is insufficient to support a refusal to treat (Sinclair, 2000).

The HIV-Positive Child

Sterken, 1995, notes that the CDC recommends that children with HIV infection remain in the classroom until they demonstrate neurological deficits or problems related to excretion. Although § 504 of the Rehabilitation Act of 1973 protects an individual against discrimination on the basis of the individual's handicap, the U.S. Supreme Court has concluded that individuals handicapped by a contagious disease who pose a significant health risk to others are not protected by § 504 (Sterken, 1995). HIV-positive children are also protected under Public Law No. 94-142 , which delineates the fundamental rights of all children with disabilities and sets forth procedures to ensure that children with disabilities receive the free and appropriate education to which they are entitled (Sterken, 1995). Sterken, 1995, notes that the NP caring for an HIV-positive child can play an important role in helping the family deal with the school system. The NP needs to remind the family that failing to disclose the information places the child at both physical and psychological risk. NPs can provide support to the family of an HIV-positive child by (1.) informing the parents of a child's right to an education, (2.) meeting with school officials and school personnel to educate them about HIV infection and appraising them of the child's individual needs, (3.) accompanying parents to school board meetings when they feel this would be supportive, (4.) providing consultation to teachers and principals in talking to other classmates about HIV and AIDS, and (5.) providing up-to-date information to the school pertaining to the child's progress once the child has entered the classroom (Sterken, 1995).

General strategies for dealing with HIV issues are listed in Box 8-5.

BOX 8-5	Strategies for Dealing With HIV Issues

Sinclair, 2000, suggests the following strategies in dealing with HIV issues:

- Maintain current knowledge about HIV and AIDS and document that information when appropriate.
- Ensure privacy and confidentiality at all times.
- Maintain written guidelines to enhance privacy and confidentiality and periodically review them with attending, per diem, and staff personnel.
- Disclose to safeguard others only when ethical and legal parameters have been met.
- Train staff concerning compliance with antidiscrimination laws regarding HIV and AIDS; make sure current information is available.
- Institute and enforce universal precautions rigorously.
- Assess the HIV risk acquisition status of patients while acknowledging the sensitive and confidential nature of the questions.
- Offer HIV testing as part of routine health promotion, being especially vigilant to encourage testing for all pregnant women and for women who have recurrent monilial vaginitis; document the offer.
- Provide cervical screening every 6 months for HIV-positive women.
- Discuss the ramifications of perinatal transmission with HIV-positive women and respect their right to make reproductive decisions.
- Refer infected persons to a comprehensive program that includes social services, psychological support, and health care. Know the programs or know the people who are familiar with the programs offered in the community.
- Ensure that patients have appropriate and sufficient information for informed consent for all procedures, treatments, and clinical research protocols.
- Teach transmission prevention by using the specific language and parlance of the patient.
- Establish institutional contact with an attorney conversant with laws relating to HIV/AIDS so that questions can be posed and suggested policies and procedures can be reviewed before implementation.

MINORS

Each state's law defines the age below which a person is considered to be a minor and thus incompetent to consent to medical treatment. In most states, this age is 18 years.

Practice areas likely to serve minors are ambulatory care, obstetrics/gynecology clinics, labor and delivery, neonatal intensive care unit, and the emergency room.

Consent for Minors

Laws in the past required parental consent before health care could be provided to a minor. This created the problem of minors not seeking care for conditions they didn't want their parents to know about. Beginning in the 1970s, federal and state legislation was passed allowing minors to consent for their own care on the basis of either their status or the category of care they were seeking. Generally when a child has reached the age of 14 years, she or he is viewed as being capable of understanding and participating in decision-making. At this age, teens should be given appropriate information about treatment options and their preferences should be included in the overall health care process. Parents or legal guardians remain the ultimate decision-makers; their judgments can override that of the child unless the child is legally capable of giving her or his own consent (Muscari, 1998).

Minors who may consent to their own care include:

- Those living apart from their parents (self-sufficient minors) 15 and older
- Married minors (ask for a copy of the marriage certificate)
- Minors in military service (regardless of age)
- Legally emancipated minors (14 and older who have been granted legal independence from parents/guardians)
- Minors who are parents of a child

The mature minor doctrine is a common law concept indicating that minors may consent for their own health care if all the following criteria are met:

- The minor is 15 years of age or older.
- The minor is capable of giving informed consent and has demonstrated maturity and decision-making capacity.
- The proposed treatment is for the minor's benefit and does not involve complex, high-risk, medical or surgical procedures.

This doctrine applies to cases where no other exceptions to parental consent apply and parental involvement is impractical or problematic (Pharris, 1997).

Category-of-care exceptions allow minors to consent based upon the type of care they are seeking; the exceptions include:

- Diagnosis and treatment of sexually transmitted diseases (STDs); age varies by state (see below)
- Health care and counseling after sexual assault or abuse
- Emergency care
- General medical care
- Abortion
- HIV/AIDS care
- Drug and alcohol treatment (no methadone or LAMM [levoal-phacetyl-methadol] without parent/guardian consent)
- Contraceptive care
- Pregnancy-related care
- Mental health services (outpatient only, no convulsive treatment, psychosurgery, or psychotropic drugs without parent/guardian consent)

Parental consent is required when:

- Patient is under age, unmarried, and no special circumstances apply
- Patient is underage, pregnant, not married, and the care is not related to prevention or treatment of pregnancy and no other special circumstances apply

Minor's Consent for Treatment of Sexual Assault

Most states neither enable nor prohibit minors' consent for this treatment. Illinois allows consent. California, Kansas, Mississippi, and Ohio allow consent but mandate parental notification. Kansas, Mississippi, and Ohio require written notification of the examination. New Jersey allows consent but requires that the parents or guardian be notified immediately unless the attending physician believes it is in the patient's best interest not to do so. Arizona and Wyoming allow consent if the parents can't be located.

Minor's Consent for Treatment of STDs

As of 1995, all states had statutes allowing adolescents to consent for diagnosis and treatment of STDs. Regarding treatment for STDs, the ages differ: in South Carolina persons 16 and older can consent; in Hawaii, New Hampshire, and North Dakota, persons 14 and older can consent; in Delaware and Vermont, persons 12 and older can consent. Connecticut law says that if the patient is under 12 years of age, the facility must report the name, age, and address of the minor to the Commissioner of Children and Families. Mississippi Code Ann. § 41-41-13 indicates that an NP who in the exercise of due care renders medical care to a minor for treatment of a venereal disease is under no obligation to obtain the consent of a parent/guardian or to inform them of the treatment. Other states don't specify a lower age limit for consent for diagnosis and treatment of STDs (Pharris, 1997).

3126 E. New Hope Cemetery Rd.
Peru, IN 46970

- - - - - - - - - - - -

PACKING SLIP:
Amazon Marketplace Item: The Advanced Practice Nurse's Legal Handbook [Paperback] by Cady,
Rebecca F...
Listing ID: 0306W873525
SKU: 148.05CC
Quantity: 1

Purchased on: 21-Apr-2003
Shipped by: bookarama@direcway.com
Shipping address:

4/21/2003

FINAL SALES!!!
1800KARAMA

Minor's Consent for Drug and Alcohol Treatment

New Hampshire Rev. Stat. Ann. § 318-B: 12-a, which is typical of statutes permitting this consent, indicates that any minor 12 or over may submit himself or herself for treatment for drug problems to any NP without consent of the parent, guardian, or any other person charged with his or her care or custody.

Minor's Consent for Pregnancy Care

Harner et al., 2001, note that in as many as two-thirds of teenage pregnancies, adult males are the fathers; in California sexual partners of pregnant California girls ages 11 to 12 were an average of 10 years older than the girls. In almost every state, pregnant teens may consent to prenatal obstetric and postpartum care; some states require the teen to be at least 14 years old (Pharris, 1997). In 11 states, providers caring for the pregnant teen may notify her parents of the pregnancy (Pharris, 1997).

Teens in most states are allowed to give consent for the adoption of their babies; however, some states require the father of the baby and both sets of grandparents to be involved in the process (Pharris, 1997).

Regarding abortion services, currently 14 states require parental notification prior to the performance of services (Pharris, 1997). Seventeen other states require written consent of at least one parent for a minor's abortion (Pharris, 1997). Nineteen states have a mandatory waiting period ranging from 1 to 24 hours after state-directed counseling before the abortion can be performed (Pharris, 1997). Arkansas, Minnesota, Colorado, North Dakota, and Mississippi have especially burdensome notification and consent laws that require both parents to have some involvement in the minor's abortion (Pharris, 1997).

Most states make some provision for the parental consent requirement to be circumvented by a judicial bypass procedure. Typically this procedure involves the child filing a petition with a local court to obtain the court's approval to have the procedure without parental notification. In the case of *American Academy of Pediatrics v. Lungren* (1994), the court found that California legislation restricting the right to procreative choice for unemancipated minors by requiring parental notification invaded their constitutionally protected right to privacy.

Minor's Confidentiality

Who "owns" the nurse–patient confidentiality protection when the patient is a minor? If a minor consents for her or his own care, confidentiality is mandatory; only the patient has access to the records unless the law requires parental notification. In this case, information cannot be disclosed without a waiver from the minor; violation of this privacy is usually a misdemeanor (Muscari, 1998). If both parent and child sign the consent form, the parent has a right to access the records. If an assault is reported to the police, parts of that record are public record and may be accessed by the parents.

In California when the parent has sought care for a minor for substance abuse and the care is received, the parents may request and receive medical information about the care even if the child objects, UNLESS the care was provided in a federally assisted program (federal law requires the child's consent prior to release of any patient information). Ideally, disclosures should not be shared unless there is a need for immediate intervention or in cases of suicidal or homicidal ideation.

Informing Parents Without the Minor's Consent
This varies by state but in general is allowed by law when

- The patient is under age, unmarried, and no special circumstances exist
- The patient is under age, no special circumstances exist, there is an emergency, and the parents are not available
- The patient is a self-sufficient minor; patient not married, pregnant, under age, care is not related to prevention or treatment of pregnancy and no other special circumstances;
- The patient is a minor receiving care for rape, sexual assault, drug/alcohol abuse, or outpatient mental health treatment.

Information likely to cause an assertion of breach of confidentiality by the minor includes sexual information including contraception, STDs, and information about sexual activity; information related to drug and/or alcohol abuse; mental health treatment information; information about homosexuality.

When dealing with a teenager who has been a long-time patient, you should discuss your facility's policy regarding consent and confidentiality as the child reaches the mid-teen years. This discussion should take place with both parent/guardian and child together to assure they receive the same information (Wildey, 1992). The parent should be reminded that at this point in time, you will not disclose the content of future visits without the teen's consent unless the teen is engaged in a behavior or situation that may be harmful to self or someone else (Wildey, 1992).

The American Academy of Pediatrics has issued the following criteria for definition of a mature minor:

1. An adolescent who initiates his or her own appointments
2. An adolescent who personally initiates health care
3. An adolescent who is able to state his or her own needs
4. An adolescent who seems able to follow through with recommendations
5. An adolescent who seems to understand both the risks and benefits of the proposed treatment (Wildey, 1992)

When presented with a situation where an established teen patient comes in on his or her own for the first time and asks that the visit be kept confidential, Wildey, 1992, recommends that the practitioner discuss with the teen before she or he leaves the office exactly what information if any will be shared with the parents. If the past pattern has involved routine calls to the parents following visits and the parents are aware of the visit (but not the reason), you should discuss with the patient the fact that failure to follow this pattern will likely lead the parents to become suspicious and may result in a confrontation. In the event that the established teen patient comes in and requests to pay and that the parents not be billed, the practitioner should accept payment from the teen for services rendered and issue an itemized bill directly to the teen (Wildey, 1992).

Required Reporting

Under the Child Abuse Prevention and Treatment Act (42 U.S.C. § 5101), all health care professionals in the United States are mandated reporters of actual or suspected child abuse or neglect. The APN will be required to violate the pregnant teen's confidentiality in cases where the teen is a victim of child abuse; however, most states do not require health care providers to report cases of statutory sexual assault (Harner et. al., 2001). In some states such as Minnesota, reporting of sexual assault is mandatory only if the perpetrator was responsible for the care of the minor, was in a position of authority over the minor, or has a significant relationship with the minor such as a family member or someone living in the same home (Pharris, 1997).

All states have laws that require certain health care professionals to report any signs of suspected child abuse. The law requires reporting signs of physical and sexual abuse as well as neglect. Components of required reporting laws include definitions of actions/ failures to act that constitute child abuse; adoption of reasonable cause as the threshold of suspicion for reporting; definitions of which providers are mandatory reporters; establishment of procedures for oral and written reports; provisions for taking x-rays and other medical tests; provisions regarding immunity of the reporting provider from liability for having reported; and penalties, which are usually fines plus action against their licenses, to providers who fail to comply. Box 8-6 discusses the required reporting laws of Pennsylvania, which are typical of this type of law. Box 8-7 gives guidelines for assessing a child for physical or sexual abuse and neglect.

In the case of *Casbohm et al. v. Metrohealth Medical Center et al.* (2000), the court confirmed that the health care provider defendants who provided reports of suspected child abuse were absolutely immune under state law from civil suit by the parents of the children, even though the parents provided evidence from other medical experts that the nurse practitioner's findings were a "gross over-interpretation of non-specific findings as being suggestive of sexual abuse" and that none of the findings were even suspicious of abuse.

BOX 8-6	Required Reporting Statute

PA code §21.501–21.507 govern required reporting in that state. §21.501 provides the following definitions of child abuse:

1. A recent (within 2 years of the date of the report) act or failure to act that causes nonaccidental serious physical injury to a child under 18 years of age,
2. An act or failure to act that causes nonaccidental serious mental injury to or sexual abuse or sexual exploitation of a child under 18 years of age,
3. A recent (within 2 years of the date of the report) act, failure to act, series of acts, or failures to act that creates an imminent risk of serious physical injury to or sexual abuse or sexual exploitation of a child under 18 years of age, or
4. Serious physical neglect constituting prolonged or repeated lack of supervision or the failure to provide the essentials of life, including adequate medical care, that endangers a child's life or development or impairs the child's functioning.

These acts may be committed by a person who is a parent of the child, a person responsible for the welfare of the child, an individual residing in the same home as a child (who is 14 years of age or older), or a paramour of a child's parent. A person responsible for the child's welfare is defined as a person who provides permanent or temporary care, supervision, mental health diagnosis or treatment, training or control of a child in lieu of parental care, supervision and control.

Serious mental injury is defined as a psychological condition, as diagnosed by a physician or licensed psychologist, including the refusal of appropriate treatment that does one or more of the following:

1. Renders a child chronically and severely anxious, agitated, depressed, socially withdrawn, psychotic, or in reasonable fear that the child's life or safety is threatened
2. Seriously interferes with a child's ability to accomplish age-appropriate developmental and social tasks

Serious physical injury is defined as an injury that causes a child severe pain or significantly impairs a child's physical functioning, either temporarily or permanently.

Sexual abuse or exploitation is defined as the employment, use of persuasion, inducement, enticement or coercion of a child to engage in or assist another person to engage in sexually explicit conduct or a simulation of sexually explicit conduct for the purpose of producing a visual depiction, including photographing, videotaping, computer depicting, or filming of sexually explicit conduct or the rape, sexual assault, molestation, incest, indecent exposure, prostitution, statutory sexual assault, or other form of sexual exploitation of children.

(continued)

BOX 8-6	Required Reporting Statute (Continued)

§21.502 requires RNs, LPNs, or CRNPs who, in the course of their employment, occupation, or practice of their profession, come into contact with children to report or cause a report to be made to the Department of Public Welfare when they have reasonable cause to suspect on the basis of their professional or other training or experience that a child coming before them in their professional or official capacity is a victim of child abuse. Reports in this state must be made orally by telephone immediately when the suspicion arises; a written report must be made within 48 hours after the oral report.

§21.507 indicates that disciplinary action may be taken against the professional license of an RN who fails to report, and that criminal penalties will also apply.

The 23 PA C.S. § 6318 provides that as a general rule, any person participating in good faith in the making of a report, cooperating with an investigation or testifying in a proceeding arising out of an instance of suspected child abuse, the taking of photographs, or the removal or keeping of a child in protective custody is immune from any civil or criminal liability for those actions.

INFERTILITY PATIENTS

Reame, 1999, notes that few states regulate the practice of assisted reproduction and assisted reproductive technologies (ART) treatments are beyond the usual hospital accreditation guidelines and standard medical licensing requirements set by public health departments. A federal law, the Fertility Clinic Success Rate and Certification Act, was designed to require clinics to report their pregnancy rates to the CDC but has had limited and disappointing impact because it seeks only voluntary com-

BOX 8-7	Assessing for Abuse and Neglect

The following are guidelines for assessing a child for physical or sexual abuse: assess whether or not the history reported to you is consistent with the injuries; document the date, time, and place of the occurrence; if the child is old enough, interview her or him separately about what happened; document any evidence of a STD; be specific when documenting injuries (ie, location, size, shape, and color of every bruise, lesion, or burn); supplement your notes with drawings, photographs and x-rays (Chiocca, 1998a).

Assessing a child for neglect includes the following actions: assess whether or not child's basic needs of food, shelter, clothing, medical care, and a clean and safe environment are being met. Examples of observations that can document neglect include lack of well child visits and immunizations, underweight for age/height, and observable signs of poor nutrition (Chiocca, 1998b).

pliance and lacks authority and budget to validate clinic data or punish those who choose not to report their pregnancy rates or provide misleading information (Katz, 1997).

In the United States, the practice of ART is subject only to minimum standards and the voluntary guidelines of its professional organizations, the American Society for Reproductive Medicine (ASRM), and its affiliate, the Society for Assisted Reproductive Technologies, groups that have no regulatory or enforcement power (Reame, 1999).

In New York, the following recommendations exist regarding minimum information needed by infertility patients for informed consent for assisted reproduction:

1. The likelihood that the patient will become pregnant, based on experience at the particular program with patients of comparable age and comparable medical conditions including the program's most recent published outcome statistics
2. The anticipated price of the procedure including charges for procedures and medications not covered in the standard fee
3. The risks associated with any drugs to be used
4. The risks associated with egg retrieval and embryo or oocyte transfer
5. The risks associated with the transfer of multiple embryos or oocytes including the likelihood of multiple gestation, the possibility that fetal reduction might be recommended as a response to multiple gestation, a clear explanation of the nature of fetal reduction and the associated risks, and the patient's right to participate in decisions about the number of embryos or oocytes to transfer
6. The reasonable psychological ramifications of the procedures
7. The program's experience performing the particular procedure
8. Alternatives to the procedure including the alternative of no treatment (Reame, 1999)

ASRM has available on its website numerous practice guidelines and policy statements (http://www.asrm.org). Laws vary widely among the states as to ART. At least 35 states have laws regarding sperm donation, but only Florida, Oklahoma, North Dakota, Texas, and Virginia regulate egg donation. Compensated surrogacy is prohibited in New York and several other states but is permitted in California. New Hampshire and Virginia have laws regarding requirements for informed consent providing for specific disclosure requirements regarding medical and psychological risks, legal rights and obligations, specific testing protocols for donated gametes, and details about the clinic's success rates (Reame, 1999).

As of 1999 it was estimated that about 81,000 births occur annually as a result of ART (Baker, 1999). The reproductive and genetic technology committee of the family law section of the American Bar Association is drafting a model act to deal legislatively with the many legal and ethical issues presented by the rapid advances in reproductive technologies over the last 10 years (Baker, 1999). As of 1996, four states (Connecticut, Georgia, Oklahoma, Oregon) had laws mandating that only a physician can perform the insemination procedure (Henry, 1996).

Informed consent for infertility patients has certain specific requirements: a detailed discussion of the nature of the infertility problem, the risks of the proposed treatment, any alternatives to the proposed treatment, the consequences of not undergoing the proposed treatment, and the potential rate of success of that particular procedure in similar patients as well as the provider's experience and educational level (Henry, 1996). For patients undergoing artificial insemination, the consent should include the material risks and consequences of the procedure, the screening procedures for donors, and any alternative treatments (Henry, 1996). For patients undergoing in vitro fertilization (IVF), informed consent requires the procedures for preservation or disposal of excess fertilized ova. For procedures involving a surrogate, informed consent should be obtained from the husband/donor, his wife, and the prospective surrogate and should include information about the surrogate screening procedures, risks, and screening for birth defects, and the risks of pregnancy for the prospective surrogate (Henry, 1996). To protect the APN in case of litigation regarding a surrogate arrangement, a copy of the surrogate agreement and written documentation of the screening procedures and the informed consent of all parties should be kept in the medical record (Henry, 1996).

Some states have created laws dealing with infertility procedures. For example, California B. & P. Code § 2260 requires a physician who removes sperm or ova from a patient for implantation in one other than the patient or his or her spouse to obtain a specific written consent. Violation of this law constitutes unprofessional conduct and will result in civil penalties if the provider fails to comply on two occasions.

New York Codes, Rules & Regs. 10 NYCRR § 52-8.3 (2000) provides that only a licensed physician, physician's assistant, or nurse practitioner may order artificial insemination. A nurse practitioner or registered nurse trained in the technical aspects of artificial insemination by a physician or physician's assistant at the insemination site may perform artificial insemination procedures.

VICTIMS OF DOMESTIC VIOLENCE

Orloff, 1996, notes that there are four common instances where the health care provider may be held liable when dealing with victims of domestic violence:

1. Reporting abuse to police without permission of an adult victim of abuse
2. Failing to identify victims of domestic violence

3. Failing to provide information and appropriate referrals to patients who have been identified as victims of domestic violence
4. Failure to warn victims about the potential for assaults against them when treating the abuser (generally this duty arises when the abuser presents a clear and present danger of harm to a specific victim or victims; some states impose a duty to warn all persons who are foreseeably endangered by the abuser's conduct with respect to all risks that make the conduct unreasonably dangerous)

The APN can play an important role in helping victims of domestic violence by

1. Identifying patients who are victims of domestic violence
2. Documenting the violence against the patient
3. Referring the patient to legal and social service providers
4. Providing emotional support for the domestic violence victim (Orloff, 1996)

APNs need to be aware of basic legal premises involved in dealing with domestic violence to better advocate for their patients who are victims of this phenomena. Civil protection orders, which are available in every state, are a type of court order that tells the abuser not to harm the victim again and provides criminal penalties against the abuser if further abuse occurs (Orloff, 1996). Victims of domestic violence can file for a protective order at any time; emergency orders are available when there is imminent danger of further abuse (Orloff, 1996). In almost all states, protective orders can be obtained when the abuser is a spouse or former spouse as well as a nonspousal family member (Orloff, 1996). The order can include the victim and the victim's children (Orloff, 1996). Under federal law, protective orders must be enforced in any state or community in the United States, regardless of where the orders were issued (Orloff, 1996). Usually these orders only last for a certain period of time; in some states, though, they can last indefinitely (Orloff, 1996). After a victim obtains an order, the recipient should get several certified copies before leaving the courthouse because she or he will need to always carry a copy, leave one copy at any location where she or he spends time, and file a copy at police stations located near home and workplace (Orloff, 1996). Unless the protective order is indefinite, the victim must follow up by bringing a family court action to permanently resolve custody and child support orders (Orloff, 1996).

ENHANCE YOUR LEARNING

1. Interview your facility's risk manager regarding policies developed to protect patient privacy.

2. Design a research study to assess the level of understanding among providers in your facility regarding HIV confidentiality laws in your state.

3. Develop a sample protocol for your practice area regarding informed consent for minors.

4. Review your facility's policies regarding the emergency exception to the requirement for informed consent.

TEST YOUR COMPREHENSION

1. Identify two pieces of information that must be provided by the health care provider to the patient during the informed consent discussion.

2. Discuss the law regarding informed consent for the incompetent patient.

3. Identify two categories of care for which minors can generally give consent.

4. Discuss the legal issues that APNs face in the treatment of victims of domestic abuse.

REFERENCES

Baker, D. (1999). Catching up to science . *American Bar Association Journal,* 88.

Brooke, P. (1997). HIV and the law: An update. *RN, 60*(5) 59-60, 63–64.

Chiocca, E. (1998). Documenting suspected child abuse, part 1. *Nursing 98,*28(8), 17.

Chiocca, E. (1998). Documenting suspected child abuse, part 2. *Nursing 98, 28*(9), 25.

Clark, G., Lucas, K., & Stephens, L. (1994, June). Ethical dilemmas and decisions concerning the do not resuscitate patient undergoing anesthesia. *Journal of the American Association of Nurse Anesthetists, 62*(3), 253–256.

Doughty, R. (1994). The confidentiality of HIV related information: Responding to the resurgence of aggressive public health interventions in the AIDS epidemic. *California Law Review, 82,* 111–184.

Gostin, L., & Webber, D. (1998). HIV infection and AIDS in the public health and health care systems, the role of law and litigation. *JAMA, 279*(14), 1108–1113.

Harner, H., Burgess, A., & Asher, J. (2001). Caring for pregnant teenagers: Medicolegal issues for nurses. *Journal of Obstetric, Gynecologic and Neonatal Nursing, 30*(2), 139–147.

Heinrich, L. (1987). Care of the female rape victim. *Nurse Practitioner, 12*(11) 9-27.

Henry, P. (1996). Overview of the legal issues pertaining to the treatment of infertility. *Nurse Practitioner Forum, 7*(2), 58–59.

Henry, P. (1993). Legal issues relating to access to medical records. *Nurse Practitioner Forum, 4*(3), 120–121.

Katz, M.A. (1997). The role of a federal regulatory agency. *Women's Health Issues, 7,* 192–194.

Kjervik, D. (1996). Assisted suicide: The challenge to the nursing profession. *Journal of Law, Medicine and Ethics,* 24(3) 237–42.

Knepper, K. (1998). The medical records maze: A construct of federal inaction and state inconsistency. *Journal of Health Law, 31*(2), 114.

Muscari, M. (1998). When can an adolescent give consent? *American Journal of Nursing,* 98(5), 18–19.

Noonan, R. & Roth, P. (1997). Genetic testing and insurance discrimination: Challenges for nurses in advanced practice. *Advanced Practice Nursing Quarterly, 3*(3), 20–30.

Opinion of Attorney General to Margie Rose, M.P.H. Branch Head. (1977). Family Planning Branch, Division of Health Services, 47 N.C.A.G. 80.

Orloff, L. (1996). Effective advocacy for domestic violence victims, role of the nurse midwife. *Journal of Nurse Midwifery, 41*(6), 473–492.

Pharris, M.D. & Ledray, L.E. (1997). Consent and confidentiality in the care of the sexually assaulted adolescent. *Journal of Emergency Nursing, 23*(3), 279–81

Reame, N. (1999). Informed consent issues in assisted reproduction. *Journal of Obstetric, Gynecologic and Neonatal Nursing, 28*(3), 331–338.

Sharon, F., & Wilkinson, W. (1988,). Drug screening in the workplace-scientific and legal issues. *Nurse Practitioner, 13*(2), 41–49.

Sinclair, B. (1999). HIV and women, understand your responsibilities; reduce your risk. *AWHONN Lifelines, 3*(6), 35–38.

Sterken, D. (1995). HIV/AIDS in the classroom: Ethical and legal issues surrounding the public education of the HIV infected child. *Journal of Pediatric Health Care, 9*(5), 205–210.

Urbanski, P. (1997). Getting the go ahead, helping patients understand informed consent. *AWHONN Lifelines, 1*(3), 45–48.

Wildey, L. (1992). Legal issues in the management of the pregnant adolescent. *Journal of Pediatric Health Care, 6*(2) 93, 111–112.

Cases

Abram v. Children's Hospital of Buffalo, 552 NE2d 178 (1989).

American Academy of Pediatrics v. Lungren, 32 Calif. Rptr.2d 546 (1994).

Anderson v. St. Francis-St. George Hospital, 671 N.E.2d 225 (Ohio 1996).

Behringer v. The Medical Center at Princeton, 592 A2d 1251 (1991).

Cannell v. Medical & Surgical Clinic, 315 N.E.2d 278 (Ill. 1974).

Casbohm et al. v. Metrohealth Medical Center et al., Ohio App. LEXIS 4184 (2000).

C.M. v. Tomball Regional Hospital, 961 S.W. 2d 236 (1997).

Cruzan v. Director, Missouri Department of Health, 497 U.S. 261 (1990).

Doe v. Roe, 599 NYS 2d 350 (1993).

Hill v. National Collegiate Athletic Association, 7 Calif. 4th 1 (1994).

Hutchinson v. St. Louis Altenheim, 858 S.W. 2d 304 (Mo. 1993).

In re Application of M.S. Hershey Medical Center, 595 A.2d 1290 (1991).

In re M.R., 638 A.2d 1274 (N.J. 1994).

Leach v. Shapiro, 469 N.E.2d 1047 (Ohio 1984).

Mathis v. Morrissey, 11 Calif. App. 4th 332 (1992).
Matter of Hughes, 611 A.2d 1148 (N.J. 1992).
Matter of Roche, 687 A2d 349 (1996).
Matter of Storar and Matter of Eichner v. Dillon, 420 N.E.2d 64 (N.Y.) 1981.
Matter of Tavel, 661 A2d 1061 (1995).
Miller v. Rhode Island Hospital, 625 A2d 778 (1993).
Munri v. Regents of University of California, 215 Calif. App. 3d 977 (1989).
Paradies v. Benedictine Hospital, 431 NYS 2d 175 (1980).
Parkson v. Central DuPage Hospital, 435 N.E.2d 140 (Ill. 1982).
Rains v. Superior Court, 150 Calif. App. 3d 933 (1984).
Truman v. Thomas, 27 Calif. 3d 285 (1980).
Urbaniak v. Newton, 226 Calif. App.3d 1128 (1991).
Vandi v. Permanente Medical Group, 7 Calif. App. 4th 1064 (1992).

Statutes

Freedom of Information Act, 45 C.F.R. § 5 (1998).
Privacy Act, 45 C.F.R. § 5b (1998).

Additional Reading: Minors

Center for Youth Law, State Minor Consent Statutes. Available from the Center for Continuing Education in Adolescent Health. (513) 559-4681.
Alan Guttmacher Institute Website, *http://www.agi-usa.org/graphics/gr030406_f1.html* provides state-specific age guidelines regarding a minor's ability to give consent for medical procedures including abortion.

Prescriptive Authority

Introduction

Like the laws regarding autonomy of practice for APNs (APNs), the laws regarding prescriptive authority vary widely among states. This chapter illustrates the range of autonomy and authority that APNs in the United States are currently granted with respect to prescriptive authority. As with all issues dependent on state laws, it is imperative that the APN understand the laws regarding prescriptive authority in each state where the APN practices. Table 9-1 provides an overview of all state laws regarding prescriptive authority for APNs. Tables 9-2 through 9-5 address specific aspects of prescriptive authority for each APN category.

TRENDS REGARDING PRESCRIPTIVE AUTHORITY FOR APNS

Naegle, 1994, reported that the majority of prescriptions written by nurse practitioners were for anti-infective agents, analgesics, respiratory agents, hormones, and vitamins/minerals. In a 1997 survey, nurses were writing prescriptions for the following medications: hormone replacement therapy, oral contraceptives, antibiotics, vaginal infection medications, creams or suppositories, pain relief, anti-inflammatories, alternative contraceptives, emergency contraception, colds or flu relief, and fertility drugs (AWHONN, 1997). Currently, all states provide prescriptive authority for nurse practitioners (NPs); about half of the states allow certified registered nurse anesthetists (CRNAs) prescriptive authority; all but 15 states allow some clinical nurse specialists (CNSs) prescriptive authority. Certified nurse midwives (CNMs) currently have prescriptive authority in all but two states.

Most states that allow CNSs to prescribe limit this authority to CNSs in certain specialties. One of those specialties is psychiatric/mental health. Psychiatric/mental health CNSs report the following major barriers to obtaining prescriptive authority: work setting limitations, personal

(text continues on page 225)

TABLE 9-1   Prescriptive Authority for APNs

STATE	CRNA	NP	CNM	CNS
Alabama	No	Yes	Yes	No
Alaska	Yes	Yes	Yes	No
Arizona	No	Yes	Yes	No
Arkansas	Yes (administration only)	Yes	Yes	Yes
California	No	Yes	Yes	No
Colorado	Yes	Yes	Yes	Yes
Connecticut	Yes	Yes	Yes	Yes
Delaware	Yes	Yes	Yes	Yes
District of Columbia	Yes	Yes	Yes	No
Florida	Yes	Yes	Yes	Yes
Georgia	Yes	Yes	Yes	Yes
Hawaii	No	Yes	Yes	Yes
Idaho	Yes	Yes	Yes	Yes
Illinois	No	Yes	Yes	Yes
Indiana	No	Yes	Yes	Yes
Iowa	No	Yes	Yes	Yes
Kansas	Yes	Yes	Yes	Yes
Kentucky	Yes	Yes	Yes	Yes
Louisiana	No	Yes	Yes	Yes
Maine	No	Yes	Yes	No
Maryland	No	Yes	Yes	No
Massachusetts	No	Yes	Yes	Yes
Michigan	Yes	Yes	Yes	Yes
Minnesota	Yes	Yes	Yes	Yes
Mississippi	Yes	Yes	Yes	No
Missouri	Yes	Yes	Yes	Yes
Montana	Yes	Yes	Yes	Yes
Nebraska	Yes	Yes	Yes	No
Nevada	No	Yes	Yes	Yes
New Hampshire	Yes	Yes	Yes	Yes
New Jersey	No	Yes	Yes	Yes
New Mexico	No	Yes	Yes	Yes
New York	No	Yes	Yes	No
North Carolina	No	Yes	Yes	No
North Dakota	Yes	Yes	Yes	Yes
Ohio	No	Yes	Yes	Yes

(continued)

TABLE 9-1   Prescriptive Authority for APNs (Continued)

STATE	CRNA	NP	CNM	CNS
Oklahoma	Yes (administration only)	Yes	Yes	Yes
Oregon	No	Yes	No	No
Pennsylvania	No	Yes	No	No
Rhode Island	No	Yes	Yes	Yes
South Carolina	No	Yes	Yes	Yes
South Dakota	No	Yes	Yes	No
Tennessee	Yes	Yes	Yes	No
Texas	Yes	Yes	Yes	Yes
Utah	No	Yes	Yes	Yes
Vermont	Yes	Yes	Yes	Yes
Virginia	Yes	Yes	Yes	No
Washington	Yes	Yes	Yes	No
West Virginia	Yes	Yes	Yes	Yes
Wisconsin	Yes	Yes	Yes	Yes
Wyoming	Yes	Yes	Yes	Yes

TABLE 9-2   Prescriptive Authority for CRNAs

STATE	CONTROLLED SUBSTANCES	PROTOCOLS REQUIRED	DISPENSING ALLOWED	FORMULARY
Alabama	Not granted	—	—	—
Alaska	Yes	No	No	No
Arizona	No	No	No	No
Arkansas	Yes	Yes	No	No
California	Not granted	—	—	—
Colorado	Yes	Yes	Yes	No
Connecticut	Yes	Yes	Yes	No
Delaware	Yes	Yes	Yes	No
District of Columbia	Yes	Yes	No	No
Florida	Yes (for administration only)	Yes	Yes	No
Georgia	Yes	Yes	Yes	Yes
Hawaii	Not granted	—	—	—
Idaho	Yes	No	Yes	No
Illinois	Not granted	—	—	—
Indiana	Not granted	—	—	—

(continued)

TABLE 9-2 Prescriptive Authority for CRNAs (Continued)

STATE	CONTROLLED SUBSTANCES	PROTOCOLS REQUIRED	DISPENSING ALLOWED	FORMULARY
Iowa	Not granted	—	—	—
Kansas	Yes	Yes	No	Yes
Kentucky	No	Yes	Yes	No
Louisiana	Not granted	—	—	—
Maine	Not granted	—	—	—
Maryland	Not granted	—	—	—
Massachusetts	Not granted	—	—	—
Michigan	No	Yes	Yes	No
Minnesota	Yes	Yes	Yes	No
Mississippi	Yes (administration only)	Yes	Yes	Yes
Missouri	No	Yes	Yes	No
Montana	Yes	Yes	Yes	No
Nebraska	Yes	No	Yes	No
Nevada	Not granted	—	—	—
New Hampshire	Yes	No	Yes	Yes
New Jersey	Not granted	—	—	—
New Mexico	Not granted	—	—	—
New York	Not granted	—	—	—
North Carolina	Not granted	—	—	—
North Dakota	Yes	Yes	No	No
Ohio	Not granted	—	—	—
Oklahoma	Yes (administration only)	No	No	No
Oregon	Not granted	—	—	—
Pennsylvania	Not granted	—	—	—
Rhode Island	Not granted	—	—	—
South Carolina	Not granted	—	—	—
South Dakota	Not granted	—	—	—
Tennessee	Yes	Yes	Yes	Yes
Texas	Yes (administration only)	Yes	No	No
Utah	Not granted	—	—	—
Vermont	Yes	Yes	No	Yes
Virginia	Yes	Yes	Yes	Yes
Washington	Yes (administration only)	Yes	No	No
West Virginia	Yes	Yes	No	Yes
Wisconsin	Yes	Yes	Yes	Yes
Wyoming	Yes	Yes	Yes	No

TABLE 9-3 Prescriptive Authority for NPs

STATE	CONTROLLED SUBSTANCES	PROTOCOLS REQUIRED	DISPENSING ALLOWED	FORMULARY
Alabama	No	Yes	No	Yes
Alaska	Yes	No	Yes	No
Arizona	Yes	No	Yes	No
Arkansas	Yes	Yes	No	No
California	Yes	Yes	Yes	No
Colorado	Yes	Yes	Yes	No
Connecticut	Yes	Yes	Yes	No
Delaware	Yes	Yes	Yes	No
District of Columbia	Yes	Yes	No	No
Florida	Yes	Yes	Yes	No
Georgia	Yes	Yes	Yes	Yes
Hawaii	No	Yes	No	Yes
Idaho	Yes	No	Yes	No
Illinois	Yes	Yes	Yes	No
Indiana	Yes	Yes	No	No
Iowa	Yes	Yes	Yes	No
Kansas	Yes	Yes	No	Yes
Kentucky	No	Yes	Yes	No
Louisiana	No	Yes	Yes	No
Maine	Yes	No	Yes	Yes
Maryland	Yes	Yes	Yes	No
Massachusetts	Yes	Yes	Yes	No
Michigan	Yes	Yes	Yes	No
Minnesota	Yes	Yes	Yes	No
Mississippi	Yes	Yes	Yes	Yes
Missouri	No	Yes	Yes	No
Montana	Yes	Yes	Yes	No
Nebraska	Yes	Yes	Yes	No
Nevada	No	Yes	Yes	Yes
New Hampshire	Yes	No	Yes	Yes
New Jersey	Yes	Yes	Yes	No
New Mexico	Yes	No	Yes	Yes
New York	Yes	Yes	No	No
North Carolina	Yes	Yes	Yes	No
North Dakota	Yes	Yes	No	No

(continued)

TABLE 9-3   Prescriptive Authority for NPs (Continued)

STATE	CONTROLLED SUBSTANCES	PROTOCOLS REQUIRED	DISPENSING ALLOWED	FORMULARY
Ohio	Yes	Yes	No	Yes
Oklahoma	Yes	Yes	No	No
Oregon	Yes	No	Yes	Yes
Pennsylvania	No	Yes	Yes	Yes
Rhode Island	Yes	Yes	No	Yes
South Carolina	Yes	Yes	No	Yes
South Dakota	Yes	Yes	Yes	No
Tennessee	Yes	Yes	Yes	Yes
Texas	No	Yes	Yes	No
Utah	Yes	Yes	No	No
Vermont	Yes	Yes	No	Yes
Virginia	Yes	Yes	Yes	Yes
Washington	Yes	Yes	Yes	No
West Virginia	Yes	Yes	No	Yes
Wisconsin	Yes	Yes	Yes	Yes
Wyoming	Yes	Yes	Yes	No

TABLE 9-4   Prescriptive Authority for CNMs

STATE	CONTROLLED SUBSTANCES	PROTOCOLS REQUIRED	DISPENSING ALLOWED	FORMULARY
Alabama	No	Yes	No	Yes
Alaska	Yes	No	Yes	No
Arizona	Yes	No	Yes	No
Arkansas	Yes	Yes	No	No
California	No	Yes	No	No
Colorado	Yes	Yes	Yes	No
Connecticut	Yes	Yes	Yes	No
Delaware	Yes	Yes	Yes	No
District of Columbia	Yes	Yes	No	No
Florida	Yes	Yes	Yes	No
Georgia	Yes	Yes	Yes	Yes
Hawaii	No	Yes	No	Yes
Idaho	Yes	No	Yes	No
Illinois	Yes	Yes	Yes	No

(continued)

TABLE 9-4 Prescriptive Authority for CNMs (Continued)

STATE	CONTROLLED SUBSTANCES	PROTOCOLS REQUIRED	DISPENSING ALLOWED	FORMULARY
Indiana	Yes	Yes	No	No
Iowa	Yes	Yes	Yes	No
Kansas	Yes	Yes	No	Yes
Kentucky	No	Yes	Yes	No
Louisiana	No	Yes	Yes	No
Maine	Yes	No	Yes	Yes
Maryland	Yes	No	Yes	Yes
Massachusetts	Yes	Yes	Yes	No
Michigan	Yes	Yes	Yes	No
Minnesota	Yes	No	Yes	No
Mississippi	Yes (administration only)	Yes	Yes	Yes
Missouri	No	Yes	Yes	No
Montana	Yes	Yes	Yes	No
Nebraska	Yes	Yes	Yes	No
Nevada	No	Yes	Yes	Yes
New Hampshire	Yes	No	Yes	Yes
New Jersey	Yes	Yes	Yes	Yes
New Mexico	Yes	No	Yes	Yes
New York	No	No	No	No
North Carolina	Yes	Yes	Yes	No
North Dakota	Yes	Yes	No	No
Ohio	Yes	Yes	No	Yes
Oklahoma	Yes	Yes	No	No
Oregon	Not granted	—	—	—
Pennsylvania	Not granted	—	—	—
Rhode Island	Yes	Yes	No	No
South Carolina	Yes	Yes	No	Yes
South Dakota	Yes	Yes	Yes	No
Tennessee	Yes	Yes	Yes	Yes
Texas	Yes	Yes	Yes	No
Utah	Yes	Yes	No	No
Vermont	Yes	Yes	No	Yes
Virginia	Yes	Yes	Yes	Yes
Washington	Yes	Yes	Yes	No
West Virginia	Yes	Yes	No	Yes
Wisconsin	Yes	Yes	Yes	Yes
Wyoming	Yes	Yes	Yes	No

TABLE 9-5   Prescriptive Authority for CNSs

STATE	CONTROLLED SUBSTANCES	PROTOCOLS REQUIRED	DISPENSING ALLOWED	FORMULARY
Alabama	Not granted	—	—	—
Alaska	Not recognized	—	—	—
Arizona	Not granted	—	—	—
Arkansas	Yes	Yes	No	No
California	Not granted	—	—	—
Colorado	Yes	Yes	Yes	No
Connecticut	Yes	Yes	Yes	No
Delaware	Yes	Yes	Yes	No
District of Columbia	Not granted	—	—	—
Florida	Yes	Yes	Yes	No
Georgia	Yes	Yes	Yes	Yes
Hawaii	No	Yes	No	Yes
Idaho	Yes	No	Yes	No
Illinois	Yes	Yes	Yes	No
Indiana	Yes	Yes	No	No
Iowa	Yes	Yes	Yes	No
Kansas	Yes	Yes	No	Yes
Kentucky	No	Yes	Yes	No
Louisiana	No	Yes	Yes	No
Maine	Not granted	—	—	—
Maryland	Not granted	—	—	—
Massachusetts	Yes	Yes	Yes	No
Michigan	No	Yes	Yes	No
Minnesota	Yes	Yes	Yes	No
Mississippi	Not granted	—	—	—
Missouri	No	Yes	Yes	No
Montana	Yes	Yes	Yes	No
Nebraska	Not recognized	—	—	—
Nevada	No	Yes	Yes	Yes
New Hampshire	Yes	No	Yes	Yes
New Jersey	No	Yes	Yes	No
New Mexico	Yes	No	Yes	Yes
New York	Not granted	—	—	—
North Carolina	Not granted	—	—	—
North Dakota	Yes	Yes	No	No

(continued)

TABLE 9-5   Prescriptive Authority for CNSs (Continued)

STATE	CONTROLLED SUBSTANCES	PROTOCOLS REQUIRED	DISPENSING ALLOWED	FORMULARY
Ohio	Yes	Yes	No	Yes
Oklahoma	Yes	Yes	No	No
Oregon	Not recognized	—	—	—
Pennsylvania	Not recognized	—	—	—
Rhode Island	Yes	Yes	No	Yes
South Carolina	Yes	Yes	No	Yes
South Dakota	Not granted	—	—	—
Tennessee	Not recognized	—	—	—
Texas	No	Yes	Yes	No
Utah	Yes	Yes	No	No
Vermont	Yes	Yes	No	Yes
Virginia	Not granted	—	—	—
Washington	Yes	Yes	Yes	No
West Virginia	Yes	Yes	No	Yes
Wisconsin	Yes	Yes	Yes	Yes
Wyoming	Yes	Yes	Yes	No

comfort with prescribing, and ability to develop a collaborative agreement with a psychiatrist (Kaas, et al., 1998). As of 1998, 33 states granted some form of prescriptive authority to the psychiatric/mental health CNS (Kaas, et al. 1998). Most of these states require the CNS to have master's preparation in the psychiatric/mental health clinical area, graduate credit in pharmacology, and certification by a national nursing certification organization and also that the CNS prescribe collaboratively with a physician through a written collaborative practice agreement developed by the CNS and the physician (Kaas, et al., 1998).

LIABILITY ISSUES REGARDING PRESCRIBING

NPs have been found to be equally competent as physicians in prescribing appropriate medications for clients' conditions (Brown, 1995). However, the APN needs to be aware of potential liability related to prescriptive practice. Two issues particular to liability related to prescribing are failure-to-warn cases and off-label prescribing. The learned intermediary rule indicates that it is the duty of the prescribing physician to be fully aware of (1.) the characteristics of the drug he or she is prescribing, (2.)

the amount of the drug that can be safely administered, and (3.) the different medications the patient is taking. It is also the duty of the prescribing physician to advise the patient of any dangers or side effects associated with the use of the drug as well as how and when to take the drug. The warnings that must accompany drugs are directed to the physician rather than to the patient because the prescribing physician is to use his or her independent judgment, take into account data supplied from the manufacturer, other medical literature, and any other sources available and weigh that knowledge against the patient's personal medical history to decide whether or not to prescribe a given drug (*Mazur v. Merck*, 1992).

This learned intermediary rule protects drug companies from lawsuits brought by patients when adequate warnings about the drug are provided to a learned intermediary (ie, a physician or APN). Some states (West Virginia, Georgia) have held that nurses may act as learned intermediaries under certain circumstances. Pennsylvania has declined to so apply this rule (*Mazur v. Merck*, 1992). Texas has applied this rule to APNs. Box 9-1 discusses the case of *Wyeth-Ayerst Laboratories Company et al. v. Medrano* (2000).

Snell, 1999, notes that once a drug has approval, the Federal Drug Administration (FDA) prohibits the manufacturer from promoting the drug for an unlabeled use. However there is no prohibition against the drug being prescribed, dispensed, or administered by a health care professional for an unlabeled use. To guard against liability for off-label use, the APN needs to inform the patient that the prescribed drug is for an unapproved indication and of the rationale used to recommend treatment and must document to show that the patient was informed and given the opportunity to ask questions (Snell, 1999). The APN does need to be aware, however, that some states specifically prohibit APNs from prescribing drugs for off-label use.

THE ISSUE OF CONTROLLED SUBSTANCES

Not all states permit the APN to prescribe controlled substances; some allow certain schedule drugs to be prescribed and others prohibit certain categories of APN from prescribing these drugs. Therefore it is imperative to be aware of the particular laws in the state where you practice regarding controlled substances. Controlled substances are grouped according to the following classifications:

Schedule I: drugs with high abuse potential without accepted medical use or lack of accepted safety measures for use. These drugs (eg, heroin, marijuana) are prescribed only for research purposes under stringent protocols.

Schedule II: drugs with high abuse potential with acceptable therapeutic use. Examples include common narcotics such as mor-

BOX 9-1	The APN as Learned Intermediary

In the case of *Wyeth-Ayerst Laboratories Company et al. v. Medrano* (2000), plaintiff was a 29-year-old mother of two. After the birth of her first child, she began to use birth control pills as her form of contraception. However, while still using the birth control pills, she became pregnant with her second child. Therefore, she decided that she needed to consider other contraceptive options. Approximately 4 weeks after the birth of her second child, she went to her doctor's office and met with Bonnie George, an advanced practice nurse (APN), concerning Norplant. During this visit, Medrano was given a booklet, shown a videotape, and spoke with nurse George regarding the Norplant System. Medrano went home, spoke with her husband, and decided that she wanted Norplant to be her method of birth control.

Approximately 3 weeks after this initial visit, Medrano returned to have Norplant inserted. At this second office visit, she and nurse George once again discussed Norplant. Nurse George explained the procedure and answered some of Medrano's questions about the potential side effects associated with this contraceptive. Before the implantation procedure took place, Medrano signed a consent form that stated she had been counseled about Norplant and understood the risks associated with the Norplant System. Medrano admitted that at the time of implantation she was aware of the potential side effects associated with Norplant and she made the decision to receive the Norplant System. Approximately 15 months after Medrano had Norplant inserted into her arm, she chose to have it removed.

In this suit, Medrano claimed that the drug company failed to adequately warn her of the potential side effects associated with Norplant by failing to communicate to her information and knowledge it had about the risks and side effects of using the Norplant System. However, she admitted that all the side effects she suffered were listed in the warning booklet in some form.

In prescription drug cases, courts have found that it is reasonable for the manufacturer to rely on the health care provider to pass on its warnings. This is reasonable because the learned intermediary understands the propensities and dangers involved in the use of a given drug, and as the prescriber, he or she stands between this drug and the ultimate consumer. Medrano contended that this doctrine should not apply in this particular instance because Medrano was not treated by a physician. It was undisputed that Medrano received counseling about the risks and side effects of Norplant; however, it was also undisputed that she did not receive this treatment from her doctor. Medrano was treated by nurse George, an APN who worked for Medrano's long-time obstetrician/gynecologist, Charles Moses.

The court noted that under Texas law, as an APN, nurse George had the right to prescribe medication and to treat patients without the supervision of a physician. The court felt that given the qualifications of an APN, it was logical that the rule should be extended to include the APN as well. Since Texas law allowed a nurse to become certified to prescribe drugs without a doctor's supervision, the law must view her or him as being capable of offering and

(continued)

| BOX 9-1 | The APN as Learned Intermediary (Continued) |

performing this individualized medical treatment. Texas law gave nurse George the authority to prescribe and implant the Norplant System. As a physician would do, nurse George counseled, informed, and advised Medrano of the risks and side effects associated with this contraceptive when she prescribed it. In other words, Medrano received individualized medical treatment. Since nurse George served the same purpose that a physician in this position would, the court refused to create an exception to the learned intermediary doctrine merely because Ms. George held the title "advanced practice nurse" rather than physician.

phine, amphetamines, and methadone. Written prescriptions are required and no telephone renewal is allowed without an emergency.

Schedule III: drugs with lower abuse potential than Schedule II drugs with acceptable therapeutic uses (eg, a narcotic with codeine). Prescriptions are required to be rewritten after 6 months or five refills but can be ordered via telephone.

Schedule IV: drugs with low abuse potential with an acceptable therapeutic use (eg, chloral hydrate and diazepam). Prescription guidelines are the same as that for Schedule III drugs.

Schedule V: drugs with lower abuse potential than Schedule IV drugs with little potential of physical or psychological dependence (eg, cough syrup with codeine). Prescription required; however, some can be dispensed without a prescription based on state regulations. (Snell, 1999).

Laws of the Selected States Regarding Prescriptive Authority

Arizona

Registered nurse practitioners (NPs and CNMs) have full prescriptive and dispensing authority if they fulfill criteria established by the board of nursing. To prescribe in Arizona, NPs and CNMs must have 1 year of documented active practice as an NP or CNM immediately prior to application and must provide evidence of at least 45 contact hours of education in pharmacology or clinical management of drug therapy or both within 2 years prior to the application, 6 hours of which must have been obtained in the 1 year prior to the application (Ariz. Board of Nursing Regs. § R4-19-507).

Ten contact hours of continuing education in pharmacology or pharmacology management or a combination of both must be obtained each calendar year to maintain prescriptive authority (Ariz. Board of Nursing Regs. § R4-19-50). Detailed instructions regarding the authority to dispense are provided in board of nursing regulations § R4-19-508. NPs and CNMs are given their own Drug Enforcement Administration (DEA) numbers and may prescribe Schedule II to V drugs (Ariz. Board of Nursing Regs. § R4-19-50). CNSs have no prescriptive authority in Arizona. According to A.A.C. § R4-19-513, CRNAs can prescribe in this state if they have

1. Current licensure as a professional nurse in Arizona in good standing
2. Graduation from an educational program accredited by the American Association of Nurse Anesthetists' Council on Accreditation of Nurse Anesthesia Educational Programs or a predecessor and that has the objective of preparing a nurse to practice nurse anesthesia
3. Initial certification by the American Association of Nurse Anesthetists' Council on Certification of Nurse Anesthetists and recertification, as applicable, by the American Association of Nurse Anesthetists' Council on Recertification of Nurse Anesthetists

A CRNA granted prescribing authority may prescribe drugs or medication to be administered by a licensed, certified, or registered health care provider preoperatively, post-operatively, or as part of a procedure performed in a health care facility, the office of a health care provider, or in an ambulance (A.A.C. § R4-19-513).

California

CNMs and NPs have a limited prescribing privilege to furnish drugs and devices. CNMs may furnish drugs and devices only in specified facilities and may not furnish controlled substances (Calif. B. & P. Code §2746.51). NPs may furnish drugs and devices including Schedule III through V controlled substances (Calif. B. & P. Code § 2836.1). Except for the NP in solo practice, there are no restrictions on sites where NPs are authorized to furnish (Calif. B. & P. Code § 2836.1).

The furnishing of drugs and devices must be in accordance with standardized procedures developed with the supervising physician and must be incidental to the provision of family planning services, prenatal care, or routine health care to essentially healthy persons (Calif. B. & P. Code § 2836.1). The procedure must specify the NPs and/or CNMs who may furnish drugs or devices, which drugs or devices may be furnished and under what circumstances, the extent of physician supervision, and the method of periodic review of the NP's or CNM's competence (Calif. B. & P. Code §2746.51; 2836.1).

CNM and NP furnishing authority is conditional upon the issuance of a furnishing number by the board of nursing (Calif. B. & P. Code §2836.3; 2746.51). To obtain this number, the CNM or NP must complete a qualifying pharmacology course and a 6-month physician-supervised experience in furnishing (Calif. B. & P. Code §2746.51, 2836.1). Assembly

Bill 1545, which became law on January 1, 2000, allows NPs to dispense drugs including controlled substances pursuant to a standardized procedure or protocol, in primary, community, and free clinics. This new law also allows an NP who functions pursuant to a standardized procedure to sign for delivery or receipt of complimentary samples of dangerous drugs or devices that have been requested in writing by his or her supervising physician. This new law requires the NP who has a furnishing number to obtain a DEA number to furnish controlled substances in Schedules III through V.

Florida

Dispensing practitioners include those advanced registered nurse practitioners (ARNPs) whose protocols permit them to dispense medications for a fee but they must register with the board of nursing (FAC § 64B9-4.011). ARNPs have prescribing privileges but are presently limited to legend drugs. ARNPs prescribe within their own scope of practice agreement (protocol) between the medical doctor and the ARNP. The protocol broadly lists the medical scope of practice within the ARNP's practice and the generic categories (ie, antibiotics, antihypertensives) from which the ARNP prescribes. The prescription contains the ARNP's and physician's name and license numbers (Pearson, 1999).

Illinois

Illinois Statutes § 65/15-20 outlines the rules regarding prescriptive authority in this state. A collaborating physician may delegate limited prescriptive authority to an APN as part of a written collaborative agreement. This authority may include prescription and dispensation of legend drugs and controlled substances in Schedules III, IV, or V. To prescribe controlled substances, an APN must obtain a mid-level practitioner controlled substance license. Medication orders must be reviewed periodically by the collaborating physician. The collaborating physician must file a notice of delegation of prescriptive authority and termination of the delegation. Upon receipt of the notice delegating authority to prescribe controlled substances, the licensed APN will be eligible to register for a mid-level practitioner controlled substance license.

Massachusetts

To prescribe in Massachusetts, a nurse must be an APN, have a minimum of 24 contact hours in pharmacotherapeutics beyond those acquired through a generic nursing education program, and have a valid registration to issue written or oral prescriptions or medication orders for controlled substances from the Massachusetts Department of Public Health and, where required, by the U.S. DEA (244 CMR 4.00 § 4.05).

In Massachusetts, CNMs, NPs, and psychiatric CNSs may issue written prescriptions and medication orders for Schedule II through VI controlled substances, provided certain requirements are met (105 CMR 700.003). The nurse must register with the Department's Division of Food and Drugs and with the DEA. The nurse must practice in accordance with written guidelines mutually developed and agreed upon by the certified nurse midwife, nurse practitioner, psychiatric nurse, and a supervising physician. These guidelines must address frequency of medication review by the nurse and the supervising physician; review of initial prescriptions or changes in medication by the supervising physician; procedures for initiating intravenous solutions; and limits, if any, on the types of medication to be prescribed, the quantity and duration of prescriptions, and the issuance of refill prescriptions. Schedule II drug prescriptions must be reviewed by a supervising physician within 72 hours of issuance. All prescriptions must be consistent with the scope of practice as defined for nurses practicing in the expanded role. The nurse may order controlled substances in Schedule V from a drug wholesaler, manufacturer, laboratory or distributor. The nurse may obtain Schedule II through V medications for dispensing only as supplied by the supervising physician or obtained through a written prescription for the patient. Telephone orders are permitted provided that the nurse clearly identifies his or her name and professional designation to the pharmacist and provides his or her registration number, work address, phone number, and the name of the supervising physician. An oral prescription must be followed up with a written prescription. The nurse may prescribe controlled substances for a patient in a health facility or other setting through use of written medication orders entered on the patient's medical record maintained at the facility, provided that the written orders meet all applicable state and federal regulations for the licensure of these facilities (10 SCMR 700.003).

243 CMR 2.10 provides detailed rules regarding physician supervision of nurses engaged in prescriptive practice. A supervising physician must review and provide ongoing direction for the nurse's prescriptive practice in accordance with written guidelines mutually developed and agreed upon with the nurse. This supervision must be provided as is necessary, taking into account the nurse's education, training, and experience, the nature of the nurse's practice, and the availability to the nurse of clinical back-up by physicians, to ensure that the nurse is providing patient care services in accordance with accepted standards of practice (243 CMR 2.10). A supervising physician must sign prescriptive practice guidelines only when able to provide supervision consistent with the rules outlined above, taking into account factors including but not limited to geographical proximity, practice setting, volume and complexity of the patient population, and the experience, training, and availability of the supervising physician and the nurse(s) (243 CMR 2.10). A supervising physician may not enter into guidelines unless the nurse has professional malpractice liability insurance with coverage of at least $100,000.00 per claim with a minimum annual aggregate of not less than

$300,000.00 and unless the guidelines limit the nurse to prescriptive practice in or on behalf of federal, state, county, or municipal health care facilities (243 CMR 2.10).

The guidelines pertaining to prescriptive practice must include a mechanism to monitor prescribing practices including documentation of review with a supervising physician at least every 3 months; include protocols for the initiation of intravenous therapies and Schedule II drugs; and specify the frequency of review of initial prescription of controlled substances. The initial prescription of Schedule II drugs must be reviewed within 96 hours and conform to the regulations of the department of public health (244 CMR § 4.22 and 4.23).

The board of nursing may request documentation of the supervising physician's review of the nurse's prescriptive practice. Failure to provide this documentation may result in disciplinary action (243 CMR 2.10).

An NP, CNM, or psychiatric/mental health CNS may also order tests and therapeutics pursuant to guidelines mutually developed and agreed upon by the nurse and the supervising physician in accordance with state regulations. The prescription must include the name of the physician with whom the nurse has developed and signed mutually agreed upon guidelines (Stat. chapt. 112 §§80E and 80G).

CNMs, NPs, and psychiatric CNSs may dispense controlled substances in a single dose or in such quantity as is essential for the treatment of the patient provided the amount of the controlled substance does not exceed the amount needed for the patient's immediate treatment and that all controlled substances required by the patient as part of treatment are dispensed by prescription to the ultimate user (Mass. Ann. Laws ch. 94C, § 9). Controlled substances may be administered by a nurse midwife only in a medical emergency and only in accordance with client-specific standing orders written by a physician. Local anesthesia for the infiltration of the perineum for episiotomy repair may be administered in accordance with client-specific standing orders written by the physician (105 CMR 142.650).

Prescription forms for CNMs and NPs must have a space for entering the name of the supervising physician (105 CMR 721.030). CNMs and NPs must maintain records and inventories of all Schedule I through III controlled substances he or she dispenses or administers (105 CMR 700.006).

Rules regarding hospice medication orders include the following: (1.) verbal medication orders must be countersigned by the NP within 72 hours, (2.) if the NP orders medications, all initial medication orders or significant changes in medications and all Schedule II drug orders must be reviewed by the supervising physician, (3.) if an NP orders medications, there must be a general review of the medications by the NP and the supervising physician (CMR 141.207).

Missouri

APNs were granted prescriptive authority (except for controlled substances) on August, 18, 1993. Under this law, the APN may prescribe medications if there is a collaborative agreement between the APN and a physician. House Bill 564 is self-executing and collaborative agreements could be entered into after the bill was signed. The law allows for propagation of rules if needed. If rules are recommended, they must have the agreement of the Board of Healing Arts, Missouri State Board of Nursing, and Pharmacy Board. Rules proposed in 1996 have created a climate of unease in APNs in that state (Thornton, 1996). These proposed rules would limit practice by

1. Regulating the number of miles allowed between the provider and the collaborative physician. This number varies from 30 to 50 miles in differing areas of the state.
2. Stipulating a calendar month internship with the collaborating physician before a collaborative agreement may be signed.
3. Stipulating that treatments be based on protocols, standing orders, or written agreements.
4. Limiting medication dispensed to cover 72 hours or less.
5. Requiring a referral if a client has a new or changed condition. The client must be seen by a physician within 2 weeks after being seen by the nurse practitioner (Missouri State Board of Nursing, 1995).

With respect to prescribing, the physician retains the responsibility for ensuring the appropriate administration, dispensation, prescription, and control of drugs pursuant to a collaborative practice arrangement (Mo. Regs. 4 CSR 200-4.200). APNs are not permitted to prescribe controlled substances. The APN may administer or dispense a controlled substance in a collaborative practice arrangement only under the direction and supervision of the collaborating physician; this will only occur on a case-by-case basis following verbal consultation between the collaborating physician and APN. The APN must record the consultation and physician's directions in the patient's chart which must be co-signed by the physician (Mo. Regs. 4 CSR 200-4.200). APNs in a collaborative practice arrangement may only dispense starter doses of medication to cover a period of time for 72 hours or less unless they work in a Title X family planning clinic or publicly funded clinic that dispenses medications free of charge (Mo. Regs. 4 CSR 200-4.200). The medications to be dispensed or prescribed by the APN must be consistent with the APN's and the physician's scopes of practice (Mo. Regs. 4 CSR 200-4.200).

New York

Callahan, 1996, notes that prescriptive privileges in New York state are liberal for nurse practitioner providers. The NP must have a practice agreement with the attending physician and have graduated from an approved graduate-level nurse practitioner program that provides 45 hours of pharmacology content and information on the prescribing laws of New York state. State certification then gives authority to practice as well as a registration number for prescribing medication. NPs in New York state also may hold DEA numbers to prescribe Schedules III, IV, and V controlled substances. Orders from NPs stand on their own merit and the NP's license to practice; physician co-signature is not required. Prescriptions for drugs, devices, and immunizing agents may be issued by an NP in accordance with the practice agreement and practice protocols. Prior to prescribing, the NP must obtain a certificate from the Department of Education upon successfully completing a program including an appropriate pharmacology component or its equivalent as established by the commissioner's regulations. The issued certificate will state whether or not the nurse practitioner has successfully completed such a program or equivalent and is authorized to prescribe (139 NYCL 6902). To the extent that the practice agreement and practice protocol provide for certified NPs prescribing drugs, state law provides them with authority to prescribe drugs independently provided that they are either registered under the Federal Controlled Substance Act or exempt from such registration (New York, 1992).

A licensed midwife may prescribe and administer drugs, immunizing agents, diagnostic tests and devices, and order laboratory tests. Prior to prescribing, a midwife must obtain a certificate from the department of education on successfully completing a program including a pharmacology component or its equivalent(140 NYCL 6951).

Tennessee

Qualifications for an APN to prescribe include current registered nurse licensure; a graduate degree in nursing (master's degree or doctorate); preparation in specialized practitioner skills at the master's, post-master's, doctoral, or post-doctoral level to include at least 3 quarter-hours of pharmacology instruction or its equivalent; and current national certification in the appropriate nursing specialty area. Those who want to prescribe controlled substances must also have a DEA number (Tenn. Comp. Rules & Regs. §1000-4-.03).

A nurse who has been issued a certificate of fitness as an APN must file a notice with the board of nursing containing:

1. Name of APN
2. Copy of the formulary describing the categories of legend drugs to be prescribed and/or issued
3. Name of the licensed physician having the supervision, control, and responsibility for prescriptive services rendered (Tenn. Comp. R. & Regs. R. 1000-4-.01 (2000))

The NP who holds a certificate of fitness is authorized to prescribe and/or issue controlled substances in Schedules II through V, subject to supervisory rules developed by the boards of medicine and nursing (TCA 63-7-123). APNs may not prescribe or issue drugs to cause an abortion (Tenn. Code Ann. § 53-10-104).

Texas

To prescribe in Texas, the nurse must complete the following requirements:

1. Be approved by the board of nursing as an APN.
2. Submit to the board of nursing the application for limited prescriptive authority and the appropriate documentation of the necessary education, training, and current skills including pharmacotherapeutics as determined by the board of nursing to carry out or sign prescription drug orders.
3. Complete courses in pharmacotherapeutics, advanced assessment, diagnosis and management of problems within the clinical specialty, and pathophysiology. These courses must be academic courses from a regionally accredited institution with a minimum of 45 clock hours per course. NPs, CNMs, CRNAs, will be considered to have met these requirements on the basis of courses completed in the advanced practice educational program. CNSs must submit documentation of successfully completing separate courses in these content areas.
4. CNSs approved as APNs by petition on the basis of completion of a non-nursing master's degree may not prescribe (22 TAC § 222.2 [2000]).

A physician may, with supervision not requiring his or her physical presence, delegate to a APN the act or acts of administering, providing, or carrying out, or signing a prescription drug order through physician's orders, standing medical orders, standing delegation orders, or other orders or protocols in treating patients at (1.) a site serving a medically underserved population or (2.) the physician's primary practice site. Prescriptions issued may only be written for dangerous drugs. No prescriptions for controlled substances may be authorized or issued. If the APN authorizes generic substitution, the protocol must provide direction to the APN as to whether or not and under what circumstances product selection will be permitted by a pharmacist. A delegating physician is responsible for devising and enforcing a system to account for and monitor prescriptions issued under his supervision (22 TAC § 193.6).

A physician's authority to delegate the carrying out or signing of a prescription drug order at his primary practice site is limited as follows. The physician may delegate three physician assistants or APNs or their full-time equivalents practicing at the physician's primary practice site.

The physician may only delegate these tasks to the patients with whom the physician has established or will establish physician–patient relationship, but this does not require the physician to see the patient within a specific period of time (22 TAC § 193.6).

In a licensed hospital or ambulatory surgical center, a physician may delegate to a CRNA the ordering of drugs and devices necessary for the CRNA to administer an anesthetic or an anesthesia-related service ordered by the physician. The physician's order does not have to be drug-specific, dose-specific, or administration technique-specific. Pursuant to the order and in accordance with facility policies or medical staff bylaws, the nurse anesthetist may select, obtain, and administer those drugs and apply the appropriate medical devices necessary to accomplish the order and maintain the patient's bodily functions (22 TAC § 193.6).

A physician may delegate to a nurse midwife the act or acts of administering or providing controlled substances to patients during intrapartum and immediate post-partum care. The physician may not delegate the use or issuance of a triplicate prescription form. The delegation of authority must be under a physician's order, medical order, standing delegation order, or protocol that must require adequate and documented availability for access to medical care. The physician's orders, medical orders, standing delegation orders, or protocols must provide for reporting or monitoring the client's progress including complications of pregnancy and delivery and the nurse midwife's administration and provision of controlled substances to his or her patients. This physician's authority to delegate is limited to

1. Three nurse midwives or physician assistants or their full-time equivalents and
2. The designated facility where the nurse midwife provides care (22 TAC § 193.6).

ENHANCE YOUR LEARNING

1. Develop a sample prescriptive protocol meeting the requirements of one state that requires protocols for prescribing.
2. Visit your state's board of nursing website to research pending changes to prescriptive authority in your state, if any.
3. Interview an APN who has practiced in two states regarding the differences in prescriptive practice.
4. Research the history of the laws regarding APN prescriptive practice in your state.

TEST YOUR COMPREHENSION

1. List the two states that do not allow CNMs to prescribe.
2. List at least two states that require protocols for NP prescriptive authority.
3. Describe the difference between Schedule I and Schedule II controlled substances.
4. Discuss the learned intermediary rule.

REFERENCES

AWHONN. (1997). Are you writing prescriptions? *Lifelines, 1*(6), 23.

Brown, S, & Grimes, D. (1995). A meta-analysis of nurse practitioners and nurse midwives in primary care. *Nurs Res, 45*, 332–339.

Callahan, M. (1996, September). The APN in an acute care setting: The nurse practitioner in adult cardiac surgery care. *Nursing Clinics of North America, 31*(3), 487–493.

Missouri House Bill No. 564: CCS SS SCS HS HCS HB 564. 87th General Assembly. Jefferson City Mo. (1993).

Missouri State Board of Nursing. (1995). *Missouri state board of nursing: Collaborative practice draft*. (Title IV, Department of Economic Development Division 200. General Rules.) Jefferson City: Mo. State Board of Nursing.

Naegle, M. (1994). Prescription drugs and nursing education: Knowledge gaps and implications for role performance. *The Journal of Law, Medicine and Ethics, 22*(3), 257–261.

New York Opinions of the Attorney General F92-2 (1992).

Snell, B.J. (1999). Issues related to the practice of prescribing. *JOGNN, 28*(5), 513–519.

Thornton, C. (1996). Nurse practitioner in a rural setting. *Nursing Clinics of North America, 31*(3), 495–505.

Cases

Mazur v. Merck & Co., Inc., 964 F.2d 1348 (1992).

Wyeth-Ayerst Laboratories Company et al., v. Medrano, 2000 Tex. App. LEXIS 5235 (2000).

Reimbursement

As with other aspects of advanced practice nurse (APN) regulation, reimbursement rules and laws vary widely among the states. APN reimbursement is also governed by various federal laws. It is important for the APN, especially one in independent practice, to have a thorough knowledge of the federal laws governing reimbursement as well as the laws of the state where the APN practices. This chapter discusses the development of federal law regarding APN reimbursement and state law regarding APN reimbursement in the selected states.

Finerfrock & Havens, 1997, note that most third–party payers recognize nurse practitioners (NPs) as qualified providers of health care. However, reimbursement and coverage policies may differ substantially and there may be significant differences between how the NP is allowed to practice under state law and the criteria the plan may impose as a precondition for payment.

FEDERAL LAW

The Rural Health Clinic Service Act was enacted in 1978 to improve primary health care for persons who are medically underserved. The act allows Medicare and Medicaid to be used as reimbursement for the services of an NP or a nurse midwife. The act stipulates that reimbursement be for services provided in a rural health clinic (RHC). The clinic may be either independent or provider-based. A provider-based RHC is a subordinate part of the provider hospital and is under the supervision of the hospital's administration (Medicare Regs., 1991).

Medicaid first reimbursed certified nurse midwives (CNMs) in 1980 (Sellards & Mills, 1995). Medicaid first reimbursed NPs in 1982 (Sellards & Mills, 1995). Congressional legislation passed in 1986 made certified registered nurse anesthetists (CRNAs) the first nursing specialty to be accorded direct reimbursement rights under the Medicare program (AANA, 2000a). Under the Omnibus Reconciliation Act (OBRA) of 1989,

239

APNs were subject to reimbursement limitations. CNMs were covered only for services throughout the maternity cycle, not for family planning or gynecological care; maternity cycle services were reimbursed at 65% of the physician fee schedule amount. NPs were required to work in collaboration with a physician; NP reimbursement was capped at a percentage of the physician fee schedule; and coverage was limited to certain NP specialties (Inglis & Kjervik, 1993). Box 10-1 illustrates the history of reimbursement for CNM services.

As of 1993, 24 states mandated by statute some level of direct third–party reimbursement for CNMs and NPs; the majority having declared that any service covered for other providers must be covered for APNs operating within their state-defined scope of practice (Inglis & Kjervik, 1993). As of 1993 APNs were eligible to receive direct third–party reimbursement in 38 states. APNs were receiving direct payment under the four federal health programs (Medicare, Civilian Health and Medical and Program for the Uniformed Services [CHAMPUS], Federal Employees Health Benefits Program [FEHBP], and Medicaid) and Medicare had been implemented for specified types of APNs in 18 states. In 42 states APNs were able to receive Medicaid reimbursement equal to or somewhat below the level of reimbursement paid to physicians (Inglis & Kjervik, 1993). As of 1995, all categories of NPs and certified nurse specialists (CNSs) were considered fully autonomous providers and were reimbursable under CHAMPUS (Sellards & Mills, 1995). Box 10-2 outlines the history of reimbursement for NP services.

As of 1996 APNs were eligible for federal reimbursement (Medicare Part B, Medicaid, CHAMPUS, FEHBP) of services but with significant limitations related to types of services reimbursable and locales of practices and with payment rates for APN reimbursement to be determined by the individual states (Spatz, 1996). As of 1997, CRNAs are eligible to receive direct reimbursement from Medicare, nearly half of all Medicaid programs, CHAMPUS, as well as private insurers and managed care organizations (AANA, 1997). As of January 1, 1998, NPs can be directly reimbursed by Medicare in all practice settings (National Association of Pediatric Nurse Practitioners [NAPNAP], 1998).

BOX 10-1	History of CNM Reimbursement

1978 RHCA allows reimbursement by Medicare and Medicaid for CNM services in rural health clinics.
1980 Medicaid reimburses for CNM services.
1993 Direct reimbursement to CNMs begins under all federal health programs.

BOX 10-2	History of NP Reimbursement

1978   RHCA allows reimbursement by Medicare and Medicaid for NP services in rural health clinics.
1982   Medicaid reimburses for NP services.
1993   NPs are directly reimbursed under all federal health programs.
1998   NPs are directly reimbursed by Medicare.

As of January, 2000, 36 states directly reimbursed CRNAs under Medicaid. CRNAs were directly reimbursed under CHAMPUS and FEHB. Twenty-two states mandated direct private insurance payment to CRNAs and 38 Blue Cross/Blue Shield entities provided direct reimbursement to CRNAs. In addition, a number of managed care organizations in Arkansas, Iowa, Kentucky, Minnesota, New Mexico, Oregon, South Dakota, Tennessee, and Wisconsin were reimbursing CRNAs (AANA, 2000b).

The current federal Medicaid statutes define covered medical services as including services furnished by a CNM (42 U.S.C. 1396[a]). The Medicaid Act requires participating states to provide CNM services and NP services (42 U.S.C. 1396d [a]). Dower, et al., 1999, note that under federal law, state Medicaid programs must pay for CNM care as long as the service provided is allowed under state law; however, states may set their own payment rates so while just over half the state Medicaid programs reimburse CNMs at 100% of the physician fee schedule for Medicaid, some states pay for CNM care at 70 to 90% of the physician fee schedule.

The Balanced Budget Act of 1997, effective January 1, 1998, removed restrictions on the type of areas and settings in which the professional services of NPs and CNSs are paid for by Medicare. As a result, payments are allowed for services furnished in all areas and settings permitted under state licensure laws but only if no facility or other provider charges or is paid any amounts for furnishing the professional services. In most cases, separate payment is allowed for NP and CNS services provided in a facility setting; NPs and CNSs must bill the Part B carrier directly for services. Separate payment for the professional services of NPs and CNSs provided in a RHC or federally qualified health center is not permitted. The act also increased the payment for NPs and CNSs to 80% of the lesser of either the actual charge or 85% of the physician fee schedule amount. For assistant at surgery services, payment is 80% of the lesser of either the actual charge or 85% of the physician fee schedule. To receive payment under the Balanced Budget Act, the NP and CNS must submit claims to the Part B carrier under her or his own billing number for professional services furnished in a facility or other provider setting except when the services are clearly facility services and are specifically included in the costs covered by the intermediary payment to the facility.

Services provided "incident to" physicians' services are not affected by the act. These services must still be provided by a physician's employees under the physician's direct supervision, and they continue to be paid for under the physician fee schedule as though the physician actually performed them. These "incident to" services may be provided by NPs, CNSs, and other nurses employed by the physician. All NPs and CNSs must have his or her own provider identification number to bill Medicare under the act (NAPNAP, 1998b; Lowe & Havens, 1998). For the first time, this act allowed NPs to be directly reimbursed for Medicare Part B services. This legislation requires NPs to have a master's degree, be licensed by the state as an NP, and be certified as an NP by a nationally recognized certifying body. In July 1999, the Health Care Financing Administration (HCFA) announced plans to modify the requirements as follows: the NP must be licensed as an NP by the state and must be certified by a nationally recognized certifying body or the NP must have been granted a Medicare billing number by December 31, 2000. The effect was that NPs who had been granted and who maintained a Medicare billing number would not lose the number solely on the basis of education and credentialing (NAACOG Certification Corporation [NCC], 1999). In the final rule published in late 1999, HCFA also indicated that nurses applying for a billing number after January 1, 2003 would be required to have a master's degree in addition to the qualifications listed above (NAPNAP, 2000). The act did not affect CNMs and CRNAs as they were already reimbursed under Medicare Part B (Hodson, 1998).

On November 2, 1998, HCFA issued the physician practice expense final rule, which redefined collaborative practice for NPs to be reimbursed by Medicare. This rule applies to NPs in states that don't require a written practice agreement. This rule requires such NPs to have an agreement with one or more physicians documenting their scope of practice and identifying ways they will work with the physician to provide the patient care needed (NAPNAP, 1998a). As of April of 2000, HCFA indicated it would remove the federal requirement that physicians must supervise CRNAs when administering anesthesia to Medicare patients. Until then, in anesthesia cases involving Medicare patients, the federal rule required supervision of CRNAs for hospitals and ambulatory surgical centers to be reimbursed for the nonanesthesia portion of the patient's care. However for the CRNAs themselves to be reimbursed, Medicare did not require supervision. The final rule was to be published in the Federal Register in June 2000 (AWHONN, 2000). However, this regulation is threatened by President George W. Bush's hold on all pending federal regulations issued late in the previous administration. In addition, bills have been introduced in the U.S. House and Senate to reinstate physician oversight of nurse anesthetists (AWHONN, 2001).

LAWS OF SELECTED STATES:

Arizona

State Health Plans

Instead of Medicaid, Arizona has the Arizona Health Care Cost Containment System (AHCCCS).

NPs AHCCCS contracts with primary care providers on a capitated basis including NPs. AHCCCS reimbursement for NPs is 60% of the physician rate (Pearson, 2000).

CNMs CNM services provided by a certified nurse practitioner in midwifery are covered services under the AHCCCS program (A.A.C. § R9-22-215 [1999]).

Private Plans

If a disability insurance contract in this state provides for reimbursement for any service within the scope of the practice of an NP, the plan must pay for the NP services. Payment can be made directly to the certified registered nurse or registered nurse practitioner (A.R.S. § 20-1406.03 [1999], A.R.S. § 20-1376.03 [1999]). If a subscription contract of a hospital and medical service corporation provides for reimbursement for any service within the scope of the practice of a registered nurse practitioner or a certified registered nurse, the corporation must pay for the services. Payment can be made directly to the certified registered nurse or registered nurse practitioner if she or he has a participation contract with the corporation (A.R.S. § 20-841.03 [1999]).

California

Medicaid

In California, the Medicaid program is called Medi-Cal. Table 10-1 summarizes Medi-Cal treatment of APNs. Reimbursement for services of a nurse midwife, a certified family nurse practitioner, or a certified pediatric nurse practitioner will be the usual charges made to the general public not to exceed the maximum reimbursement rates for the same service (22 C.C.R. 51503.2 [2000]). Reimbursement will be the lesser of the billed amount or the established rates. Claims for payment for APN services must include:

1. The APN's name and license or certificate number
2. The location where the service was rendered
3. The name of the supervising or attending physician

Reimbursement for APN services is limited to those defined as Medi-Cal reimbursable services and within the scope of practice of nurse midwives and NPs (22 C.C.R. 51503.1 [2000]). Reimbursement for nurse anesthetist services will be the usual charges made to the public not to

TABLE 10-1   Medi-Cal Treatment of APNs

APN	SERVICES COVERED	DIRECT REIMBURSEMENT
CRNA	Yes	Yes
CNS	No	No
NP	Yes	Yes
CNM	Yes	Yes

(22 CCR 51051; 22 CCR 51503.2; Welfare & Institutions Code §14132.4, 14132.41.and 14115.3).

exceed the maximum reimbursement rates. No fees will be paid to nurse anesthetists for anesthesia services when the nurse anesthetist is compensated on a salary or other contract basis for performing the same or similar services (22 C.C.R. 51505.2 [2000]).

State Health Programs
The Department of Public Social Services may enter into contracts with NPs and CNMs acting within their scopes of practice(Calif. Wel. & Inst. Code § 14088.14 [2000]). 10 C.C.R .2699.300 (2000) indicates that under the Access for Infants and Mothers program, the basic scope of benefits rules do not preclude direct reimbursement of nurse practitioners or other advanced practice nurses in providing covered services.

Private Plans
California Insurance Code § 10353 (2000) indicates that every policy of disability insurance issued, amended, or renewed on or after January 1, 1992, that offers coverage for perinatal services must provide for direct reimbursement to CNMs and NPs for perinatal services. The CNM or NP may collect payment for any unpaid portion of his or her fee as provided for under the plan for other providers.

Third–party payers are required to reimburse psychiatric-mental health nurses for qualifying services (Pearson, 2000).

Florida

In Florida, ARNPs receive Medicaid, Medicare, CHAMPUS, and third–party reimbursement. Medicaid reimburses ARNPs at 80% of physician amounts and pays 100% if an on-site physician countersigns the chart within 24 hours. Private insurers must reimburse nurse midwife services if the policy includes pregnancy care (Pearson, 2000).

Florida Statute § 641.3923 (1999) indicates that a health maintenance organization must not discriminate against any APN licensed and certified in the state, who is acting within the scope of their license and certification, solely on the basis of the license or certification. However, a plan may include providers only to the extent necessary to meet the needs of the plan's enrollees or establish measures designed to maintain quality and control costs consistent with the plan's responsibilities.

Illinois

Medicaid

Illinois law recognizes pediatric nurse practitioners and family nurse practitioners and authorizes them to render services. Therefore the state must offer direct Medicaid reimbursement to pediatric nurse practitioners and family nurse practitioners (Illinois, 1993).

State Health Programs

The Department of Public Aid will pay clinics for RHC and federally qualified health center services of NPs and nurse midwives (89 Ill. Adm. Code 140.462 [2000]). Box 10-3 lists non-reimbursable APN services. The Department of Public Aid's medical programs require nurses to bill the Medical Assistance Program at the same rate they charge patients who pay their own bills and patients covered by other third–party payors. In addition, a nurse may bill only for services he or she personally provides or that are provided under his or her direct supervision in his or her office by his or her staff. A certified pediatric nurse practitioner or certified family nurse practitioner may bill only for the services personally provided. A nurse may not bill for services provided by another nurse (89 Ill. Adm. Code 140.400 [2000]). Payments will be made according to a schedule of statewide pricing screens established by the Department of Public Aid. However, pediatric nurse practitioners, family nurse practitioners, and nurse midwives will be reimbursed for covered services at 70% of the established screen (89 Ill. Adm. Code 140.400 [2000]). Table 10-2 outlines requirements for APN reimbursement under state health plans. 89 Ill. Adm. Code 142.400 (2000) outlines services provided by a managed care entity under the state's Mediplan Plus program to include nurse midwife services.

BOX 10-3	Non-Reimburseable APN Services

- CNM services provided to recipients of General Assistance, Aid to the Medically Indigent, or the Migrant Medical Program
- NP services provided to recipients of General Assistance, Aid to the Medically Indigent, or the Migrant Medical Program
- Consultations between CNMs or between a CNM and a physician
- Hospital outpatient and clinic services of NPs and CRNAs

(89 Ill. Adm. Code §140.436 and §148.140)

TABLE 10-2   Requirement for APN Reimbursement

	CNM	PNP	FNP
State RN licensure	Yes	Yes	Yes
National certification	No	Yes	Yes
Completion of accredited program	Yes	Yes	Yes
State authorization to practice as an APN	Yes	Yes	Yes
Physician practice agreement	Yes	Yes	Yes

(89 Ill. Adm. Code Section 140.435).

The physician agreements required for reimbursement of APN services must meet certain requirements. The agreement must explain the physician's oversight of the nurse and authorize the specific procedures or categories of procedures that may be performed by the nurse. The services to be provided must be services that the physician generally provides his or her patients in the normal course of his or her medical practice. The agreement must specify which procedures do not require a physician's presence while being performed. The agreement must specify the parameters and details of all authorized procedures that may be carried out. A copy of this signed agreement must be on file with the state and must be updated annually (89 Ill. Adm. Code 140.400 [2000]). The APN services must not conflict with the Illinois Nursing Act of 1987 or the Medical Practice Act of 1987 and their implementing regulations (89 Ill. Adm. Code 140.400 [2000]).

Under 89 Illinois Administrative Code 148.60 (2000), services not covered or reimbursed as hospital services include nurse anesthetist services. Payment for general anesthesia services will be made only to hospitals that qualify for these payments under the Medicare Program (Title XIII) and will be made when services are provided by a hospital-employed CRNA.

Private Plans
There is no legislation in this state mandating or prohibiting third–party insurers' reimbursement of APRN services.

Massachusetts
State Health Plan
The state's medical assistance program will pay either an independent NP or CNM or the physician employer of a nonindependent NP or CNM for services when

1. The services are limited to the NP's or CNM's scope of practice

2. The NP or CNM has a current license to practice in Massachusetts

3. The NP or CNM has a current collaborative arrangement with a physician or group of physicians; this requirement is deemed to be met for nonindependent NPs or CNMs employed by a physician (130 CMR 433.433 and 130 CMR 433.419 [2000]).

These laws also outline independent NP and CNM provider eligibility. Only an independent NP or CNM may enroll in MassHealth as a provider. Any NP or CNM applying to participate must submit documentation that he or she

- Is a member of a group practice of physicians and other practitioners and is compensated by the practice in the same manner as the physicians and other practitioners
- Is a member of an NP group practice or CNM group practice or is in private practice (130 CMR 433.433 and 130 CMR 433.419 [2000]).

The collaborating physician must be a MassHealth provider who engages in the same type of clinical practice as the NP or CNM. The NP or CNM must practice in accordance with written guidelines developed in conjunction with the collaborating physician. The NP or CNM must provide the state with documentation of the collaborative arrangement including guidelines and any written agreement signed by the NP or CNM and the collaborating physician(s). The guidelines must specify what services the NP or CNM is authorized to perform and the established procedures for common medical problems. Consultation between an independent NP or CNM and a collaborating physician is not reimbursable as a separate service (130 CMR 433.433 and 130 CMR 433.419 [2000]). Any NP or CNM who does not meet the above requirements is nonindependent and is not eligible to enroll in MassHealth as a provider. As an exception, an individual physician (who is neither practicing as a professional corporation nor is a member of a group practice) who employs a NP or CNM may submit claims for services provided by the NP or CNM employee (130 CMR 433.433 and 130 CMR 433.419 [2000]).

NP The state division of health care finance and policy will pay for an individual medical visit by an NP at 100% of the 1995 Federally Qualified Health Center rate (114.6 CMR 11.06).

CNM Under division of medical assistance rules, when an independent CNM is the primary provider and a cesarean section is done by the collaborating physician, the CNM may claim payment for the prenatal visits on a fee-for-service basis (130 CMR 433.424). In addition, this division will pay for delivery by a CNM when the CNM is a contractor or employee of a community health center if the CNM is not receiving a salary from a hospital or other institution to perform the same service (130 CMR 405.422). Community health centers (CHC) may bill for services provided by a nurse midwife that relate to pregnancy, labor, birth, and the immediate postpartum period when the nurse midwife is contractor or employee of the CHC (130 CMR 405.427 [2000]). Box 10-4 lists the conditions that apply to CNM reimbursement.

Prenatal or postpartum care provided by a nurse midwife in the patient's home is not reimbursable. A nurse midwife on the staff of a CHC must have successfully completed a formal educational program for nurse midwives as required by the Massachusetts Board of Registration in Nursing. A nurse midwife who has completed these educational requirements may provide services prior to the first certification examination for which the nurse midwife is eligible. If the scheduled examination is missed or if the CNM fails to pass the exam, the nurse midwife must immediately cease providing services. After passing the examination, the nurse midwife must be certified to practice by the Board of Registration in Nursing. When certification expires or is suspended, the nurse midwife must immediately cease providing services (130 CMR 405.42 [2000]).

CRNA Anesthesia services provided by a nurse anesthetist are reimbursable by the state medical assistance program only if the nurse anesthetist meets the following conditions:

1. Is authorized by law to perform the services for which payment is sought

---

BOX 10-4   **Massachusetts Conditions for CNM Reimbursement**

1. The services must be limited to the CNM's scope of practice.
2. The nurse midwife must meet the educational and certification requirements mandated by state law.
3. The nurse midwife must enter into a formal collaborative arrangement with a physician or group of physicians as required by state law or regulation.
4. The immediate postpartum period during which nurse-midwife services may be provided is defined as a period of time not to exceed 6 weeks after the date of delivery.
5. Deliveries by a nurse midwife must occur in facilities licensed by the Department of Public Health for the operation of maternity and newborn services.

(130 CMR 405.427).

2. Is a full-time employee of the physician and is not a salaried employee of the hospital
3. Performs the services under the direct and continuous supervision of the physician. The physician must be in the operating suite and responsible for no more than two operating rooms. Availability of the physician by telephone does not meet the supervision requirement (130 CMR 433.454 [2000]).

For state medical programs, the rates of payment for physician-provided anesthesia service only apply to anesthesia service rendered by a nurse anesthetist if the conditions listed in Box 10-5 exist.

Private Plans

Any contract between a subscriber and a non-profit hospital service corporation under an individual or group hospital service plan, any subscription certificate under an individual or group medical service agreement, and any accident and health insurance policy or health service contract must cover CRNA and NP services if the services rendered are within the scope of the CRNA's license or NP's authorization to practice and the policy or contract currently provides benefits for identical services rendered by any other provider of health care (Mass. Ann. Laws ch. 176A, § 8S ; ch. 176B § 4T, ch. 175 § 47Q [2000]).

Massachusetts Ann. Laws ch. 175, § 47E (2000) indicates that any blanket or general policy of insurance or any policy of accident and sickness insurance that provides hospital and surgical expense insurance

---

BOX 10-5 | Conditions to be Met for CRNA Payment at Physician Rates

a. The nurse anesthetist is a full-time employee of the eligible physician provider and is not a salaried employee of the hospital.
b. The nurse anesthetist is authorized to perform the services for which payment is sought.
c. The nurse anesthetist performs the services under the direct, personal, and continuous supervision of the eligible physician provider.
d. The eligible physician provider customarily includes the charges in his bill to patients other than publicly-aided and industrial accident patients. To provide direct, personal, and continuous supervision, the physician need not be in the room where the services are being performed at all times but must be close by and available to provide immediate personal assistance and direction. Availability by telephone does not meet this requirement.

(114.3 CMR 16.04 [2000])

must cover CNM services if the services are reimbursed when performed by any other licensed practitioner and if the services are within the CNM's lawful scope of practice.

Massachusetts Ann. Laws Ch. 176G, § 4 (2000) indicates that any health maintenance organization contract must cover CRNA and NP services, subject to the terms of a negotiated agreement between the health maintenance organization and the provider.

Massachusetts Ann. Laws Ch. 176B, § 7 (2000) indicates that every nurse midwife has the right to enter into a written agreement with a medical service corporation doing business where the nurse midwife resides or has a usual place of business to perform midwifery services. The corporation may place no restriction on its participating nurse midwives as to methods of diagnosis or treatment. A corporation may terminate its agreement with any participating nurse midwife (a.) for failure to comply with the reasonable rules and regulations of the corporation including rules and regulations governing the keeping of accounts, records, and statistics, the making of reports and proof of services rendered, or (b.) for presenting any fraudulent, unreasonable, or improper claim for payment or compensation. The agreement may not be terminated by the corporation unless it first gives the CNM a written statement of the charges against him or her, an opportunity for hearing, a reasonable notice of the time and place of hearing, and a written decision accompanied by a statement of the reasons for the decision. A CNM may terminate his or her agreement with the corporation at any time upon giving at least 1 year's notice in writing to the corporation and each of his or her patients to terminate as of a specific date, provided that the CNM must not terminate any patient relationship until arrangements have been made for appropriate referrals, continuation, and follow-up care. The corporation may not discriminate in any way against participating nurse midwives in furnishing midwifery service.

Physicians, chiropractors, and nurse midwives have right to contract with medical service corporations, while other classes of health care providers have such contracts only if the medical service corporation in its discretion chooses to include their services (*Blue Shield of Massachusetts, Inc. v. Board of Review*, 1986).

Missouri

Medicaid

The Missouri State Board of Nursing website provides detailed instructions and contact information for APNs to enroll as Medicaid and Medicare providers in this state.

13 CSR 70-55.010 (2000) outlines Medicaid Program Benefits for nurse midwife services. To be eligible for participation in the Missouri Medicaid Nurse Midwife Program, a provider must meet the following two criteria:

1. Have current licensure as a registered nurse
   - A nurse midwife who practices in Missouri must be a currently licensed RN in Missouri.
   - A nurse midwife who provides services to Missouri Medicaid recipients in a state other than Missouri must be a currently licensed RN in that state and be legally authorized under that state's law to practice as a nurse midwife
2. Hold current certification by the American College of Nurse-Midwives

Medicaid reimbursement for nurse midwives is limited to the following types of care:

1. Complete care, management and monitoring of a woman absent medical complications and her unborn/newborn infant throughout the course of the normal cycle of gestation including pregnancy, labor, and delivery and the initial postpartum period not to exceed 6 weeks
2. Routine post-delivery care of the neonate including physical examination of the baby and conference with parents (13 CSR 70-55.010 [2000])

Nurse midwives may be reimbursed by Medicaid for services performed in inpatient hospital, outpatient hospital, office, and home settings (13 CSR 70-55.010 [2000]).

Medicaid reimbursement for services rendered will be the lower of the provider's usual and customary charge to the general public or the Medicaid maximum allowable amount (13 CSR 70-55.010 [2000]).

Medicaid reimbursement is made to APNs enrolled as Missouri Medicaid fee-for-service providers and to Medicaid-enrolled APNs associated with a Federally Qualified Health Care and/or RHC facility at the same rate as physicians (Pearson, 2000).

State Plan
The Uninsured Parents' Health Insurance Program covers services of APNS and CNMs (13 CSR 70-4.090 [2000]). Under this state's public health and welfare rules, payment will be made for the services of a certified pediatric or family NP to the extent that the services are provided in accordance with the Nurse Practice Act and its regulations regardless of whether the NP is supervised by or in association with a physician or other health care provider (Mo. Rev. Stat. §208.152).

Private Plans
Health insurers, nonprofit health service plans, and HMOs in this state must reimburse a claim for services provided by an APN if the services are within the APN's scope of practice (Mo. Rev. Stat. 376.407).

New York

State Plan

NP Callahan, 1996, notes that in her New York practice, fees for inpatient NP services are capitated; this is unlike fees for nurse midwives or nurse anesthetists. Occasionally patients need to be seen beyond the period of capitated coverage. Often these visits go without charge or are billed as limited office visits for reimbursement to the practice. The NP does not receive any percentage of these receipts.

NPs in New York state can enroll as service providers under the state medical care program (18 N.Y. C.R.R. § 504.1). NPs are authorized to provide health care services to eligible medical assistance recipients within their scope of practice. For an NP to provide health care services to eligible medical assistance recipients, he or she must enroll with the Department of Social Services. The physician in collaboration with the NP must also enroll with the Department of Social Services. As a condition of enrollment, the NP and the collaborating physician must agree to make their practice agreements and protocols available for inspection by staff of the Department of Social Services (DSS) (10 N.Y. C.R.R. § 85.43 [2000]).

18 New York Code of Rules and Regulations § 505.32 (2000) outlines rules regarding state medical assistance payments for NP services. Written practice agreements and practice protocols between NPs and their collaborating physicians must contain provisions for the collaborating physician's review of patient records at least every 3 months. The physician's review of patient records is not a billable service under the Medical Assistance (MA) program. The NP must make the written practice agreements, practice protocols, and evidence that the collaborating physician has reviewed patient records available to the state. The NP must submit the name of and other identifying information concerning the collaborating physician with his or her enrollment application. Payment for NP services provided by an NP who is paid a salary by a medical facility reimbursed under the MA program for its services on a rate basis will be made on a fee-for-service basis only if the cost of the nurse practitioner services is not included in the facility's cost-based rate. Payment will be made for medically necessary ancillary services covered under the MA program and that the nurse practitioner orders for an MA recipient. Payment will only be made for prescription drugs when prescribed by a nurse practitioner with the authority to write prescriptions.

18 New York Code of Rules and Regulations § 505.32 9 (2000) outlines the Preferred Physicians and Children Program (PPAC) under which a written agreement is entered into by a provider and the Department of Social Services pursuant to which the department pays enhanced fees for certain medical services provided to children under the age of 21 who are eligible for MA. This section has detailed requirements for the NP to participate in this program.

CNM New York Consolidated Laws Service Public Health § 2523 (2000) indicates that prenatal care service providers are eligible to participate in the prenatal care assistance program if they satisfy the standards for providing services established by the state, have not been disqualified from participation in the medical assistance program, agree to serve eligible service recipients, and are certified nurse midwives practicing on an individual or group basis. Services provided by a nurse midwife who is salaried by a medical facility that is reimbursed for services on a cost-related basis will not be reimbursed on a fee-for-service basis if the cost for the nurse midwife's salary is included in the facility's cost-based rate. Services provided by nurse midwives have been eligible for payment and state reimbursement since January 1, 1984 (18 N.Y. Code of Rules and Regulations § 505.8 [2000]).

Private Plans

Laws regarding health maintenance organizations (HMOs) in this state are provider-neutral, applying equally to physician and non-physician providers (Pearson, 2000).

Tennessee

Medicaid

Services to be provided by the state Medicaid program include:

1. Services by nurse anesthetists who are registered by the board of nursing, have completed an advance course in anesthesia, and hold a current certification from the American Association of Nurse Anesthetists
2. Nurse midwife services performed by a person who is licensed as a registered nurse and certified by the American College of Nurse Midwives
3. Services provided by certified pediatric nurse practitioners and certified family nurse practitioners as required by federal law (Tenn. Code Ann. § 71-5-107 (1999))

Medicaid reimbursement to CNMs for covered services is the lesser of the billed amount or 90% of the maximum amount paid to physicians statewide for similar maternity and newborn services (Tenn. Comp. Rules & Regs. R. 1200-13-1-.06 [2000]). Except for an emergency, delivery will not be reimbursed unless provided in a hospital or in an ambulatory surgical center classified to provide maternity services (Tenn. Comp. Rules & Regs. R. 1200-13-1-.06 [2000]). CRNA services provided with medical direction are reimbursed the lesser of billed charges or 44% of what would have been paid to a physician for similar services. CRNA services provided without medical direction are reimbursed the lesser of billed charges or 80% of that paid to a physician for similar services (Tenn. Comp. Rules & Regs. R. 1200-13-1-.06 [2000]). The CRNA who performed the service must be identified on claims submitted for payment except when the claim is submitted by an individual CRNA for services she or he personally performed (Tenn. Comp. Rules & Regs. R. 1200-13-1-.06 [2000]).

Tennessee Comp. Rules & Regs. R. 1200-13-1-22 (2000) provides rules regarding Medicaid coverage of services of CNMs. In each joint practice situation, written protocols jointly developed by the nurse midwife and physician must be executed outlining delegated medical tasks and drug management used in patient care. Protocols must be reviewed, revised annually, and, signed and dated by the physician and the certified nurse midwife. Maternity services performed by the nurse midwife may not include the assisting in childbirth by any artificial, forcible, surgical, or mechanical means not addressed in the protocol. Newborn services are limited to routine newborn care. For a nurse midwife to obtain a Medicaid provider number and receive reimbursement, the requirements outlined in Box 10-6 must be met. Medicaid-covered services provided by nurse midwives are limited to diagnoses and procedures related to an uncomplicated maternity cycle, an uncomplicated delivery, and routine newborn care (Tenn. Comp. Rules & Regs. R. 1200-13-1-.06 [2000]).

In the Medicaid program, at the option of the physician, required visits after the initial visit may alternate between visits by the physician and an NP working under the physician's delegation (Tenn. Comp. Rules & Regs. 1200-13-1-.05). Under the state Medicaid program, psychiatric evaluations are covered when ordered and billed by a psychiatrist and performed by a NP (Tenn. Comp. Rules & Regs. 1200-13-1-.07). Advanced practice RNs and NPs engaged in the delivery of primary health care are defined as primary care providers under the TennCare program (Tenn. Comp. Rules & Regs. 1200-13-12-.08).

Private Plans

Whenever any contract, plan, or policy of insurance issued in Tennessee provides for reimbursement of any service within the lawful scope of

---

BOX 10-6	**Tennessee Requirements for CNM Medicaid Reimbursement**

a. Completion and submission of an enrollment form that includes a copy of the certification issued by the American College of Nurse-Midwives and a copy of a current Tennessee Registered Nurse license
b. Submission of a nurse-midwife consultation and referral agreement with a physician engaged in the practice of obstetrics and participating in the Tennessee Medicaid program
c. Execution of a Medicaid provider agreement

(Tenn. Comp. R & Regs. R. 1200-13-1-.22).

practice of a nurse midwife, NP, CRNA, or CNS, the insured or other person entitled to benefits under the contract, plan, or policy is entitled to reimbursement for these services whether the services are performed by a physician or by the APN (Tenn. Code Ann. § 56-7-2407 and § 56-7-2408 [1999]).

Texas

Medicaid

Pursuant to 25 Texas Administrative Code § 29.2101 (2000), anesthesia services provided by a CRNA are covered by the Texas Medical Assistance (Medicaid) Program. To be payable, the services must meet the requirements outlined in Box 10-7. The program will not reimburse the CRNA for equipment or supplies, which are the responsibility of the facility where the services are provided. If the equipment and supplies are covered and reimbursable by the program, payment may be made to the facility if the facility is approved for participation in the program (Tenn. Code Ann. § 56-7-2407 and § 56-7-2408 [1999]).

To participate in the Texas Medical Assistance Program, a CRNA must meet the requirements listed in Box 10-8. Medicaid services include services performed by APN if the services

1. Are within the scope of practice for advanced nurse practitioners
2. Are consistent with rules and regulations of the Texas State Board of Nurse Examiners

BOX 10-7	Texas Requirements for Medicaid Payment of CRNA Services

1. Services are within the CRNA's scope of practice
2. Services are reasonable and medically necessary
3. Services are prescribed and supervised by a physician (MD or DO), dentist, or podiatrist, who must be licensed in the state in which he or she practices
4. Services are provided under one of the following conditions:
   A. No physician anesthesiologist is on the medical staff of the facility where the services are provided
   B. No physician anesthesiologist is available to provide the services
   C. The physician, dentist, or podiatrist performing the procedure requiring the services specifically requests the services of a CRNA
   D. The eligible recipient requiring the services specifically requests the services of a CRNA
   E. The CRNA is scheduled or assigned to provide the services in accordance with policies of the facility in which the services are provided
   F. The services are provided by the CRNA in connection with a medical emergency

(25 Texas Administrative Code § 29.2101).

BOX 10-8	Texas Medicare Requirements for CRNA Participation

1. Be an RN who is approved as an advanced nurse practitioner by the state in which he or she practices and is currently certified by either the Council on Certification of Nurse Anesthetists or the Council on Recertification of Nurse Anesthetists
2. Comply with all applicable federal and state laws and regulations governing the services provided
3. Be enrolled and participating in Medicare
4. Be enrolled and approved for participation in the Texas Medical Assistance Program
5. Sign a written provider agreement with the department or its designee
6. Comply with the terms of the provider agreement and all requirements of the Texas Medical Assistance Program
7. Bill for services covered by the Texas Medical Assistance Program in the manner and format prescribed

(25 Texas Administrative Code § 29.2102 [2000])

3. Would be covered if provided by a physician (medical doctor or doctor of osteopathy) (25 Texas Administrative Code § 29.2501 [2000])

To be payable, services must be reasonable and medically necessary. APNs employed or paid by a physician, hospital, facility, or other provider must not bill the program directly for their services if that billing would result in duplicate payment for the same services. If the services are covered by the program, payment may be made to the physician, hospital, or other provider (if the provider is approved for participation) who employs or reimburses advanced nurse practitioners (25 Texas Administrative Code § 29.2501 [2000]).

Texas Administrative Code § 355.8221 (2000) outlines reimbursement rules for CRNAs under the state Medicaid program. Payment for covered anesthesia services provided by a participating CRNA is limited to the lesser of the actual charge or 85% of the rate reimbursed to a physician anesthesiologist for the same service. Reimbursement for covered CRNA services may be made to the CRNA actually performing the services or, provided that federal requirements related to reassignment of claims are met, to a hospital, physician, dentist, podiatrist, group practice, or ambulatory surgical center with which the CRNA has an employment or contractual relationship. CRNA services are reimbursed only when the services are submitted for payment under a CRNA provider number.

25 Texas Administrative Code § 29.2401 (2000) outlines benefits available under the Texas Department of Health, in federally qualified health

centers (FQHC) to eligible Medicaid recipients to include nurse practitioner services. To be a provider of Medicaid-covered services, a NP must

1. Be licensed by the Texas State Board of Nurse Examiners
2. Be recognized by the state as an APN
3. Comply with all applicable federal and state laws and regulations governing the services provided
4. Be enrolled and approved for participation in the Texas Medical Assistance Program
5. Sign a written provider agreement with the department or its designee
6. Comply with the terms of the provider agreement and all requirements of the Texas Medical Assistance Program
7. Bill for services covered by the Texas Medical Assistance Program in the manner and format prescribed (25 Texas Administrative Code § 29.2502 [2000])

In a Medicare skilled nursing facility (SNF), with certain exceptions a physician may (while providing supervision) delegate tasks to an NP or clinical nurse specialist (CNS) (40 Texas Administrative Code § 19.1205 [2000]). A task may not be delegated when the regulations specify that the physician must perform it personally or when the delegation is prohibited under state law or by the facility's own policies. In a Medicaid nursing facility, any required physician task may also be satisfied when performed by a NP or CNS who is not a facility employee but who is working in collaboration with the physician. The APN providing care to a pediatric resident must have training and expertise in the care of children with complex medical needs (40 Texas Administrative Code § 19.1205 [2000]).

1 Texas Administrative Code § 355.8281 (2000) governs reimbursement under Medicare for NPs. Covered services provided by NPs are reimbursed on the basis of the lesser of actual charge or maximum fee established by the Texas Department of Health or its designee. The maximum fee is 85% of the rate paid to a physician (medical doctor or doctor of osteopathy) for the same service. APNs are reimbursed at the same reimbursement level as physicians for laboratory services, x-ray services, and injections.

To be reimbursable by the Medicare program, birth attendant services must be provided by a physician (medical doctor or doctor of osteopathy) or CNM who is enrolled and participating in the program. If the birthing center uses or refers the mother or child to a physician, CNM, and/or hospital that does not participate in the program or that has not agreed to bill the program for services provided, the birthing center must inform the recipient in advance of the recipient's potential financial responsibility (1 Texas Administrative Code § 355.8181, [2000]). Nurse midwife services under Medicaid must be provided by a CNM enrolled and approved for participation in the Texas Medical Assistance (Medicaid) Program. Nurse midwife services are covered if the services:

1. Are within the CNM's scope of practice
2. Are consistent with rules and regulations promulgated by the Board of Nurse Examiners for the State of Texas
3. Would be covered if provided by a physician (medical doctor or doctor of osteopathy) (25 Texas Administrative Code § 29.1601 [2000])

Deliveries by a CNM must be done in a hospital or facility licensed and approved by the appropriate state licensing authority for the operation of maternity and newborn services and approved for participation in the Texas Medical Assistance Program. Home deliveries performed by a CNM are reimbursable with prior authorization. The CNM must submit a written request for prior authorization during the recipient's third trimester of pregnancy. That request must include a statement signed by a licensed physician who has examined the recipient during the third trimester and determined that at that time she is not at high risk and is suitable for a home delivery (25 Texas Administrative Code § 29.1601 [2000]).

To be directly reimbursed by Medicaid, a CNM who manages the medical aspects of a case under a physician's control and supervision must perform the services according to the written protocols required by the State Board of Nurse Examiners and the services must not be duplicative of other charges to the Medicaid program. The Medicaid program does not reimburse the CNM for conducting childbirth education classes (25 Texas Administrative Code § 29.1601 [2000]).

25 Texas Administrative Code § 29.1602 (2000) outlines CNM conditions for participation in the Medicaid program. A CNM must be a licensed registered nurse who is approved as an advanced nurse practitioner in nurse midwifery and who is also certified by the American College of Nurse-Midwives. To participate in the Medicaid program, a CNM must identify a licensed physician or group of physicians with whom an arrangement has been made for referral and consultation in the event of medical complications. If the collaborating physician or group is not participating in the Texas Medical Assistance Program, the CNM must inform recipients of their potential financial responsibility. If and when the arrangement is changed or cancelled, the CNM must notify the state in writing of the identity of the new physician or group within 2 weeks after the cancellation or change.

Medicaid payment for covered nurse midwife services is limited to the lower of the customary charge or the maximum allowable fee, rate, or reimbursement schedule, if any, as established by the state. The state reimburses only the CNM actually performing or directing the covered service unless federal requirements related to reassignment of claims have been met. A nurse midwife is not reimbursed directly by the Medicaid program for services provided if she or he is employed, salaried, or reimbursed by a hospital, nursing facility, other institution, or if the facility includes the nurse midwife's payment for services in the reimbursement formula or vendor payment to the hospital, facility, institution, or other provider. Certified nurse midwives employed by or paid by a physician, health maintenance organization, hospital, or other facility may not bill the Medicaid program directly for nurse midwife services if that billing would result in duplicate payment for the same services. If the services are covered and reimbursable by the Medicaid program, payment may be made to the physician, hospital, or other provider who employs or reimburses the nurse midwife (25 Texas Administrative Code § 29.1603 [2000]).

State Plan

Texas Health & Safety Code § 61.0285 (2000) indicates that in addition to basic health care services provided under the state Indigent Health Care and Treatment Act, a county may provide other medically necessary services that the county determines to be cost-effective including services provided by NPs, CNMs, CNSs, and CRNAs.

25 Texas Administrative Code § 14.201 (2000) indicates that under the county indigent health care program, counties are required to provide rural health care clinic primary care services to eligible households by reimbursing providers of services who meet the requirements of the Indigent Health Care and Treatment Act. The services include those of an NP, a nurse midwife, or other specialized nurse practitioner as well as annual physical examinations with associated testing by an APN if those services are within the scope of practice in accordance with the standards established by the Board of Nurse Examiners. Optional services under this program include:

1. Federally Qualified Health Center NP services
2. APN and CNM services that must be medically necessary and provided within the scope of practice of an APN or CNM and covered in the Texas Medicaid program when provided by a physician
3. CRNA services that must be medically necessary; provided within the CRNA's scope of practice; and prescribed and supervised by a physician, dentist, or podiatrist licensed in the state where they practice
4. Psychotherapy services that must be medically necessary based on an APN referral if the referral is within the scope of the APN's practice in accordance with the standards established by the Board of Nurse Examiners (25 Texas Administrative Code § 29.1603 [2000])

Private Plans

Although HMOs and preferred provider organizations (PPOs) are prohibited from discriminating against APNs based solely on licensure, actual reimbursement practices vary greatly by company and type of APN (Pearson, 2000).

ENHANCE YOUR LEARNING

1. Review your own health insurance policy to determine whether APN services are included as a benefit.
2. Interview an APN regarding his or her experiences with public and private reimbursement.
3. Visit one website listed at the end of the chapter to review current information regarding reimbursement legislation.
4. Interview the head of the billing department at your facility regarding APN reimbursement issues.

TEST YOUR COMPREHENSION

1. Discuss the limitations placed on NPs by the Omnibus Reconciliation Act of 1989.
2. Discuss the changes in APN reimbursement created by the Balanced Budget Act of 1997.
3. List two requirements for claims for APN services in California.
4. Discuss the rules for CRNA reimbursement under Medicare in Texas.

REFERENCES

American Association of Nurse Anesthetists (AANA). (1997, January). Nurse anesthetists—Providing anesthesia into the next century executive summary. Available at http://www.aana.com/library/execsummary.asp.

American Association of Nurse Anesthetists (AANA). (2000a). Nurse anesthetists at a glance. Available at http://www.aana.com/information/crnas.ataglance.asp.

American Association of Nurse Anesthetists (AANA). (2000b). Nurse anesthesia reimbursement. Available at http://www.aana.com/library/reimbursement.asp.

AWHONN. (2001). *AWHONN Legislative News and Views*. Washington, D.C.

AWHONN. (2000). Nurse anesthetists no longer need physician supervision. *Legislative News and Views*.

Callahan, M. (1996). The advanced practice nurse in an acute care setting: The nurse practitioner in adult cardiac surgery care. *Nursing Clinics of North America, 31*(3), 487–493.

Dower, C.M., Miller, J.E., O'Neil E.H., & the Taskforce of Midwifery. (1999, April). *Charting a course for the 21st century: The future of midwifery*. San Francisco: Pew Health Professions Commission and the University of California San Francisco Center for the Health Professions.

Finerfrock, W., & Havens, D. (1997, May/June). Coverage and reimbursement issues for nurse practitioners. *Journal of Pediatric Health Care, 1*(3), 139–143.

HCFA. (1991). Medicare Regulations, Part 491, Certification of Certain Health Facilities, Subpart A Rural Health Clinics, Conditions for Certification. *1991 Medicare and Medicaid guide*. Chicago, Ill.

Hodson, D. (1998, May). The evolving role of advanced practice nurses in surgery. *AORN Journal, 67*(5), 998–1006.

Illinois Opinion of the Attorney General 93-022, 1993.

Inglis, A., & Kjervik, D. (1993, Summer). Empowerment of advanced practice nurses: Regulation reform needed to increase access to care. *The Journal of Law, Medicine and Ethics, 21*(2), 193–205.

Lowe, M. & Havens, D. (1998, May/June). Hot issues for NPs in 1998. *Journal of Pediatric Health Care, 12*(3), 161–163.

National Association of Pediatric Nurse Practitioners (NAPNAP). (1998). Medicare reimbursement. *Legislative News Archive.* Available at http://www.napnap.org/archives/legnews-archive/legnews-19980107.html.

National Association of Pediatric Nurse Practitioners (NAPNAP). (1998a, January 25). Collaboration/supervision requirements. Legislative News Archive. Available at http://www.napnap.org/archives/legnews-archive/legnews-19990125.html.

National Association of Pediatric Nurse Practitioners (NAPNAP). (1998b, June 25). HCFA issues BBA guidelines. *Legislative News Archive.* Available at http://www.napnap.org/archives/legnews-archive/legnews-19980625.html

National Association of Pediatric Nurse Practitioners (NAPNAP). (2000, January 29). HCFA final rule on nurse practitioner qualifications. *Legislative News.*

NCC (NAACOG Certification Corporation). (1999/2000, Winter). New Medicare rules affect nurse practitioners. *NCC News,* p. 4.

Pearson, L. (2000, January). Annual legislative update, how each state stands on legislative issues affecting advanced nursing practice. *The Nurse Practitioner, 25*(1), 16–68.

Sellards, S., & Mills, M. (1995, May). Administrative issues for use of nurse practitioners. *Journal of Nursing Administration, 25*(5), 64–70.

Spatz, D. (1996, June). Women's health: The role of advanced practice nurses in the 21st century. *Nursing Clinics of North America, 31*(2), 269–277.

Cases

Blue Shield of Massachusetts, Inc. v. Board of Review, 22 Mass. App. 160, 492 NE2d 99 (1986).

Additional Resources

Websites that provide timely information on legislative matters including reimbursement issues

American Academy of Nurse Practitioners http://www.aanp.org.

American College of Nurse Practitioners http://www.nurse.org.

National Association of Pediatric Nurse Practitioners http://www.napnap.org.

Health Care Financing Administration (HCFA) documentation guidelines for evaluation and management services are available from HCFA's website at www.hcfa.gov in the professional/technical section of the Medicare subheading.

Business Considerations

Many advanced practice nurses (APNs) feel like the proverbial fish out of water when dealing with the non-clinical aspects of their careers. It is important for APNs to be aware of business issues even if they are not in independent practice because issues can arise even for the employee APN. The scope of the information available on this subject is vast, so this chapter outlines considerations for the APN related to the business aspects of practice and provides a list of resources for APNs to consult when addressing issues related to the business of their practice.

Issues for Advanced Practice Nurses in Independent Practice

SETTING UP THE PRACTICE

Lambert & Lambert, 1996, have written a comprehensive article about starting an independent practice. They note that nurses in independent practice are the owners or proprietors of the enterprise that provides the client service, are financially and legally responsible for all aspects of the client service provided, define and control the nature of the services provided, possess the autonomy of the practice, determine the nature of the client relationship, are fully accountable for the quality of the relationship, and are responsible for the actions occurring during that relationship. Box 11-1 identifies steps to be taken when starting an independent practice.

One of the most important decisions the APN makes in setting up a practice is the type of business structure to be used. Ideally this decision should be made only after consulting a business attorney experienced in the setup of medical practices in your area and after consulting a tax attorney experienced in the issues pertaining to medical practices.

BOX 11-1	Steps to Starting an Independent Practice

- Determine the mission of the service to be provided; mission must be focused, well-defined, and within the nurse's area of expertise.
- Identify short and long term goals for the practice.
- Assess community need, including the need for the proposed practice, analyzing potential and existing competitors, deciding on the most desirable location for the practice, identifying referral sources, and identifying the community's receptivity to the type of service to be offered.
- Decide upon a business structure.
- Identify legal considerations, including state law and insurance.
- Select a physical space for the practice.
- Finance the practice.
- Develop an advertising strategy.
- Develop a marketing strategy.
- Develop a plan for acquisition of clients.
- Develop procedures regarding recordkeeping.
- Develop procedures and sources for reimbursement.

(Lambert & Lambert, 1996)

The most common types of business structures for APN practice are the partnership, the corporation, and the sole proprietorship. Buppert, 1996, provides a review of these legal entities. A sole proprietor is singly responsible for the business, makes all decisions, and gets all the rewards but retains all legal liability and responsibility for taxes. In a partnership, each partner shares profits and liabilities and each pays taxes on his or her own earnings. Each partner is personally liable for debts and judgments against the business and has an equal say in how the business runs. Corporations can take different forms depending on the state's law. Usually APNs must form a professional service corporation, which leaves liability for malpractice with the APN. In a corporation, the bylaws describe the chain of command within the company; if not incorporated, the APN should have an agreement with any partners specifying the decision-making process (Buppert, 1996).

RAINMAKING

Lawyers refer to the activities leading to the acquisition of new clients as rainmaking. These activities are essential for any APN starting out in independent practice, as well as for the APN who has been in independent practice. Effective rainmaking helps to grow the client base and compensates for the inevitable loss of existing patients through death, relocation, etc. There are many ways the APN can "sell" his or her services in the community. Ward, 1998, suggests the following public relations actions:

- Advertise in local phone books.

- Direct mail to target groups.
- Distribute flyers describing the APN's and/or the practice's services, philosophy, and credentials.
- Distribute appointment calendars with the practice's name and address.
- Volunteer to give community presentations.
- Provide free care for a homeless shelter.
- Provide free Pap smears on an occasional basis to a womens' clinic.
- Join leadership groups such as the chamber of commerce.
- Offer to teach sex education courses.
- Ask your patients to refer their friends and relatives.
- Have patient-friendly office hours including evenings and weekends.

LEGAL CONSIDERATIONS

Legal considerations for independent practice are extremely important and will require consultation with an experienced business attorney. To find an attorney, the APN can consult the county bar association in his or her town as well as any local lawyer referral services. It is also a good idea to get recommendations from other APN practices or from physicians' groups about the attorneys they use. It is imperative that the APN select an attorney with experience negotiating contracts on behalf of health care providers and in the business issues faced by medical practices.

CONTRACTS

Among the contracts the APN in independent practice may encounter are collaborative agreements, contracts for rental or purchase of office space, contracts with employees or independent contractors, and contracts with insurance companies. Henry, 1996, reminds us that a collaborative agreement should define the organizational structure, role identification, and the responsibility of each member of the collaborative practice. Buppert, 1998, recommends the NP negotiating a managed care organization (MCO) contract be sure to cover the following issues:

- Which services are included in primary care?
- What is the fee schedule or capitation rate?
- If capitated payment applies, which services are included in the capitated rate?
- What is the turnaround time between billing and payment?
- Will the MCO withhold part of the capitation, and if so, under what circumstances?
- Are specific office hours required?
- Who covers hospitalized patients?
- What are bonuses based on?

- Under what circumstances can the MCO or the provider terminate the agreement?
- In what directories will the provider be listed?

EMPLOYEES

If the APN decides to hire employees, the APN will be faced with having to withhold taxes for Social Security and Medicare, report employee income, obtain workers' compensation coverage, insure for liability as a result of employee actions, and develop employee policies and procedures. It is much simpler for the APN to avoid employees by using independent contractors to perform any needed work. Buppert, 1996, warns APNs of the potential for being considered an employer when arranging for services from other providers and recommends that the APN instruct the independent contractor provider to

1. Bill the APN periodically on the contractor's business stationery for work done.
2. Bill the APN varying amounts.
3. Not work at the APN's place of business.

INSURANCE

It is imperative that the APN maintain liability insurance for him or herself as well as any employees. In addition, if the APN has employees, it is necessary to insure against workers' compensation claims. Also, the APN should have premises liability insurance to guard against claims such as slip and fall accidents that may occur on the APN's business premises.

RECORDS

The APN needs to be aware of laws regarding record-keeping in his or her state as well as record-keeping requirements for tax and employee issues. The advice of a competent attorney is essential for this aspect of independent practice. Some states have specific laws regarding APN practice record-keeping and procedures for the records if the practice closes or the APN dies. Box 11-2 discusses an example of these types of laws.

Issues for Advanced Practice Nurses Who Are Employees

The main business issue for APNs who are employees is employment contracts. Although nurses have not traditionally been contract employees, this practice is becoming more common especially for APNs.

BOX 11-2	Laws Regarding Record Keeping

64B9-11.002, F.A.C. requires each advanced registered nurse practitioner (ARNP) engaged in private practice who maintains possession of client/patient medical records when terminating or relocating practice in so as to no longer be reasonably available to clients/patients, to notify each client/patient of the termination or relocation and unavailability. The notification must consist of at least causing to be published, in the newspaper of greatest general circulation in each county in which the nurse practices or practiced, a notice that must contain the date of termination or relocation and an address at which medical records may be obtained. The notice must be published no less than four times over a period of at least 4 weeks. In addition, the nurse must place in a conspicuous location in or on the facade of his or her office, a sign, announcing the termination or relocation of the practice. The sign must be placed at least 30 days prior to the termination or relocation and must remain until the date of termination or relocation. Both the notice and the sign must advise patients of their opportunity to transfer or receive their medical records. In addition, the ARNP must see that patient records are maintained and may be obtained by the patient for a minimum of 2 years after the termination or relocation of practice.

64B9-11.001, F.A.C. requires each ARNP engaged in private practice who maintains possession of patient medical records to ensure that their executor, administrator, personal representative, or survivor will arrange to maintain those medical records in existence upon the death of the ARNP for a period of at least 2 years from the date of death. Within 1 month from the date of death of the ARNP, the executor, administrator, personal representative, or survivor must cause to be published in the newspaper of greatest general circulation in the county where the ARNP practiced a notice indicating to the patients of the deceased ARNP that the nurse's medical records are available to the patients from a specific person at a certain location. At the conclusion of a 22-month period of time from the date of death of the ARNP, the executor, administrator, personal representative, or survivor must cause to be published once during each week for 4 consecutive weeks in the newspaper of greatest general circulation in the county where the ARNP practiced a notice indicating to the patients of the deceased nurse that patient records will be disposed of or destroyed 1 month or later from the last day of the 4th week of publication of notice.

EVALUATING AN EMPLOYMENT CONTRACT

Buppert, 1997, identifies three parts of an employment contract that are very important for the APN to be aware of: restrictive covenants, bonus formulas, and termination-without-cause clauses. Restrictive covenants prohibit an employee from practicing within a set number of miles from an employer's business for a set period of time after the employee leaves the employer's business. Buppert, 1997, suggests that when negotiating the terms of a restrictive covenant, one needs to consider the circumstances of the job offer, the severity of the restriction, the potential hardship imposed, the availability of health care providers in the area, and the availability of other practice opportunities.

When dealing with bonus formulas, the APN needs to know the different types. Productivity-based formulas are based on the number of patient visits per year and which calculations make sense for practices operating under a fee-for-service model. Under capitated reimbursement, bonuses should be given on the basis of demonstrating quality care as evidenced by a documented quality measurement tool. Profit-based formulas must have clear methods for determining profits and the NP must have the right to audit financial records (Buppert, 1997).

Termination-without-cause clauses allow the employer to terminate the APN for any reason with 30 days notice and basically defeat the purpose of an employment contract (Buppert, 1997). In negotiation of an employment contract, Buppert, 1997, recommends the following:

1. The APN should state clearly what he or she has contributed to the practice in the past year and have the figures to prove it.
2. The APN should have a basic knowledge of how the practice gets its revenues.
3. The APN should decide what terms are essential and what can be given up.
4. The APN should anticipate any drawbacks that the employer may raise in negotiations and be prepared to defend or minimize them.
5. While the APN should do the negotiating, he or she should also have the contract reviewed by an attorney with experience in reviewing contracts of health care providers including APNs.

JOB OFFERS WITHOUT CONTRACTS

To make an appropriate decision, every nurse needs to know how to evaluate a situation in which he or she is being offered a position without a written contract. The main risks of accepting a position without a contract are that the employee is not guaranteed the right to remain in the position, and the employer can unilaterally change the compensation arrangements and required duties. Buppert, 1997, discusses the advantages of employment contracts:

- Negotiation forces the parties to discuss issues.
- The contract records the agreement and can be referred to as needed to refresh memories about agreement details.
- Contracts provide assurance of some degree of job security.
- Contracts offer protection against an employee leaving the practice and taking patients with them.

- Contracts clarify issues regarding lifestyle and work style preferences.
- Contracts can specify problem-solving procedures.

Generally when a person is employed without a written contract and there is no agreement about how long the employment will last, the employment is known as "at will" employment. This means that the employment may be terminated at the will of either party on notice to the other (Calif. Labor Code § 2922). This "at will" doctrine traditionally has been the way that the law in the United States has dealt with non-contractual employment. In the last 10 or so years, courts have begun to place limitations on this theory. "At will" employment is not necessarily bad and it does not always result in problems for the employee. State and federal laws now provide protection from certain employers' abuses even when there is no written employment contract. Freitag, 1995, notes that "at will" employment does not just benefit the employer by allowing him or her to terminate employment relationships that are not benefiting the employer; it also benefits employees who have an interest in maintaining the privilege to terminate employment at will free from threat of suit, lest employers be supplied with a new weapon to harass key employees wishing to change jobs.

Absent an employment contract, there are few exceptions to the general rule of employment "at will" where an employee will have a claim for wrongful discharge. The first occurs where the discharge is in clear violation of a well-recognized and defined public policy; the second occurs where there are statutory exceptions created by federal or state legislatures (Freitag, 1995). Additionally a public employee's rights may be violated if the employee is terminated for exercising his or her First Amendment right to free speech, if the employee's speech is protected. For the speech to be protected, the speech must involve a matter of public concern. The employee's interest in expressing herself or himself on this matter must not be outweighed by any injury the speech could cause to the interest of the state as an employer (Freitag, 1995).

STATE LAW PROTECTIONS AGAINST EMPLOYER ABUSE

State laws provide certain protections for employees who do not have written employment contracts. In California and most other states, implied contracts are recognized by law. An implied contract is a contract whose existence and terms are manifested by the conduct of the parties (Calif. Civil Code § 1621). An express contract is one in which the terms are stated in words (Calif. Civ. Code § 1620). The distinction between express and implied-in-fact contracts relates only to the manifestation of assent; both types are based on the expressed or apparent intention of the parties. The true implied contract, then, consists of obligations arising from a mutual agreement and the intent to promise where the agreement and promise have not been expressed in words (*Varni Bros. Corp. v. Wine World, Inc.*, 1995). This means that even if you don't have a written contract, to a certain extent the law will recognize a contract implied by the actions of the parties. The following case provides an example of how the concept of implied contracts has been used by the courts in the health care setting. A student nurse was held to be an "employee" within the meaning of the Workmen's Compensation Act at the time she sustained an injury by falling off of a stool at a hospital. The court found her to be an employee for the following reasons:

1. She performed numerous functions that benefited the hospital.
2. Although the nursing school she attended received the hourly amount paid by the hospital for her work, this payment represented a substantial benefit to her and to other students at the school.
3. The hospital profited from the services rendered by the students.
4. It could be reasonably inferred that the students' institutional privileges could be terminated by the hospital for any infraction of its rules or for unsatisfactory services.

The court felt that based on the above factors, an implied contract of employment existed between the hospital and applicant. The contract's existence and terms were manifested by the conduct of the respective parties (*Anaheim General Hospital v. Workmen's Compensation Appeals Board*, 1970).

For a court to find that the employment was not "at will," there must be a promise, express or implied, of a guarantee of continued employment so long as there is satisfactory service. A contract for permanent employment is interpreted as a contract for an indefinite period and, in the absence of statutory provisions or public policy considerations, is terminable at the will of either party for any reason whatsoever (*Newfield v. Insurance Co. of West*, 1984). One court held that this law creates a presumption of "at will" employment. That presumed employment may be overcome by evidence that, despite the absence of a specified term, the parties agree that the employer's power to terminate would be limited in some way such as by a requirement that termination be based only on good cause. Evidence that may be considered in determining the existence of an implied-in-fact contract to terminate only for good cause includes the employer's personnel policies or practices, the employee's longevity of service, the employer's actions or communications reflecting assurances of continued employment, and the practice of the industry in which the employee is engaged (*Haycock v. Hughes Aircraft Co.*, 1994).

However, not all employees are successful in proving implicit contracts. In one case of a hospital employee against her employer for wrongful discharge based on breach of an alleged oral contract of employment, the court held that, despite 4 years of employment, fairness indicated there should be cause for dismissal. The plaintiff's complaint disclosed she was not employed for a specified term (whether 1 month or any longer) within the meaning of § 2922; therefore, the court found no cause of action as a result of her termination (*Santa Monica Hospital v. Superior Court*, 1985).

In another case involving a wrongful termination action, plaintiff's evidence of positive performance reviews, commendations, and salary increases was not sufficient to create a triable issue of fact as to whether the parties had implicitly agreed that the defendant (former employer)'s right to terminate plaintiff would be limited, because the court felt that most of those factors are natural occurrences for an employee who remains with an employer for a substantial length of time (*Horn v. Cushman & Wakefield Western, Inc.*, 1999).

FACILITY POLICIES AND HANDBOOKS AS EMPLOYMENT CONTRACTS

Some states recognize that the terms of a facility's personnel manual can become terms of an employment contract. According to the Arizona Supreme Court, a hospital's representations in its personnel manual can become terms of an employment contract and can limit the employer-hospital's ability to discharge employees. A nurse who was fired by the hospital contended that a hospital's personnel manual (which in this case was represented to the employee as part of her employment contract with the hospital) may be part of the employment contract even in an employment relationship that is otherwise terminable at will. The hospital contended that the personnel manual was nothing more than a unilateral expression of policy by which employees can guide their conduct and better understand the hospital's expectation of performance. However, the hospital insisted that if the manual were part of the employment contract, it complied with all necessary provisions. It also claimed that the manual section concerning dismissal did not imply that an employee could be terminated only for unsatisfactory service or for one of the ten listed violations.

Furthermore, the hospital claimed that the manual did not provide for an appeal from a termination by the hospital's chief executive. In agreeing with the nurse, the court noted that whether or not any particular personnel manual modifies any particular employment-at-will relationship and becomes part of the particular employment contract is a question of fact. The court added that evidence relevant to this factual decision includes the language used in the personnel manual as well as the employer's course of conduct and oral representations regarding it. However, the court specifically denied that the ruling dictated that all personnel manuals would become part of employment contracts.

The court sent the case back to the trial court for further proceedings to determine whether or not the policies contained in the manual were incorporated into and became a part of the terms of the employment contract. This court action directed that a jury determine if the manual was or was not part of the contract between the nurse and hospital. If the jury decided that the manual was not part of the contract between the nurse and the hospital, then the nurse was an at-will employee and her discharge was proper. If the jury determined that the manual did form part of the terms of the employment contract, then the jury must also determine what the terms of the employment contract were (*Joan Leikvold v. Valley View Community Hospital*, 1984).

Other states take an opposite approach. The Supreme Court of Ohio affirmed a lower court order granting the defendant hospital's summary judgment and dismissing plaintiff employee's suit alleging wrongful termination. The court held the hospital's distribution of an employee handbook did not create an express or implied employment contract. In this case the plaintiff was an employee at defendant hospital for numerous years. The defendant hospital distributed an employee handbook to plaintiff 2 months before she was fired. Plaintiff acknowledged receipt of the handbook by signing a receipt that explicitly stated the handbook was provided for informational purposes only and did not constitute an employment contract, either express or implied. Subsequently, plaintiff submitted a vacation leave request for 2 weeks. Plaintiff's supervisor denied plaintiff's request for the second week because a second employee had requested a military leave during that time. Plaintiff questioned her supervisor as to the consequences of taking the second week anyway. She was informed that failure to return on the scheduled date would lead to termination. Although plaintiff attempted to return on the scheduled date, she became ill and did not return until the following day. Plaintiff was terminated. She filed suit alleging that the employee handbook created an employment contract. The trial court granted the defendant hospital's motions for summary judgment. The plaintiff appealed.

The court found that the plaintiff was not a contractual employee for the following reasons:

1. Plaintiff signed a receipt acknowledging her employment was "at will."
2. Plaintiff admitted in deposition that the handbook did not result from negotiations between herself and defendant.
3. Plaintiff admitted in deposition that she never viewed the handbook as a binding contract.

Thus the court concluded the handbook did not serve as an employment contract (*Karnes v. Doctors Hospital*, 1990). As a result of cases like these, many facilities include a disclaimer page in the employee handbook stating that the handbook is not intended to be a contract of employment. Some facilities even require employees to sign an acknowledgment that the handbook does not create an employment contract.

Employees can use policy manuals to assert the existence of an employment contract. In *Wojcik v. Commonwealth Mortgage* (1990), the court determined the traditional "at will" employment relationship had been altered not by the employee handbook (which contained a clear disclaimer) but by a separate policy manual that had also been disseminated to employees. The court identified the following language of the policy manual as problematic: "In no event will the hiring of an employee be considered as creating a contractual relationship between the employee and the company. Their relationship is defined as 'employment at will' where either party, with appropriate notice, may dissolve the relationship" (*Wojcik v. Commonwealth Mortgage*, 1990). Despite the clear disclaimer of contractual intent in the handbook, the Wojcik court held this paragraph ambiguous. The noted paragraph along with other statements in the policy manual regarding corrective discipline provided a clear promise that an employee could reasonably rely on the belief that a contractual offer of employment had been made (*Wojcik v. Commonwealth Mortgage*, 1990).

In addition, the court held that despite a disclaimer, the employer's policy manual contained enforceable promises that required the employer not only to give his employees appropriate notice prior to discharge but also to give employees the opportunity to correct performance deficiencies before effecting the discharge (*Wojcik v. Commonwealth Mortgage*, 1990). The court based its decision on the following handbook language: "Appropriate measures for correcting performance problems are coaching, memoranda outlining specific steps for improvement, and probation. Termination for performance issues occurs only after the employee has been given the opportunity and support necessary for improvement" (*Wojcik v. Commonwealth Mortgage*, 1990).

Employee handbooks that include a laundry list of offenses that may result in discipline including discharge may create a contractual claim for continued employment. In *Montgomery v. Association of American Railroads* (1990), the court held that an employee handbook policy, which stated that an employee could not be disciplined after a probationary period without just cause, created a contractual right for an employee who was discharged (*Montgomery v. Association of American Railroads*, 1990). In *Thomas v. Garrett Corporation* (1989), the court held that an employer was entitled to summary judgment in an employee handbook breach of contract action because the employee had failed to exhaust both the formal and informal grievance mechanisms set forth in the handbook. The court analogized the employee's situation to that of a bargaining unit member with a collective bargaining agreement (*Thomas v. Garrett Corporation*, 1989). Just as the union employee must exhaust his or her contractual remedies, including arbitration, before bringing a lawsuit, employees who bring breach of contract actions based on hand-books must also exhaust the internal grievance mechanisms contained in the handbook (*Thomas v. Garrett Corporation*, 1989).

Withdrawal of a Job Offer

Employees also have recourse if the employer withdraws an oral job offer. In *Comeaux v. Brown & Williamson Tobacco* (1990), a prospective employee whose job offer was withdrawn was entitled to recover dam-ages for his detrimental reliance on the company's job offer. The plaintiff had completed several interviews with the company and was offered a sales representative job on the following conditions: (1.) a successful physical exam; (2.) relocation to California; and (3.) 1 week notice to cur-rent employer. After fulfilling all three conditions, the plaintiff and his wife moved to California and he prepared to report for work as sched-uled. On his start date, however, a company representative informed the plaintiff that there were "problems" with his employment. After com-pleting a credit check without the plaintiff's knowledge, the company rescinded his employment offer because of a poor credit history (*Comeaux v. Brown & Williamson Tobacco*,1990).

The Ninth Circuit reversed the lower court's grant of summary judg-ment for the employer. The court determined the plaintiff could recover damages based on his detrimental reliance on the company's offer and the express conditions placed on his employment. According to the court, the company deprived him of making an informed decision prior to accepting his offer and leaving his present employment, to his detri-ment, in reliance on the company's offer. The court also rejected the employer's argument that the plaintiff had waived his right to damages by signing an employment application that stated his employment was "at will" and terminable at any time by either party (*Comeaux v. Brown & Williamson Tobacco*, 1990).

Contracts Can Be Broken

It is important to note that even if a contract exists, the parties can still break the terms of the contract. This may cause the party breaking the contract to be liable to the other party for damages. Except as otherwise provided by the articles or bylaws, corporate officers are chosen by the board of directors and serve at the pleasure of the board, subject to the rights, if any, of an officer under any contract of employment. Any offi-cer may resign at any time by giving written notice to the corporation without prejudice to the rights, if any, of the corporation under any con-tract to which the officer is a party (Calif. Corp. Code § 312). Courts have held this statute to create a presumption of an "at -will" employment relationship. However, courts have also held that this presumption can be overcome by evidence of any contract of employment, whether an express written contract or an implied one. One court noted, "In enact-

BOX 11-3 | CRNA Contract Dispute

In the case of *Main v. Skaggs Community Hospital et al.* (1991), the plaintiff, a CRNA, sued the hospital, alleging breach of the CRNA's employment contract. The contract's provisions included the following language:

The Hospital agrees to appoint the Nurse Anesthetist for an indefinite period and the Nurse Anesthetist agrees to serve in such capacity for such period subject to the terms and provisions of this agreement, providing, however, that either party may terminate this agreement, with just cause, by giving sixty days' written notice by registered mail.

Plaintiff claimed that he performed all his contractual duties and fulfilled all conditions precedent, but the hospital breached the contract by discharging him without just cause. The trial court held the hospital was entitled to judgment as a matter of law in that the contract provided that the employment of plaintiff would be for 'an indefinite period' of time thereby creating an "at will" employment relationship that entitled the hospital to terminate plaintiff without cause, notwithstanding the language of paragraph one of the contract that provided `that either party may terminate this agreement, with just cause, by giving sixty days' written notice by registered mail.' Plaintiff argued the contract limited the reasons for which the hospital could discharge him by giving each party the right to terminate the agreement "with just cause." Plaintiff asserted this meant the hospital could not discharge him without just cause. Consequently, plaintiff maintained he was not an "at will" employee. The appellate court disagreed, holding that the contract was not limited to a fixed period of time nor did it terminate upon completion of one or more specific undertakings or upon the occurrence of some event. It was, by its own terms, "for an indefinite period," and purported to grant plaintiff the right to perpetual employment by the hospital unless his performance became deficient enough to constitute "just cause" for firing him. The court therefore held that it was a contract imposing an obligation in perpetuity, which was illegal under previous court rulings, and that under the contract here, plaintiff was an employee "at will"; consequently, the hospital had the right to discharge plaintiff without cause.

ing the statute, the Legislature did not limit its application to written or even express contracts. Nor is the concept of an implied contract alien to the corporate world. "Any" means "every" and "all" and thus encompasses more than contracts reduced to writing." (*Bell v. Superior Court*, 1989). Box 11-3 discusses the case of *Main v. Skaggs*, (1991).

ENHANCE YOUR LEARNING

1. Interview an APN in private practice regarding how he or she conducts rainmaking.

2. Review ads in your local phone book for APN services, and design one for your own practice.

3. Interview an attorney who has assisted APNs in setting up a partnership.
4. Review the law in your state regarding corporate forms available for APN practices.

TEST YOUR COMPREHENSION

1. Indentify three steps to take when starting an independent practice.
2. Indentify two ways an APN can "sell" his or her services in the community.
3. Define restrictive covenant.
4. Compare and contrast the three types of bonus formulas.

REFERENCES

Buppert, C. (1996). Nurse practitioner private practice: Three legal pitfalls to avoid. *Nurse Practitioner, 21*(4), 32–37.
Buppert, C. (1997). Employment agreements: Clauses that can change an NP's life. *The Nurse Practitioner, 22*(8), 108–119.
Buppert, C. (1998). Reimbursement for nurse practitioner services. *The Nurse Practitioner, 23*(1), 67, 70–76, 81.
Freitag, J. (1995). Termination for speech in health care employment: When is discussion of health care a matter of public concern? *Journal of Health Law, 28*(3), 182.
Henry, P. (1996). Analysis of the nurse practitioner's legal relationships. *Nurse Practitioner Forum, 7*(1), 5–6.
Lambert, V., & Lambert C. (1996). Advanced practice nurses: Starting an independent practice. *Nursing Forum, 31*(1), 11–21.
Ward, R. (1998). Public relations for advanced practice nurses. *AWHONN Lifelines, 2*(5), 47–48.

Cases

Anaheim General Hospital v. Workmen's Compensation Appeals Board, 3 Calif. App. 3d 468, 83 Calif. Rptr. 495 (4th Dist. 1970).
Bell v. Superior Court, 215 Calif. App. 3d 1103, 263 Calif. Rptr. 787 (2nd Dist. 1989).
Comeaux v. Brown & Williamson Tobacco, 915 F.2d 1264 (9th Cir. 1990).
Haycock v. Hughes Aircraft Co., 22 Calif. App. 4th 1473, 28 Calif. Rptr. 2d 248 (2nd Dist. 1994).
Horn v. Cushman & Wakefield Western, Inc., 72 Calif. App. 4th 798, 818, 85 Calif. Rptr. 2d 459 (1st Dist. 1999).
Karnes v. Doctors Hospital, 51 Ohio St. 3d 139, 555 N.E.2d 280 (1990).
Leikvold v. Valley View Community Hospital, Ariz. S. Ct. 17121 (1984).
Main v. Skaggs Community Hospital et al., 812 S.W.2d 185 (Mo. 1991).
Montgomery v. Association of American Railroads, 741 F. Supp. 1313 (N.D. Ill. 1990).

Newfield v. Insurance Co. of West,156 Calif. App. 3d 440, 203 Calif. Rptr. 9 (2d Dist. 1984).

Santa Monica Hospital v. Superior Court, 182 Calif. App. 3d 878, 218 Calif. Rptr. 543 (2d Dist. 1985).

Thomas v. Garrett Corporation, 744 F. Supp. 199 (D. Ariz. 1989), aff'd without opinion, 904 F.2d 41 (9th Cir. 1990).

Varni Bros. Corp. v. Wine World, Inc., 35 Calif. App. 4th 880, 41 Calif. Rptr. 2d 740 (5th Dist. 1995).

Wojcik v. Commonwealth Mortgage, 732 F. Supp. 941, 942 (N.D. Ill. 1990).

Additional Reading

Buppert, C. (1999). *Nurse practitioner's business practice and legal guide.* Gaithersburg, MD: Aspen.

Glaister, J., Sapp, A., & Esparza, E. (1996). Nurses practicing nursing independently. *Nursing and Health Care: Perspectives on Community, 17,* 128–132.

Lachman, V. (1996). Positioning your business in the marketplace. *Advance Practice Nurse Quarterly, 2,* 27–32.

Towers, J. (1990), Practice characteristics and marketing activities of nurse practitioners. *Journal of the American Academy of Nurse Practitioners, 2,* 164–167.

Complementary and Alternative Medicine

These days many patients are turning to alternative means of managing both chronic and acute medical conditions, often without the knowledge of their health care providers. This chapter explores the issues of complimentary and alternative medicine (CAM) as they pertain to the advanced practice nurse's practice and provides references to the small numbers of state laws that currently govern CAM.

Defining CAM

Approximately $13.7 billion is spent annually on alternative therapies ranging from harmless to dangerous (AWHONN, 1997) In 1993, it was reported that one of every three persons uses some sort of unconventional therapy ranging from acupuncture to meditation and prayer for all types of health conditions (Cook, 1997). Alternative therapies also have potential for use in women in labor, including inducing labor, correcting malpresentation, and managing labor pain (Cook, 1997). Vincler and Nicol, 1997, note that the increasing availability of CAM through insurance programs is likely to fuel the public's requests for such care, making it crucial for practitioners and hospitals to institute CAM policies and procedures.

CAM can be divided into four main categories based on the nature of treatment used: spiritual and psychological; nutritional; drug and biologic; physical forces and devices (Cook, 1997). The spiritual and psychological category includes therapies administered by faith healers, psychics, and mystics as well as psychological treatments such as mental imaging and hypnosis. The nutritional category includes herbal, vitamin, and dietary supplements, and promotion of specific foods or diets. The drug and biologic category includes homeopathy and the use of chemicals, serums, and vaccines. The physical forces and devices category includes therapies applied by chiropractors, massage and touch therapists, and acupuncturists in addition to other electrotherapies.

Vincler and Nicol, 1997, note that even the proponents of this definitional scheme, however, recognize that four broad categories are insufficient to describe other alternative practices such as aromatherapy and iridology (diagnoses based upon examination of the iris). In April 1995, the Office of Alternative Medicine of the National Institutes of Health impaneled a working group to produce a definition and description of CAM (Vincler and Nicol, 1997). This panel (consisting primarily of CAM practitioners) defined CAM, in part, as "a broad domain of healing resources that encompasses all health systems, modalities, and practices and their accompanying theories and beliefs, other than those intrinsic to the politically dominant health system of a particular society or culture in a given historical period." The panel noted, "Boundaries within CAM and between the CAM domain and the domain of the dominant system are not always sharp or fixed." Slagle, 1996, indicates that alternative therapies range from reflexology, therapeutic touch, massage therapy, ingested substances, energy balancing, psychic and spiritual counseling, and healing. Many modalities focus on belief in the body's own healing energies, power, and the interrelationship of the body, mind, and spirit.

Research Regarding CAM

The federal government is stepping up its efforts to provide a scientific basis for the use of botanicals in health care. In late 1997, a National Institutes of Health (NIH) consensus panel concluded that there is clear evidence that needle acupuncture can be effective for postoperative and chemotherapy nausea and vomiting, nausea in pregnancy, and postoperative dental pain. The panel also acknowledged that, although less medical evidence exists about acupuncture's effectiveness with the following conditions, the technique can help addiction, stroke rehabilitation, headache, menstrual cramps, tennis elbow, fibromyalgia, low back pain, carpal tunnel syndrome, and asthma (AWHONN, 1997a). Acupuncture is a family of procedures, the most well known involving penetration of specific anatomic locations on the skin, called acupuncture points, by thin solid generally metallic needles. As of 1997, there were approximately 10,000 acupuncture specialists in the United States; 3,000 of those were physicians (AWHONN, 1997a). As of 1997, 34 states licensed or otherwise regulated the practice of acupuncture by nonphysicians and have established training standards for certification to practice acupuncture (AWHONN, 1997a).

The NIH Office of Dietary Supplements is working with the National Center for Complementary and Alternative Medicine (NCCAM) to establish the first "Dietary Supplements Research Centers," which are expected to advance the scientific base of knowledge about botanicals, including issues of safety, effectiveness, and biological action (AWHONN, 2000). In another study, the NCCAM and the National Institute on Aging have awarded a 6-year cooperative agreement to the University of Pittsburgh School of Medicine to coordinate a multicenter study of the effectiveness of ginkgo biloba extract in preventing dementia in older individuals (AWHONN, 2000a). Extracts from the leaves of the ginkgo biloba tree have been used for centuries by practitioners of Chinese medicine to treat a variety of medical conditions; in Europe and Asia, this extract is routinely taken to treat a wide range of complaints including Alzheimer's disease (AWHONN, 2000a). A 1997 study suggested that this extract may be of some help treating symptoms of Alzheimer's disease and vascular dementia; however, some recent case studies imply that daily use of this extract may cause side effects such as excessive bleeding, especially when combined with daily use of aspirin (AWHONN, 2000a).

Risk Management Issues Related to CAM

A significant concern is whether or not providers are even aware of their patients' use of CAM. A study published in 1993 found that 72% of the persons who used CAM did not inform their physicians they had done so (Vincler & Nicol, 1997). A later study found that nearly 10% of the U.S. population (approximately 25 million people) saw a practitioner in 1994 for at least one of these four categories of service: chiropractic, relaxation techniques, massage, and acupuncture (Vincler & Nicol, 1997). The authors also made the following recommendations regarding history-taking in eliciting information about patients' use of CAM:

- Ask direct, nonjudgmental questions to learn about the patient's use of CAM.
- Inquires should include specific reference to various therapies, especially herbal preparations. Otherwise, many patients may fail to report use of herbs because they do not consider "natural" products to be a form of medicine. This is especially true because these products are sold as dietary supplements and their sale and manufacture is largely unregulated by the federal Food and Drug Administration (FDA).
- Do not make disparaging remarks about CAM; encourage patients to fully disclose their use of alternative therapies.

Vincler and Nicol, 1997, note that some medical commentators recommend specific steps to improve physician–patient communication when a patient's use or request for CAM stems from of a culturally based preference. These commentators recommend a four-step approach for a provider presented with such a scenario. These four steps are: (1.) identify the culturally relevant values, principles, and concepts; (2.) discern the meaning of those principles and concepts; (3.) gain insight into the culturally accepted approach; and (4.) begin to understand the larger context (social, political, historical) in which the cross-cultural situation/relationship is embedded. These steps help to ensure that the provider fully considers the treatment plan from the patient's perspective and, when medically feasible, incorporates the patient's preferences. The steps also help to clarify assumptions the provider may be making based on cultural norms rather than criteria genuinely based on standard of care parameters.

David Eisenberg, M.D. of Beth Israel Deaconess Medical Center in Boston believes there is a moral imperative to ask patients if they use alternative therapy in order to safeguard them, understand and honor their values, and promote a relationship-centered approach to their care (AWHONN, 1997). In dealing with the issue of alternative therapy, Eisenberg recommends that

- Providers should help patients identify suitable licensed CAM providers.
- Patients should be given a list of initial questions.
- Follow-up visits should be scheduled to monitor patients' treatment plans and responses to treatment.

Eisenberg stresses patient safety, documentation within the patient's record, and shared decision-making. Vincler and Nicol, 1997, recommend that providers explore the reasons for a patient's use of these therapies to reveal the concern or problem the patient is attempting to treat, which will help to evaluate the patient's request and may suggest a conventional therapy that could address the patient's needs. Additionally, the dialogue demonstrates a respect for the patient's needs and beliefs, thereby opening the door for a more meaningful relationship.

Slagle, 1996, notes that when a client uses alternative therapies, with or without the knowledge of the NP, there may be physiological, ethical, and legal implications. If the APN decides to incorporate alternative therapies into his or her practice, there are several important points to keep in mind: the advanced practice nurse (APN) must be sure that the laws in the state of practice are broad enough to permit the use of alternative therapies by the APN; options of treatment and expected outcomes should be discussed with the client, followed by informed consent; the APN must be aware of potential hazards of some alternative therapies including increased risk of harm when using ingested substances, variable assimilation and excretion modes of substances, possible toxicity or injury as a result of a contaminant or improper use, interference or interaction with concurrent, traditional treatment and variability in efficacy, delay of possibly more appropriate, and more effective, conventional care (Slagle,

1996). Vincler and Nicol, 1997, recommend that before the provider recommends CAM therapy, he or she should consider a number of questions:

1. Why should the treatment be ordered? What is the expected benefit?
2. What, if any, conventional treatment is not being given as a result?
3. What treatment would other providers provide in the same circumstances?
4. What are the known or possible risks of the CAM therapy?

In terms of risk management activities for the APN involved in alternative medicine treatments, Slagle, 1996, recommends the following: consultation with or referral to medical and or alternative health specialists; recommendation for the client's participation in experimental treatment programs conducted by conventional medical investigators; consultation with in-house counsel and review of policies; ongoing documentation of all known factors regarding the client including the NP's assessment, recommendations, and counseling of the client; consultation with other health-related sources; and documentation of the client's preferences and decisions about his or her health care. Vincler and Nicol, 1997, make the following recommendations regarding documentation about CAM therapies. When a provider either recommends or approves a patient's request for CAM therapies, he or she should at least enter a note in the patient's medical record. This documentation should include

- The provider's general understanding of the CAM therapy and how it applies to the particular patient
- All relevant information conveyed by the patient to the provider
- Any pertinent information the provider gave to the patient
- Some demonstration, if the patient is hospitalized, that hospital polices or procedures were followed

Vincler and Nicol, 1997, suggest that to fulfill the provider's obligations to the patient regarding CAM, at a minimum the provider should attempt to obtain information regarding basic questions of efficacy and safety such as (1.) is the remedy better than a placebo or doing nothing? (2.) is the remedy as safe as a placebo or doing nothing? (3.) does potential benefit exceed the potential harm? However, they acknowledge that much of this information may be unavailable. They also note that there may be some instances in which CAM therapy and allopathic medicine diverge, leaving no middle ground, such as when the provider reasonably believes that the patient's use of CAM is harmful and inconsistent with conventional therapy. Ultimately, if a patient insists on receiving CAM in such circumstances against medical advice, the provider may elect to terminate the provider–patient relationship. Termination, however, is generally a decision of last resort and made only in extreme circumstances where the patient's non-cooperation prohibits the provider from delivering adequate care. Moreover, a provider electing to terminate the relationship must do so in a manner that does not constitute actionable "patient abandonment."

In terms of informed consent for CAM therapies, Vincler and Nicol, 1997, suggest that the provider develop and use a form in which the patient assumes the risk of CAM therapy. Assumption of the risk allows an individual to accept responsibility for actions or decisions while acknowledging potential risks associated with those choices. Using an assumption of the risk form to document the patient's knowledge of the risks helps demonstrate that the patient made a knowing decision to proceed with a particular CAM therapy. It also it gives patients a greater role in choosing whether or not to receive CAM therapies of uncertain benefit without exposing hospitals or providers to increased liability risks. Vincler and Nicol, 1997, recommend using a consent-to-assume-risks form for patients receiving CAM therapy. That form should include acknowledgment that the patient has been informed by the provider that

- Use/receipt of this alternative therapy is of unknown benefit
- Use/receipt of this alternative therapy creates unknown risks
- Use/receipt of this alternative therapy may be harmful
- If the alternative therapy involves ingestion of a substance (herbal products, nutritional supplements), these substances may not be FDA regulated for medicinal purposes and may contain unknown quantities of active ingredients and may potentially contain contaminants.

The form should acknowledge that the patient is aware there may be very little scientific information available about this alternative therapy; there may be unanticipated side effects/symptoms as a result of this alternative therapy; it is the patient's responsibility to let the physician and other healthcare providers know if any side effects/symptoms occur; and if such side effects/symptoms occur, the provider may advise or direct the alternative therapy be stopped.

The provider should counsel the patient to stop CAM therapy if any of the following conditions exist:

- The patient has a serious condition making her use of CAM potentially dangerous
- The CAM therapies may lessen the efficacy of conventional care.

If the patient persists in using CAM, the provider should ask the patient's permission to contact the CAM provider in an effort to resolve the difficulties (Vincler and Nicol, 1997).

REVIEW OF PERTINENT STATE LAW

Louisiana

This state's nursing board has recognized that acupressure, moxibustion, hypnosis, and massage therapy are within the registered nurse's scope of practice. Pursuant to the Law R.S. 37:3553 as amended in the 1997 legislative act, if the registered nurse (RN) uses the title "Massage Therapist," the said RN must hold a current massage therapy license. RNs may employ and initiate complementary therapies for patients seeking such therapies as part of an overall plan of nursing care to meet nursing and patient goals such as comfort, relief of pain, relaxation, improved coping mechanisms, reduction or moderation of stress, and increased sense of well-being provided the patient has given informed consent. In all practice settings, written policies must be in place that provide for the registered nurse to perform such modalities (Louisiana Board of Nursing, 1999).

Nevada

This state recognizes practitioners of homeopathy via granting a certificate to practice as an advanced practitioner of homeopathy (NAC 630A.420). Qualifications for this certificate include:

1. A baccalaureate degree from a college or university approved by the board or equivalent qualifications as determined and approved by the board of nursing.
2. Successful completion of at least one of the following training programs approved by the board: (a.) a program to become certified or licensed to practice as a nurse practitioner, a chiropractor, or an acupuncturist or doctor of oriental medicine; (b.) a program to receive a degree from a domestic or foreign medical school approved by the board, a homeopathic medical school approved by the board, or a school of naturopathy approved by the board, or (c.) any other medical training approved by the board
3. Successful completion of not less than 6 months of training in homeopathy
4. Successful completion of the examination administered by the board (NAC 630A.420)

ENHANCE YOUR LEARNING

1. Visit your local health foods store and review the types of herbal supplements available.
2. Interview a CAM provider regarding his or her practice.

3. Determine whether your state's laws permit CAM practice by APNs.

4. Develop a consent form for CAM to be used in your practice.

TEST YOUR COMPREHENSION

1. Identify the four main categories of CAM.

2. Identify three conditions that can be helped by acupuncture.

3. List 2 ways to elicit information about a patient's use of CAM.

4. Identify two risk management activities for the APN involved in alternative medicine treatment.

REFERENCES

AWHONN. (1997). Helping patients choose alternative therapies. *AWHONN Lifelines, 1*(4), 23.

AWHONN. (1997). NIH panel comes to consensus on acupuncture. *AWHONN Lifelines, 1*(6), 20.

AWHONN. (1999). Research centers to study herbs. *AWHONN Lifelines, 3*(6), 12.

AWHONN. (1999). Multicenter study on ginkgo biloba funded. *AWHONN Lifelines, 3*(6), 14.

Cook, A, & Wilcox, G. (1997). Pressuring pain: Alternative therapies for labor pain management. *AWHONN Lifelines, 1*(2), 36–41.

Louisiana Board of Nursing. (1999, August, 25). Declaratory statement regarding the role and scope of practice of registered nurses performing holistic nursing practice and complimentary therapies.

Slagle, M. (1996). The nurse practitioner and issues of alternative therapies. *Nurse Practitioner, 21*(2), 16–19.

Vincler, L., & Nicol, M. (1997). When ignorance isn't bliss: What healthcare practitioners and facilities should know about complimentary and alternative medicine. American Health Lawyers Association *Journal of Health Law, 30*(3), 160.

Suggestions for Further Reading

Alternative Medicine

Auckett, A. (1989). *Baby massage: Parent child bonding through touching.* Newmarket Press.

Beinfield, H., & Kongold, E. (1992). *Between heaven and earth: A guide to Chinese medicine.* Ballentine Books.

Flaws, B. (1993). *The path of pregnancy.* Paradigm publications.

Greenwood, S. (1996). *Menopause, naturally: Preparing for the second half of life.* Vo lcano Press.

Kaptchuk, T. (2000). *The web that has no weaver: Understanding Chinese medicine.* Congdon & Weed, Inc.

Love, S. (1998). *Dr. Susan Love's hormone book: Making informed choices about menopause*. Random House.

Lowe, R. *Acupuncture in gynecology and obstetrics*. Thorsons Publishing Group.

National Center for Complementary and Alternative Medicine website *http://nccam.nih.gov*.

National Institutes of Health Consensus Development Program website *http://consensus.nih.gov*.

Northrup, C. (1998). *Women's bodies, Women's wisdom: Creating physical and emotional health and healing*. Bantam Books.

Ojeda, L. (2000). *Menopause without medicine*. Hunter House.

Sheehy, G. (1998). *The silent passage: Menopause*. Pocket Books.

The PDR for herbal medicines (1998). Medical Economics. Available by calling 800-678-5689.

Tyler, V.E. *The honest herbal: A sensible guide to the use of herbs and related remedies*. Pharmaceutical Products Press.

Weed, S. *Menopausal years: Wise women ways*. Ash Tree Publishing.

Weil, A. *Women's Health*. Ivy Books.

Zhejiang College of traditional Chinese medicine. (Ed.) *A handbook of traditional Chinese gynecology*. Blue Poppy Press.

Other Resources

The American Academy of Medical Acupuncture (323) 937-5514
http://www.medicalacupuncture.org

The American Association of Naturopathic Physicians (877) 969-2267; (703) 610-9037

The American Herbalists Guild (770) 751-6021

The American Osteopathic Association (800) 621-1773 *http://www.aoa-net.org*

The Chiropractors Association (800) 423-4690 *http://www.chiropractic.org*

The National Center for Complimentary and Alternative Medicine Clearinghouse (888) 644-6226

Index

Page numbers followed by f indicate figure:
those followed by t indicate table.